Random Waterford History

Colm Long

2013

Published in 2013

ISBN 978-0-9927283-0-4

Copyright © Colm Long

All rights reserved

No part of this publication may be copied, reproduced, stored in a retrieval system, broadcast or transmitted in any form or by any means, electronic, mechanical, photocopying, recording or otherwise without prior permission from the author.

Front Cover:
- Waterford coat of arms as depicted on the side wall of the Waterford Credit Union building in Colbeck Street
- Reginald's Tower, French Church & Christ Church Cathedral taken from Ferrybank

Acknowledgements

I would like to thank all my followers on Twitter, who by their encouragement and engagement led me to write this book.

I would also like to thank my wife's aunt Patricia Fanning, former Waterford City Librarian, who first introduced me to Waterford history many years ago by giving me a present of her original copy of Egan's *History of Waterford* (1894).

A special thanks goes to Declan McGrath for his guidance and expertise throughout all aspects of this publication.

Thanks also to Dr. Peter Crooks, TCD for his advice and permission to use extracts from the Irish Chancery Project.

Finally, this book would not have happened without the encouragement and support of my wife Jenifer, and my children Deirdre, Brendan and Stephen.

INTRODUCTION

The origin of this book comes from my use of the social media service Twitter. For those readers unfamiliar with it, Twitter allows a user to send short text-based messages, called tweets, to your followers. Having been introduced to Twitter by my son in 2011, I quickly found myself tweeting about Waterford and following people from Waterford. As I was reading some Waterford history books at the time, I began to tweet interesting historical facts, especially if I came across something which happened on that particular day. In order to introduce a common theme, I always started with the heading *Random #Waterford History* (the use of the hashtag # enables other users to easily find tweets relevant to Waterford). The only difficulty was that by its nature Twitter limits you to 140 characters per entry, so my entries for each day were short and sweet. A typical tweet was similar to the following for the 30th of April:

> *Random #Waterford History: 30 April 1793. Construction of 1st bridge across Suir began. Became known as Timbertoes. A toll bridge till 1907.*

I began scouring history books to find references for more dates, and before I knew it I had a database of entries for most days of the year. It was a logical step to consider publishing this in book form. Although I had been collecting Waterford history books for a number of years, I began to scour auction catalogues, eBay, Amazon and Abebooks for more sources of information.

The Local Studies room in Waterford City Library was an invaluable source. The foresight by the then City Librarian Patricia Fanning in setting up the *Waterford Room* back in 1977 with the assistance of Stan Carroll RIP has ensured that the historian (amateur or otherwise) has access to a virtual goldmine of material relating to Waterford history, including microfiche copies of old Waterford newspapers.

Although a number of authors have published chronologies of Waterford history from the earliest times up to the present day, I found only one book which deals with anniversaries for each day of the year. This was compiled by M. J. Hurley and published in 1900 with the very long title:

> *Links and Landmarks being a Calendar for the year 1900, recording curious and remarkable events in the History of Waterford City from the earliest times to the present day.*

However it is missing a lot of dates and each entry consists of only a single sentence.

Waterford is extremely lucky to have numerous history books of excellent quality. Besides the standard histories of Waterford published some hundred years ago (see entry for January 1st), there have also been some books of great scholarship published in recent years. For example *Waterford Treasures* by Eamonn McEneaney in 2004, *The Royal Charters of Waterford* by Julian Walton in 1992 and *Shipbuilding in Waterford* by Bill Irish in 2001, just to mention a few. Of course the *Decies* journal, with its wide range of articles, has contributed enormously to the study of Waterford history.

The website of Waterford County Library has an extensive selection of journals, books and newpapers available to view online. In addition the online resource at Irishnewsarchive.com not only gave back issues of national newspapers but also back issues of the Munster Express.

There are four books with original source material published by The Irish Manuscript Commission which deal specifically with Waterford. These were invaluable sources, and are:

- *The Civil Survey A.D. 1654-1656 County of Waterford,* Editor Robert C Simington (1942)

- *The Council Books of the Corporation of Waterford,* Editor Seamus Pender 1662 – 1700 (1964)

- *The Great Parchment Book of Waterford,* Editor Niall J. Byrne (2007)

- *The Council Book for the Province of Munster 1500 – 1649*, Editor Margaret Curtin Clayton (2008)

Quite by chance, a newspaper article in May 2012 led me to another source. This was *A Calendar of Irish Chancery Letters c. 1244 – 1509*. This amazing project by researchers in TCD involves reconstructing the Rolls of the Irish Chancery. These rolls were the formal records of decisions reached or orders made on behalf of the King from 1244 to 1509. Unfortunately the originals were destroyed in 1922 in the burning of the Four Courts. By collating all known transcripts throughout the world this ongoing project attempts to reconstruct the records. There are numerous references relating to Waterford in the letters.

There are two points I wish to bring to the attention of the reader.

- Firstly, while putting together all my research, an issue that emerged was the inconsistency in some dates amongst different historians, especially in the earlier years. Where this occurred, I have used my own judgment to balance the number of references against the track record of the author.

- Secondly, my own decision to include just one entry for each day has meant that this book can never be a complete history of Waterford. Many events in history occur on the same day, albeit in a different year. Where this has occurred, I have purposely left out events which are well known to the reader and about which other authors have written extensively. As the title suggests, this is very much a random history of Waterford.

Finally, as an amateur historian, this is not an academic work. This book is based entirely on the work of others as listed in the bibliography. I pay tribute to all of these authors. The phrase "standing on the shoulders of giants" comes to mind.

1 JANUARY

Waterford Historian

There is a vast range of books published on the history of Waterford. The following gives a flavour of the chronology of the main ones:

- 1746: *The ancient history and present state of the County and City of Waterford* – Charles Smith
- 1824: *The history, topography and antiquities of the County and City of Waterford* – Richard Ryland
- 1870: *History of Waterford* – Joseph Hansard
- 1894: *History guide and directory of the County and City of Waterford* – P.M. Egan
- 1914: *The Story of Waterford* – Edmund Downey
- 1990: *History of Waterford City and County* – Patrick C. Power

All of these books can be found in the Waterford Room of Waterford City Library in Lady Lane. Indeed this room is a virtual treasure trove of books on Waterford history.

The author of *The history, topography and antiquities of the County and City of Waterford*, published in 1824, was the Reverend Richard Hopkins Ryland. Born in Dungarvan in 1788, he was the descendant of 16th century Protestant planters. Generations of his family were Church of Ireland ministers. He married Isabella Fleury who was the daughter of the Archdeacon of Waterford and had eight children. An amateur historian, he saw himself as a successor to Charles Smith, whose book on Waterford history had been published seventy-eight years previously. Ryland provided updated information on the intervening period as well as correcting mistakes he found in Smith's book. Reverend R. H. Ryland died on the 1st of January 1867.

1867

2 JANUARY

Traffic Lights

The first set of traffic lights in Waterford City went into operation on this date in 1962. The location was the junction of Parnell Street and John Street. For years before this, a garda was on point duty at this junction directing traffic. As a result these gardaí became the best known in the city. Some well-known names included Garda Pat Costello and Garda Con Crowley.

The lights were officially switched on by the City Engineer Mr. Stan Carroll. Coincidentally, a few years later when Mr. Carroll retired, he was to provide invaluable assistance to the City Librarian in the setting up of the Waterford Room (see entry for January 1st). The lights themselves cost £2,000 and were operated by detector pads on the road. The public were reassured that they could be switched off "on the occasion of a procession or a funeral". Further traffic lights were envisaged at the Mall, the Clock Tower and Bridge Street.

The junction of Parnell Street and John Street was (and still is) known as the Carstand. This was the spot where jarvey cars lined up waiting for a fare outside the old established grocery and licensed premises of Dower's. This premises was replaced by Winstons & Besco store, which opened in August 1964. Since its closure in the summer of 1984, the building has had a number of uses including a betting shop, a video rental shop and nightclubs, (Jazbah, Rubys and lately The Foundry).

1962

3 JANUARY

Henry Denny

Henry Denny, founder of Henry Denny & Sons, bacon manufacturers, died on the 3rd of January 1870. Henry Denny was born in Waterford in 1798, the son of a boot-maker, while his grandfather was a cooper. He originally started trading as a provisions merchant in Waterford in 1820, when he entered a partnership with a long-established general merchant by the name of Simon Max. In the early 1830s the partnership was dissolved and he began trading on his own. Initially he traded from Bridge Street, and then Queen Street (now the Bridge Street end of O'Connell Street). When he died in 1870 he employed over 400 people and had branched out from Waterford to Cork and Limerick. At the time there were three other large bacon factories in the city: F.E. Barnes in Summerhill, Matterson's in the Glen (later became the Forum Cinema) and J. J. Richardson in Morgan Street.

In 1880 Henry's youngest son Edward set up Edward Denny & Co. in London and began expanding internationally; between 1885 and 1900 it had operations in Germany, Denmark and America. In 1898 Denny bought the rival firm of J. J. Richardson in Morgan Street. In 1932 they were the largest bacon curers in Europe. In 1933 Denny was awarded a gold medal for making the finest sausages at an international food fair in Manchester (this medal is now on display in Waterford Museum of Treasures).

On the 3rd of March 1972 the Denny factory at Morgan Street closed with the loss of 240 jobs. The Hypermarket was built on the site. Kerry Foods bought out the Irish operation in 1982.

1870

4 JANUARY

Strangman's Brewery

Strangman's Brewery in Mary Street closed on the 4th of January 1950 after 158 years, having opened originally in 1792. The following advertisement appeared in The Waterford Herald on the 11th of February 1792:

> *Strong Beer Brewery, Mary Street, Waterford. William Strangman & Company inform their friends and the public that they have commenced the Strong Beer and Ale brewing with hops, from the quality of their drink and attention to Orders, to all our general satisfaction to those who are pleased to favour them with their custom.*

Within a few years it had become Davis Strangman and Company. Egan, in his *History of Waterford* (1894) states:

> *A visit to the Brewery, situated at the further side of the Bridge from the Terminus, will repay the visitor. The engine-house, with its great beam-condensing engine, the hop-stores, the malt stores, the mill-room, with its huge cylindrical malt-screen and archimedian screw, are all small wonders to the usual visitor.*
>
> *The strong beer will require a strong head to imbile freely; the agreeable flavour of the stout is another characteristic of the products.*

It continued trading under the name Davis Strangman and Co. until its closure in January 1950. Four years later in 1954 Cherry's Brewery took over the building and started brewing Phoenix and later Hoffmans (see entry for June 4th).

1950

5 JANUARY

Martial Law

During the War of Independence in August 1920 the British Government enacted *The Restoration of Order in Ireland Act* to address the collapse of the British civilian administration. On the 10th of December 1920 martial law was proclaimed in Cork, Kerry, Limerick and Tipperary. On the 5th of January 1921 this was extended to Waterford in addition to Clare, Kilkenny and Wexford. Two days later the Pickardstown Ambush took place (see entry for January 7th).

The proclamation by General Macready, Commander-in-Chief of the military forces in Ireland, stated:

> *A state of armed insurrection exists, that any person taking part therein, or harbouring any person who has taken part therein or procuring, inviting, aiding or abetting any persons to take part therein is guilty of levying war, against his Majesty the King, and is liable on conviction by a Military Court to suffer death.*

However, an armistice existed until the 11th of January. Any person holding arms or ammunition could hand them into a priest with no questions asked. The proclamation went on to state:

> *After that date an unauthorised person found in the possession of arms, ammunition or explosives or wearing military or police uniform, or similar clothing likely to deceive, will be liable, on conviction, to the death penalty.*

1921

6 JANUARY

Gardaí in Cathedral

An unusual event took place in the Cathedral of the Most Holy Trinity on Sunday the 6th of January 1935 when a large Garda force took up position inside the Cathedral while mass was in progress. The reason for this was to prevent any disturbance while Bishop Jeremiah Kinnane read his pastoral letter defending the proposed sacking of Frank Edwards from his teaching position in Mount Sion Primary School.

The background to this sacking was that Edwards had become leader of the Waterford branch of the Republican Congress in 1934. However the Catholic Church condemned the organisation and saw membership as contrary to Catholic teaching. Edwards refused to resign from the Republican Congress and in October 1934 he was issued with three months notice of dismissal. Despite the intervention of the Irish National Teachers Organisation, the dismissal went ahead.

The sacking divided public opinion in the city for many years, but eventually all public bodies, including Waterford Corporation, adopted resolutions of loyalty to the Bishop. Even the Waterford News refused to publish a letter to the editor by Frank Ryan on the matter, stating: *Owing to the pronouncement made by the Bishop, addressed to all under his jurisdiction in this diocese, and binding on all Catholics, we are precluded from publishing Mr. Ryan's comment.*

Edwards later joined the International Brigade in the Spanish Civil War. He died in June 1983. Note: His brother Jack was shot and killed in Kilkenny Jail during the Civil War in 1922.

1935

7 JANUARY

Pickardstown Ambush

On the evening of Friday the 7th of January 1921 the Pickardstown ambush took place. The IRA plan was to lure a party of British military out of the city by means of a feint attack on the Tramore Police Barracks, but all did not go as expected. Firstly, the British Command sent out a much larger force than expected, (four crossley tenders with about forty soldiers). Secondly, the British force arrived out on the Old Tramore Road rather than the new main road, and finally a shot was fired too early which allowed the troops to take cover. Two IRA volunteers, Michael McGrath and Thomas McGrath, were killed.

In later years the Tramore GAA club was named after the two dead IRA men.

An interesting but distorted account of the ambush was told second hand by a Major General Stone who had served as a junior officer in the Devonshire Regiment at the time. In an interview held decades later he claimed that a friend of his, a Captain Valentine, was involved in the ambush and *using his revolver as a humane killer – killed about a dozen of them*. He also related the tale of a former soldier who visited Waterford in 1939 and mentioned in a pub that he had served with the Devons. A man with a photograph of Captain Valentine approached him saying, *if you see him, tell him we're still after him.*

1921

8 JANUARY

Mayor's Salary

Probably the first benchmarking exercise in Ireland was carried out as a result of a decision made on this date in 1833. The *Parliamentary Reform Act of 1832* had introduced wide-ranging changes to the electoral system (in addition to increased Irish representation at Westminster). Following this, attention was drawn to local government. A commission was appointed to investigate the country's corporations. Waterford Corporation decided to anticipate some reform and on the 8th of January 1833 it set up a committee to ascertain if any reduction in salary costs could be obtained without injury to public services. The committee reported in February and reduced the Mayor's salary from £276.18s.6d to £230. Similar reductions were made to the offices of Sheriff and Recorder.

This did not prevent the arrival of the commissioners in December of that year, and following fourteen days of evidence, the final commission report was scathing in its conclusions.

The report stated that in general, corporations were *in many instances, of no service to the community, in others injurious; in all, insufficient and inadequate to the proper purposes and ends of such institutions.*

In relation to Waterford Corporation it concluded that it was *a totally unrepresentative body, and a self-perpetuating clique.*

Eventually the *Municipal Corporation Act of 1840* reformed ten corporations in Ireland, including Waterford, and replaced them with more democratic and representative authorities.

1833

9 JANUARY

Gallipoli

Readers will be familiar with the song *The Band played Waltzing Matilda*, which deals with the terrible battles which occurred in Gallipoli in Turkey during the First World War, leading to the deaths of 44,000 Allied soldiers. Many associate this great loss of life with Australian and New Zealand armies. However, over 3,000 Irish soldiers lost their lives in Gallipoli fighting either in Australian, New Zealand or British uniform, and twenty-six of the dead were from Waterford. Most were in their twenties, and more than half of them have no known grave.

John Barron, Kilmacthomas
Michael Barry, Kilmanahan
Joseph Bluett, Cappoquin
Paul Bregan, Cappoquin
William Brien, Portlaw
Richard Brown, Waterford
John Burke, Waterford
Albert Douch, Waterford
James Dunne, Dungarvan
Vivian Fausset, Waterford
John Field, Waterford
Patrick Fraher, Waterford
Patrick Hayes, Waterford

Thomas Jackman, Waterford
William Lemmon, Waterford
Francia McGarry, Dungarvan
John Moore, Clonea
James Moran, Waterford
Thomas O'Regan, Ballybricken
Bertie Pope, Waterford
Patrick Power, Tramore
John Sheehan, Faws
Andrew Smith, Ballybricken
James Sullivan, Waterford
Peter Sullivan, Crooke
Thomas Whitty, Waterford

While the initial invasion began in April 1915, the bloody campaign lasted for the following eight months. The final evacuation of Gallipoli took place on the 9th of January 1916.

1916

10 JANUARY

Pere Charles

This is a very sad day in Waterford history, as it was on the 10th of January 2007 that the fishing trawlers *Pere Charles* & *Honey Dew II* were lost off the Waterford coast.

The *Pere Charles* had departed Dunmore East with a crew of five at about 10am that Wednesday morning, and was fishing for herring south of Hook Head. The vessel was with another trawler, the *Suzanna G*. Shortly after 6pm as both trawlers were making their way back to Dunmore, the skipper of the *Pere Charles* radioed, *she's breached on me …stand by us*. This was the last contact with the trawler.

All five crew on board the *Pere Charles* were lost: Billy O'Connor from Dunmore East, Tom Hennessy and his uncle Pat Hennessy, both from Kerry, Andre Dyrin from Ukraine and Pat Coady from Wexford. Of particularly poignant note was that Pat was the third generation of his family to be lost at sea. His father drowned while fishing off Cornwall the previous year, and his grandfather drowned off Kilmore Quay in 1985.

Within a few hours, the *Honey Dew II*, out of Kinsale, sank. The Irish skipper, Ger Bohan, and a Polish crewman, Tomasz Jagla, were lost while two Lithuanian crewmen, Viktor Losev and Vladimir Kostvr, were picked up later, having survived in a life raft on the raging sea for seventeen hours.

Despite massive searches and the raising of the *Pere Charles* from the seabed, none of the bodies were ever found.

2007

11 JANUARY

St. Martin's Gate

In December 1982 builders started work on a new £500,000 building for St. Martin's School at Lady Lane / Spring Garden Alley. However in early January it became clear that the work had stumbled on a major archaeological find, specifically a gate with flanking towers on the old city walls. A campaign for their retention grew overnight and Spring Garden Alley became the Waterford equivalent of Dublin's Wood Quay.

Coincidentally the Waterford Literacy and Historical Society was having its annual luncheon on Sunday the 10th of January 1983. This was attended by the Minister for Agriculture Austin Deasy TD, and also by Eddie Collins, Minister for State at the Department of Industry. Both ministers spoke out strongly in support of preserving the site. On the following day, Monday the 11th of January 1983, a specially convened meeting of Waterford City Council unanimously decided that building should stop and the site be preserved.

This led to consternation from the parents of children in St. Martin's School, who had been fundraising for many years and finally thought a new school was imminent. Following much discussion and consultation, a number of different proposals were considered. These included: building over the site, moving the school to the local convent garden or moving to a new site completely. An offer by Waterford Corporation of a new site in Ballytruckle was accepted in May 1983 and the sod was turned on the new school on the 15th of April 1986.

The remains of St. Martin's Gate can be seen today. A typical 13th century gate, it had a portcullis flanked by twin towers.

1983

12 JANUARY

Glass Technology

Late in 1946 Karel Bacik arrived in Waterford with the intention of reviving the Waterford glass industry (see entry for June 25th). However, as a graduate of a technological university, he recognised that technical education and skills were necessary if he was to succeed. He approached the City of Waterford VEC with a view to starting a course in glass technology at the Central Technical Institute (CTI). The Department of Education was quick to give its approval. With Miroslay Havel teaching design and Bacik teaching glass technology, the course began on the 12th of January 1948.

Due to work commitments Bacik himself withdrew from the course the following year. However Havel continued his association for the next forty years. In 1950 when Waterford Glass was taken over by the McGrath - Griffin consortium, the course was restructured into a pre-apprentice course. Students spent one year on the course followed by a five-year apprenticeship.

John M. Hearne tells of a further link between the CTI and Waterford Glass in his book *Waterford Central Technical Institute 1906 – 2006, A History*. In the early fifties a large number of skilled artisans from Germany were recruited for the factory. Most of these did not speak English. Following a request by the German Legation in Ireland, the CTI set up a special language class for these German families.

1948

13 JANUARY

Council Meetings

As mentioned in the introduction, the Irish Manuscripts Commission published a book in 1964 entitled *Council Books of the Corporation of Waterford 1662 – 1700*. As the following excerpt from the minutes of a meeting of the Corporation held on the 13th of January 1670 show, non-attendance at a meeting was not something taken lightly:

> *Then ordered and concluded by general vote, that every member of this council (being summoned in person or notice left with his wife or chief servant of the time and place) neglecting to appear at council without leave from Mr. Mayor shall pay for every such offence, each alderman two shillings and each common councilman one shilling at the next time they appear, without any favour.*

The attendance at this meeting included a number of Aldermen and Councillors who had, or would hold the office of Mayor: Andrew Richards (1658 & 1666), Thomas Christmas (1664), Thomas Exton (1667), John Heaven (1668 & 1669), William Hurst (1670), and Zachart Clayton (1680).

1670

14 JANUARY

The Munster Packet

Down through the years there was a wide variety of newspapers published and printed in Waterford, with such titles as: *Waterford Newsletter, Waterford Chronicle, Waterford Journal, Waterford Herald, Waterford Advertiser, Waterford Mirror, Waterford Mail,* and numerous others.

Another title was *The Munster Packet*, the first edition of which appeared on the 14th of January 1788. It was printed and published by Matthew Doyle in Peter Street. This newspaper appeared twice weekly and cost two and a half pence. In keeping with the general size of nearly all Irish papers at the time, it was about 18 inches by 12 inches.

It is not known how long this newspaper continued to be published, but in 1801, a related newspaper called *The Waterford Mirror and Munster Packet* was established. This was set up specifically to help in the election of Sir John Newport as MP for Waterford (see entry for February 9th). This paper was published three times weekly. Two years later the reference to the *Munster Packet* in the title was dropped and the *Waterford Mirror* continued in existence until 1843.

Another newspaper with the word Packet in its title was the *Carey's Waterford Packet* which was published for a very short time in 1791.

1788

15 JANUARY

First Female Councillor

The 15th of January 1912 saw the election of the first female Councillor, Dr. Mary Strangman, to Waterford Corporation.

Mary Strangman was born on the 16th of March 1872 into an old Waterford Quaker family that lived in Carriganore House. Her grandfather was John Strangman, founder of Strangman's Brewery. In 1891 she entered the Royal College of Surgeons in Dublin, at a time when this was the only medical school in the United Kingdom to admit women on the same terms as men. On graduation she spent some time in England before returning to Waterford in 1902 and setting up practice at 19 Parnell Street. She became known as Waterford's first lady doctor. In 1908 she became active in the WNHA (Women's National Health Association). This body aimed to stamp out consumption and reduce infant mortality.

In December 1911, *The Local Authorities (Ireland) (Qualification of Women) Act* came into force. This allowed women to be eligible for election to local authorities for the first time. At the local elections held a few weeks later on the 15th of January, Dr. Mary Strangman was elected as the first female Councillor in Waterford. With the support of the WNHA, she was elected from the Tower Ward, an area that included the best and worst of Waterford's living conditions, from the affluence of the Dunmore Road to the slums of Miller's Marsh. She vacated the seat in 1920. In 1923 she was appointed physician at the Waterford City and County Infirmary. Dr. Mary Strangman died in 1943. She is buried in the Quaker burial grounds in Newtown.

1912

16 JANUARY

Waterford Bicycle Club

At a meeting held in the residence of Mr. J.B. Cherry on William Street on the 16th of January 1880, the Waterford Bicycle Club was founded. It is reputed to be the second oldest such club in Britain and Ireland, the Dungarvan Club being the oldest. One of the earliest supporters was Sir William Goff of Glenville, who claimed to be the first man in Waterford and the second man in Ireland to ride the high-wheeled bicycle (see entry for November 23rd). It was Sir William who funded the construction of the cycle track in the People's Park in November 1880 (known as the Goff track). For years this track was considered to be the best racing track in Great Britain and Ireland.

Another cycling club, the Waterford Cycling Club, which was run by the RIC (Royal Irish Constabulary) was founded in the city in 1883.

In 1894 Sir William Goff gifted a silver trophy called the Goff Challenge Shield for cycle racing at the Goff Track. Engraved on the shield were scenes from around Waterford City showing the Clock Tower, the GPO, City Hall and Reginald's Tower. The Waterford Bicycle Club was dissolved in 1914 at the outbreak of World War I and a Mr. Gerald Kelly held the Goff Shield in trust. In 1929, having consulted with the Goff family, the shield was presented to Waterford Boat Club. In 2004 Waterford Boat Club gave its collection of old cups and trophies, including the Goff Shield, to Waterford Museum of Treasures. It is now on display in the Bishop's Palace.

1880

17 JANUARY

Shipwrecks

Waterford, in common with all maritime counties in Ireland, has had its share of shipwrecks down through the centuries. While there are various accounts of these shipwrecks, a comprehensive list was published in 2002 (*Shipwreck Index of Ireland, B. Teresa & R. Larn*). Using a wide variety of sources, the authors have managed to give an account of each shipwreck including dates and locations. This shows that for the coastline of Waterford alone, some 274 shipwrecks have been identified (of which 172 occurred during the 19th century).

To illustrate the details compiled by the authors of this book, the following shipwrecks occurred off the Waterford coast on the 17th of January of various years:

> 17th January 1748: SS Mary on voyage from Jamaica to Swansea.
> Cargo - wood. Master – Whitlow.
> Foundered off Waterford coast, but crew saved.
>
> 17th January 1800: SS Tonyn on voyage from Jamaica to Liverpool.
> Cargo – wood. Master – Towers.
> Sunk in Waterford harbour, fully rigged ship, with six 4-pounder cannons.
>
> 17th January 1809: SS Appledore. Stranded in Tramore Bay.
>
> 17th January 1809: SS Trusty on voyage from Bristol to Tobago.
> Cargo – wood.
> Totally wrecked on Brazen Head Rocks at entrance to Tramore Bay.
> 16 lost, 7 saved

1748 - 1809

18 JANUARY

Timbertoes

The first bridge across the River Suir, known as Timbertoes, was opened on the 18th of January 1794. Designed by Lemuel Cox, construction took a little over nine months, having begun on the 13th of April 1793. Waterford Corporation had no role in the project. The building was organised by a consortium of private citizens, who each invested £100 into the venture on the basis that tolls would be charged.

Originally there was no opening for ships to pass through. In 1800 a small 20-foot drawbridge was opened near the south side. In 1854 a larger 40-foot opening was created at the centre of the bridge to allow paddle steamers through. By the middle of the 19th century, the toll bridge was making substantial profits. Examples of some of the tolls in 1853 are:

Pedestrian 1/2d   *Unladen horse 1d.*   *Laden horse 2d.*
Horse drawn carriage with 6 horses 2s 6d.
Dozen fowl 3d.   *Score of sheep 10d.*   *Score of Cattle 3s 4d.*

Funerals were allowed free passage, which meant the cortege expanded enormously as it went to cross the bridge.

Eventually on the 19th of December 1907 the Corporation purchased the bridge for £63,000. It was declared free of tolls on the 31st of December 1907.

By 1909 it was decided to replace the old wooden bridge with a steel structure. As the new bridge was to be built at the exact same location, a temporary bridge was built twenty yards upstream and opened on the 30th of March 1911. The demolition of Timbertoes began the following day.

1794

19 JANUARY

Waterford Chronicle

The names of a number of old Waterford newspapers were mentioned on the 14th of January. Many of these are available to view on microfiche in the Waterford Room at the City Library in Lady Lane. As yet only a few are available to view online. The Irish Newspapers Archive includes copies of the Munster Express from 1908, however it is a subscription site. The Waterford County Library website includes copies of the Dungarvan Observer from 1918 and the Dungarvan Leader from 1943. The jewel in the crown is nineteen years of issues of *The Waterford Chronicle*, the earliest being from 1811. *The Chronicle* devotes much of its four pages to reports from London and elsewhere. Short news items and advertisements on its front page give a good snapshot of Waterford life at the time.

The following appeared on Saturday the 19th of January 1811:

> ROBBERY AND REWARD
> *Whereas our Stores at the Old Sugar House were entered by some Persons early this morning when Seven Quarter Pound Barrels and several pieces out of another barrel, Prime Mess Beef were feloniously stolen and carried away – We hereby offer FIFTY GUINEAS REWARD for the Apprehension and Conviction of the thieves concerned in said robbery, within the space of six months. Private Information whereby said Robbers or Beef can be discovered shall be proportionally rewarded. Waterford, 18th Jan 1811.*
> *KING AND JONES*

The article continued with a list of eighteen other named individuals, including the Mayor Cornelius Bolton, who added various amounts to the reward to bring the total to 185 guineas.

1811

20 JANUARY

Sebastian Munster

Sebastian Munster was a German cartographer whose book *Cosmographia*, published in 1544, was the earliest German description of the world. The book had numerous editions in many different languages and included a large number of maps.

In the now famous map of Europe by Munster dated 1550, Waterford is the only city in Ireland marked on the map. This was in recognition of the importance of the port by international mariners. Waterford is marked as *Garaforda* on this map. The other cities marked on the map are Edinburgh in Scotland and London, Oxford and Dover in England. A reproduction of this map can be seen on the inside cover of the book *Waterford Treasures* (Ed. Eamonn McEneaney).

Sebastian Munster created an earlier map of the "British Isles" in 1538. Known as the *Angliae Triquetra Descriptio* it again showed Waterford as the only city in Ireland. This time it is marked as *Vatford*. There are four cities shown in England: London, Canterbury, York, and Oxford. This was the earliest printed map to show Wales as a distinct entity.

Sebastian Munster was born on the 20th of January 1488.

1488

21 JANUARY

Teresa Deevy

Teresa Deevy, one of Waterford's most famous playwrights, was born on the 21st of January 1894. While at university she developed Meniere's disease and lost her hearing. In 1925 she began to submit plays to the Abbey Theatre and on the 18th of March 1930 her three-act play *Reapers* opened at that theatre. For the next ten years her plays were regularly performed at the Abbey. Her most successful play was *Katie Roche,* the story of a fiery young servant girl living a quiet life in rural Ireland while harbouring dreams of grandeur. Originally produced by the Abbey in 1936, it was revived in 1949, 1975 and 1994. A US tour began in New York in 1937, and a London production was presented in 1938. Her plays were also performed on Radio Éireann.

Teresa Deevy died in Maypark Nursing Home on the 19th of January 1963.

In recent years her work has tended to be forgotten. However in 2010, the New York based Mint Theatre Company began a three-year project to bring her plays back to the stage. In 2010 *Wife to James Whelan* was produced, the following year *Temporal Powers* was staged and in 2013 *Katie Roche* was presented. An article published in The New York Times in August 2010 stated the following:

> *In the first half of the 1930s Teresa Deevy, a deaf writer from a small city in the southeast of Ireland, was one of the most prolific and acclaimed female playwrights in the world.*

1894

22 JANUARY

Shipwrecks

On the 22nd of January 1862 a massive storm hit the Waterford coast. Five ships were lost on that day alone.

The *Tiger*, a fully rigged ship on a voyage from Boston to Liverpool, was lost on Creaden Head. Twenty-two crew survived, and two were lost.

The schooner *Sophia* was also lost at the same location. All the crew were saved.

The barque *Queen of Commerce,* on a voyage from Antwerp to Liverpool, was lost off Ballymacaw with no loss of life.

In Bonmahon the schooner *Active* foundered offshore with the loss of its five crew.

In Dungarvan, the schooner *Sarah Ann* sank with the loss of its five crew.

The following day, the Italian ship the *Angelicia,* sailing from Queenstown to Newcastle, was also wrecked at Creaden Head, while a day later, the *Nairn* was lost at Brownstown Head.

1862

23 JANUARY

James Power

Municipal elections took place in Waterford on the 15th of January 1903. On the following night the drapery shop of James Power (a candidate for mayor) caught fire. James and two of his employees were sleeping on the second floor. As the stairs were impassable, the second-floor window was the only means of escape. James lowered the two employees to safety from the window by sheets tied together to the leg of a bed. Unfortunately, the fire took hold and he was forced to jump a 30-foot drop. He was rendered unconscious and brought to the infirmary where he remained for six weeks.

On the 23rd of January he was driven from his hospital bed to the Council chamber for the mayoral election. There were three candidates - himself, Maurice Quinlan and John Higgins. Following the vote, Power was elected. He then returned to hospital.

Later that year Mayor Power welcomed Andrew Carnegie to Waterford when he laid the foundation stone for the library in Lady Lane (see entry for October 19th). James Power continued to serve three years as Mayor from 1903 to 1906. He was Mayor during the visit of King Edward VII to Waterford in May 1904, and was knighted by the King as he left the city (see entry for May 2nd).

1903

24 JANUARY

Bridget Redmond

On the 24th of January 1933 Bridget Redmond (wife of the late Captain William Redmond) was elected TD for Waterford. This continued a Redmond tradition in Waterford that was ongoing since her father-in-law, John Redmond, first secured the seat in 1891. When John Redmond died in March 1918, his son Captain William Redmond took the seat and held it until he died in April 1932. There was no immediate by-election for this vacancy, and the seat remained unfilled until a snap general election was held on the 24th of January 1933. Although Bridget did not top the poll on the first count, she was the first candidate to be elected after the third count.

Born in Co. Kildare in 1904, Bridget Redmond (nee Mallick) attended the Ursuline Convent in Waterford from 1916 to 1922. She married William Redmond (eighteen years her senior) on the 18th of November 1930. However she was widowed within seventeen months. Like her late husband and father-in-law she never lived in the city, preferring instead to visit frequently to give account of her stewardship. Her politics was an unusual mix of both left and right wing. While she was opposed to de Valera's economic war with Britain she was also a committed Blueshirt. She represented Cumann na nGaedheal, (later Fine Gael) during seven consecutive general elections.

Bridget died in May 1952, and so ended the Redmondite flame in Waterford.

1933

25 JANUARY

Civil War Executions

Three months after the outbreak of the civil war in 1922, the Free State Provisional Government introduced *Army Emergency Powers*, which had the effect of instituting martial law for the duration of the conflict. This legislation allowed for the execution of men captured bearing arms against the state. Seventy-seven people in total were executed during that period.

Only two such executions took place in Waterford. These occurred on the 25th of January 1923. Two Youghal men, Michael Fitzgerald and Patrick O'Reilly, were found guilty of possession without proper authority of arms and ammunition at Clashmore on the 4th of December. Both were sentenced to death. On the morning of Thursday the 25th of January the two men were marched from Ballybricken prison to the parade square of the burnt-out Infantry Barracks in Barrack Street where they were executed.

Thirty years later, two of the streets on the Cork Road were named Fitzgerald Road and O'Reilly Road in honour of the men.

The Commander in Chief of the national army at that time was Richard Mulcahy, who was born in Waterford in 1886 (see entry for May 10th). The legacy of these executions during the Civil War was to last for years. In 1948 Mulcahy was leader of Fine Gael, but had to step aside and allow his colleague John A. Costello to take the post of Taoiseach, as many of the coalition parties never forgave him for his role in the Civil War executions.

1923

26 JANUARY

Great Lewis Sank

On the 26th of January 1645 the *Great Lewis*, the flagship of the Cromwellian fleet, sank off Duncannon Fort.

In 1642 the Civil War began in England, while in Ireland the Confederation of Kilkenny was formed to oppose Cromwell and the parliamentary forces. The soldiers in Duncannon Fort declared for Parliament while the Irish confederate forces were loyal to the King. Cromwell sent four ships to relieve the fort. These were the *Great Lewis* (the 400-ton flagship of the parliamentary forces), the *Madeline*, the *Mayflower* and the *Elizabeth*. The Confederates who were besieging the fort attacked the ships. Three managed to cut their cables and get away. The *Great Lewis*, however, was caught in an unfavourable tide and was prevented from moving off. Having come under heavy fire its masts broke and she drifted out of range. The ship was so seriously damaged that she sank two days later, on the 26th of January 1645.

The wreck remained undisturbed for over 350 years until 1999, when Waterford Port discovered ship's timbers during dredging work. Following a number of dives by Dúchas, the exact position of the wreck was established, and it is now a protected site. She lies eight metres below the surface of the water in the main shipping lane of Waterford Harbour.

Note: Dúchas has never been able to definitively say that the wreck found is actually the *Great Lewis*. The Archaeology Heritage Guide states, *having considered the location of the wreck, underwater archaeological results and historical research, the prime candidate is the HMS Great Lewis.*

1645

27 JANUARY

Corporation By-Laws

Two interesting decisions were made by Waterford Corporation at its meeting held on the 27th of January 1682:

That any carman that hereafter shall be found to drive his horse or suffer him to go alone in the streets without leading him by the head shall forfeit the sum of one shilling sterling, whereof half to the informer and the other half to the poor of the parish where the offence shall be discovered.

Also that the carman of the city do carry away the dirt, dung and rubbish of the city at one penny per load in close carts, upon pain that any carman refusing to do so shall not be suffered to work or carry anything in their carts on the Quay or any other part of the city. And no carman do carry any water for sale from any conduit of the city upon pain of one shilling each hogshead, whereof half to the informer and the other half to the poor of the parish.

1682

28 JANUARY

King William of Orange

The early years of the 1690s saw the beginning of the Penal Laws following the end of the Williamite Wars. The Battle of the Boyne occurred in 1690 and the Flight of the Wild Geese occurred after the Treaty of Limerick in 1691. The extent to which Waterford Corporation accepted this new state of affairs can be seen by the tone of the following letter sent to King William of Orange on the 28th of January 1695, following the death of his wife Mary II:

We your majesties most dutiful, loyal and in peculiar manner obliged subjects, the mayor, sheriffs, and citizens of Waterford in your majesties kingdom of Ireland, being deeply affected with the sense of God Almighty heavy displeasure against us (for our own great unthankfullness and grievous sins) in depriving your majesty and these kingdoms of your most gracious and pious princess the queen, do in all humble manner console with your majesty and the rest of your loyal and good subjects that great and surprising loss. And under the like sense of our unworthiness (to enjoy so great a blessing as the continuance of your most sacred person in life and safety manage all the malice and contrivances of your majesties implacable enemies to be still the bullwork of our religion, liberties, and properties) do most sincerely offer up our unfeigned prayers and thanksgivings to the divine goodness for so singular and unparalleled mercy, humbly prostrating ourselves, our lives, and fortunes at the feet of your most sacred majesty with our most cordial and inalterable resolutions to stand by your majesty against all malicious attempts of any persons whatsoever to oppose your majesties government over the nations of Great Britain and Ireland; for the long and prosperous continuance whereof in all possible success and safety, honour and renown shall always be the devout prayers of us your majesties most faithful subjects, Attested under our common seal at the council chamber in your majesties said city of Waterford, the twenty-eighth day of January in the sixth year of your majesties reign.

1695

29 JANUARY

Advertisements in 1926

There are a number of old Waterford newspapers which are available online. These are a treasure trove of information about life in the 19th or 20th century. In many issues the advertisements give a clear snapshot of life at the time. The local papers for the weekend of the 19th of January 1926 include the following:

Doyle and Dillion at 76 The Quay had *the best selection of Lucky Wedding, Keeper and Engagement Rings*.

William Aylward, family grocer, tea, wine and spirit merchant at O'Connell Street and Thomas Street announced that he had the *finest new season's teas*. The advertisement also mentioned that *Stabling accommodation was free to customers*.

M. Doyle, Gaelic Outfitting Stores at 39 the Quay was offering *Suits to order from £3 15s 0d* and customers were invited to call for patterns.

The City and County Loan Company at O'Connell Street was offering loans of £10 upwards to *Ladies, Gentlemen, Farmers, Shopkeepers, Government Officials and all responsible persons on approved personal security – note of hand alone and without publicity*.

What is notable also is the number of advertisements placed by British concerns in Liverpool, Manchester, and Birmingham seeking *rabbit, game and poultry consignments*. Another advertisement placed by a London firm was seeking *rabbit, fox, otter, and badger skins* in addition to *horse hair*.

1926

30 JANUARY

Seahorse

In late January 1816 the troopship *Seahorse* left Ramsgate in Kent on her voyage to Cork. On board were 16 officers, 287 soldiers, 33 women and 38 children. In addition to the Master of the vessel, the crew consisted of 17 men. The officers and soldiers were members of the 2nd Battalion of the 59th Regiment assigned to garrison duty in Cork.

By the 29th of January, poor weather conditions had set in. They identified their position at close to Ballycotton Island in Co. Cork, but by the following morning they had drifted off Minehead in Co. Waterford. The weather deteriorated further, and many of its sails were then in ribbons. An attempt to drop anchors off Brownstown Head failed and eventually the *Seahorse* grounded about a mile from shore in Tramore Bay on the 30th of January. The pounding seas soon wrecked the vessel. Of the 393 people on board only 30 survived.

Dead bodies were washed up on shore over the following weeks. Most of these bodies were buried in three mass graves on the beach or in Drumcannon Churchyard. A memorial originally located at the crest of the beach was repositioned to the Doneraile Walk in 1912.

After the tragedy Lloyds of London funded the building of pillars, including the erection of the Metal Man, to prevent similar calamities. The two pillars at Brownstown Head and the three pillars at Newtown Head were erected in 1821. The Metal Man was positioned on one of the Newtown towers in 1823.

1816

31 JANUARY

Tramway

At various times throughout history the cities of Cork, Dublin and Galway have had town tramway systems, whether horse drawn, steam or electric. Waterford has never had such a system. However, a horse drawn tramway system was planned in the late 19th century. On the 31st of January 1878 Waterford Corporation adopted a report from their Railway Committee approving the application from the Waterford, Dungarvan and Lismore Railway Company for the construction of a double line of tramway from Gibbet Hill in Gracedieu to Adelphi Quay. It was assumed at the time that any future urban expansion would occur on the Gracedieu side of the city.

Hand in hand with the proposed tramway was a proposal to link the main railway network to it. At that time the terminus for the Dungarvan and Lismore line was at Waterford South Station which was located at Bilberry. A link railway was to be built from this Bilberry station by tunnelling through Bilberry Rock to a city centre terminus at Bridge Street. Although an Act of Parliament was obtained to allow this to take place, the railway company never proceeded with the link railway. Without this connection to the main railway network the proposed tramway would have been a financial disaster and was therefore abandoned.

1878

1 FEBRUARY

Council Books of Munster

Between 1570 and 1672 the Province of Munster was administered by a council whose chief officer was called the Lord President. This council oversaw the first major plantation in Ireland in the 1580s. However the province suffered a number of armed conflicts, including the Desmond revolt of 1579, the rebellion of 1598 and the Battle of Kinsale in 1601. This resulted in most of the settlers leaving the countryside. A renewed council led by Sir George Carew re-constituted the plantation. The only surviving record of this council is the register for the period 1599 to 1649. This is preserved in the British Library.

In 1999 Margaret Curtis Clayton began transcribing the manuscript and in 2008, the Irish Manuscripts Commission published it in book form as *The Council Book for the Province of Munster 1599 – 1649*. As mentioned earlier, the Irish Manuscripts Commission had already published the *Council Books of the Corporation of Waterford 1662 – 1700* in 1964.

The Council Book for the Province of Munster is full of interesting nuggets of relevance to Waterford.

For example on the 1st of February 1601 the President of Munster, Sir George Carew, authorised the payment of £2043 6s 3d to the Mayor of Waterford for expenses incurred in the landing of over 900 soldiers at Waterford, and also for supplies to Her Majesty's Army then in camp in Kinsale. This was seven months before the Battle of Kinsale in September 1601.

1601

2 FEBRUARY

City Hall

On this date in 1816 Waterford Corporation moved its headquarters from the Exchange building on the Quay to the Assembly Rooms (now City Hall) on the Mall. The Exchange was at the present site of the Ulster Bank (see entry for August 22nd).

City Hall itself was not originally built as a city hall, but as Assembly Rooms and Playhouse. It was built by a group of Waterford's leading merchants. While originally designed in 1783 by John Roberts, it appears to have taken a number of years to finish the building between 1784 and 1788. The Playhouse opened in 1784, the Assembly Rooms in 1785 and the Great Ball Room, also known as the Grand Banqueting Room, in 1788 (a number of different authors give conflicting dates for these).

At the very first meeting of the Council in the new venue, it was decided that the room where they assembled be called the Council Chamber, and the building be called the Town Hall.

Ryland in his *History of Waterford*, published eight years later in 1824, describes the Town Hall as follows:

> *The new Town Hall is a fine building, situated on the Mall, contiguous to the Bishop's Palace, and having a view of the river Suir. The front, faced with stone, presents a good appearance, and is admired for its just proportions and the simplicity of its style. The principal entrance opens into a public hall, or exchange, which was formerly the resort of merchants, who assembled here to make contracts, and transact other commercial business. Under the same roof with the town-hall, is a very neat theatre, and also a handsome suite of rooms for public entertainments.*

1816

3 FEBRUARY

Val Doonican

Val Doonican, singer and Freeman of Waterford, was born on the 3rd of February 1927. The youngest of eight children, the family home was in 10 Passage Road, just around the corner from St. Alphonsus Road. When his father died he left De La Salle and obtained a job in Graves (building suppliers). He gradually worked his way into the music business, first by getting a summer gig in Courtown Harbour. He then featured in a Radio Éireann show sponsored by Donnellys. By 1951 he was in the resident band at the Olympic Ballroom in Dublin, after which he moved to London.

As a result of a performance on *Sunday Night at the London Palladium* he was offered his own show on BBC, a show which lasted for twenty years. In 1964 his recording of *Walk Tall* entered the UK charts and was followed by numerous other hits. In 1970 he was the subject of a television programme *This Is Your Life* with Eamonn Andrews.

He stopped touring in 2009 at the age of 82. The same year he was Grand Marshall for the Waterford St. Patrick's Day Parade. He was awarded the Freedom of Waterford on the 17th of June 2011 (the same day that Brendan Bowyer was also awarded the Freedom of the City).

1927

4 FEBRUARY

Tops of the Town

From 1975 to 1996 the Irish equivalent of the X-Factor was the John Player Tops of the Town. The national finals were televised live each June and attracted massive audiences. It was on the 4th of February 1962 that the original Tops of the Town was first produced in the Theatre Royal.

Devised as a fundraising event for De La Salle Stephen Street School in 1961, it started life as a talent competition. A framework and rules were devised where each participating group would be drawn from a particular industry and would present a one-hour variety show in the Theatre Royal. Twelve groups entered for that first Tops of the Town. These included Ironfounders, Denny's, Modern Bakeries, John Hearne & Sons, Sack & Bag Co., Snowcream, Waterford Glass, St. Otteran's and the L&N. Two shows were presented each night over six consecutive Sunday and Thursday nights, with the first show on the 4th of February. The semi-finals were held at the end of March, with the final on the 5th of April. The winners were the Ironfounders who defeated the Glass by a very small margin.

The Tops went nationwide in 1964 when John Player came on board as sponsors. In 1975 RTÉ commenced broadcasting the national finals and for the next twenty years thousands of performers and back stage helpers participated. However the Tops became a victim of its own success. In an attempt to become bigger and better the productions got progressively more expensive until the cost of producing shows became prohibitive without major sponsorship. The last televised final was held in 1996 and the Tops petered out after that.

1962

5 FEBRUARY

The Rockabill

On the 5th of February 1931 the new Clyde Shipping Co. steamer *Rockabill* arrived in Waterford on her maiden voyage from Liverpool. Built by Henderson and Co. from Glasgow, she was 270 feet in length. She had accommodation for only 12 passengers, but had pens for a total of 410 cattle and 32 horses. While her main and lower decks were fitted out for the carriage of cattle, she also had a refrigerated hold for the conveyance of butter and perishable goods.

Over the next thirty-one years the *Rockabill* carried over half a million cattle and a million tons of cargo between Waterford and Liverpool. She continued sailing for most of the war years, but was requisitioned by the Admiralty for eighteen months from September 1943.

The *Rockabill* was involved in a number of minor accidents, many of which occurred when she was entering or leaving dock in Liverpool. In June 1941 she ran aground at the entrance to Waterford harbour. She was towed off by the coaster *Mayflower* and suffered little damage. On the 15th of December 1956, as she pulled out from the North Wharf, she was caught in the strong current of the incoming tide and struck a wooden structure attached to Redmond Bridge. She had to wait for about four hours until the tide turned before she could free herself.

The *Rockabill* was retired in April 1962.

1931

6 FEBRUARY

Freedom of City

The concept of Freeman goes back to the original King John Charter of 1215 (see entry for February 22nd). However the modern version of honorary Freedom was established by the *Municipal Privilege Act 1876* which put it on a more regular footing throughout Ireland.

On the 6th of February 1877, Waterford conferred its first honorary Freedom on Isaac Butt.

Isaac Butt was born in Co. Donegal in 1813. Having trained as a barrister, he was elected MP for Youghal from 1852 to 1865. He was later to become MP for Limerick from 1871 to 1879. He is best remembered as the founder of the Home Rule League, or Home Rule Party, in 1873. Butt died in 1879.

The Irish Parliamentary Party replaced the Home Rule Party in 1882. In 1913 John Redmond described Butt as *the father of Home Rule*.

However, Waterford Corporation seemed to reward Butt for other things, as the actual citation reads:

> *in recognition of services rendered ... in restoring this Corporation the privilege of nominating the gentlemen to act as High Sheriff of this ancient municipality.*

Coincidentally Isaac Butt was also the first recipient of Freedom of Dublin City on the 16th of October 1876, and also of Limerick City on the 1st of January 1877.

1877

7 FEBRUARY

SS Thompson Hankey

The history of shipbuilding in Waterford has been fully explored by Bill Irish in his excellent book *Shipbuilding in Waterford 1820-1882*. Some interesting facts from that book include:

- Over 100 ships were built in the city between 1820 and 1882
- The first iron steam ship to sail into a Russian port was built in Waterford
- Five transatlantic passenger liners were built in Waterford for the London - Le Havre - New York line

There are many anniversaries of ship launches. The *Thompson Hankey* was launched on Saturday the 7th of February 1853. This was the first fully rigged ship built by White's shipyard in Ferrybank. At 682 tons, she was ordered for the London - Mauritius trade by James Blyth, a London ship owner based in Mauritius.

White's yard had by this time developed an international reputation for wooden shipbuilding. Following the launch of the *Thompson Hankey*, White's received orders for two more fully rigged ships from James Beazley of Liverpool. The *Madge Wildfire*, at 778 tons, was launched in 1854 and the *Merrie England*, at 1045 tons, was launched in 1856. The *Merrie England* was the largest wooden sailing ship built in Ireland.

In the 1860s White's wooden shipyard went into decline due to the increased demand for iron steam ships. The shipyard eventually closed in 1873.

1853

8 FEBRUARY

City Charter

During her reign Elizabeth I granted three charters to Waterford. The first was dated the 8th of February 1568. Unfortunately this Charter has not survived.

However her second Charter dated 1574 has been preserved and is on display in the Medieval Museum. This is an extremely important document in the development of Waterford as it completely separated the city and county administration. Although prior to this the city had been governed by a mayor and two bailiffs, it now had the authority to elect sheriffs instead of bailiffs. The first elected sheriffs were James and John Sherlock.

The 1574 Charter is also important as it illustrates for the first time the inclusion of the three galleys surmounted by the three lions in the coat of arms. This remained the official coat of arms for the city until 1953 (see entry for February 16th).

1568

9 FEBRUARY

Sir John Newport

One of the most prosperous and influential families in Waterford in the late 18th and early 19th centuries was the Newport family. Originally of Dutch origin, John Newport first came to Carrick on Suir in 1670 where he set up a woollen factory. His son Simon was admitted a Freeman of Waterford in 1719. His grandson, again called Simon, was founder of the Newport Bank, which for a time was the largest bank in Waterford.

In the realm of politics, the Newport family took centre stage. Between 1727 and 1841 the office of Mayor was held ten times by a member of the family. In 1782 when Sir Simon Newport (nephew of the bank's founder) was Mayor, three other members of the family were Aldermen: Sir John, Simon and William Newport. Indeed their control over city affairs was so tight that in 1818 a secret agreement was made between the Newport and Alcock families which effectively divided up the various offices between them. The power of ruling families such as the Newports and the Alcocks was not destroyed until the Municipal Reform Act in the 1840s.

Sir John Newport, son of the Waterford banker, was born in October 1756. He was made a baronet in 1789. In 1802 he unsuccessfully ran for the Waterford seat in the general election. However, he successfully appealed the result on the basis that the Alcock faction had created over one hundred new Freemen the day before the election. He remained MP for Waterford until 1832. In 1806 he was made Chancellor of the Irish Exchequer and was Comptroller-General of the Exchequer from 1834 to 1839.

Sir John Newport died on the 9th of February 1843, age 87.

1843

10 FEBRUARY

Redmond Bridge

It was on this date in 1913 that the Redmond Bridge was opened by John Redmond himself (see entry for September 1st). The first bridge across the River Suir, known as Timbertoes, opened in 1794 (see entry for January 18th) and was a toll bridge. Waterford Corporation purchased the bridge in 1907 and it was declared free of tolls on the 31st of December 1907.

By 1909 it was decided to replace the old wooden bridge with a steel structure. It was to be constructed of ferro-concrete by the firm Kinnear, Moodie and Co. from Glasgow. A temporary bridge 60 feet upstream was completed on the 30th of March 1911 and the demolition of Timbertoes began the following day, 117 years after its original opening. The first pile was driven on the 5th of June 1911, with 208 piles driven in total. The new bridge was 700 feet long and 48 feet wide with an opening span of 80 feet. The total cost was £71,000. It was certified complete on the 6th of February 1913 and it was opened to traffic on Monday the 10th of February 1913.

The day of the opening was declared a half-holiday by Waterford Corporation. John Redmond MP and leader of the Irish Parliamentary Party, arrived by train at 1.30pm after which he was paraded down the Quay by marching bands with a large following procession. At 3 o'clock Redmond, the Mayor, and members of the Corporation went to the bridge entrance and the opening ceremony took place with approximately twenty-five thousand spectators.

The John Redmond Bridge lasted only 70 years however, and work commenced on the modern bridge in 1982, eventually opening to traffic in 1986.

1913

11 FEBRUARY

New Theatre Royal

The 18th and 19th centuries saw the opening of a number of theatres in Waterford. These included:

- Blackfriars Theatre 1764
- Assembly Rooms and Playhouse 1785
- Market-House Little Theatre 1816
- Theatre Royal Beresford Street 1840
- Bailey's New Street Theatre 1842
- Theatre Royal 1876

Another theatre was the New Theatre Royal in Bolton Street. This theatre opened on the 11th of February 1835. Five years earlier in 1830 the Waterford Equestrian Arena opened on the corner of Beau Street and Bolton Street. Known as the Royal Hibernian Arena, it was sometimes used as a theatre but a stage had to be erected each time. In late 1834, it was taken over by a Mr. Seymour who converted it to a theatre in early 1835. On opening night on the 11th of February 1835, a play called *The Mountaineers* was presented.

The world famous Waterford-born actor Charles Keane performed in a play there in April 1835. Unfortunately the theatre had a short life as it burned down on the 8th of April 1837.

1835

12 FEBRUARY

Ambrose Congreve

On this date in 1740 Waterford Corporation was formally notified that the Lord Justices and Privy Council had not approved of the election of Ambrose Congreve as Mayor. The Congreve family had first settled in the Waterford area in the 17th century when his father the Rev. John Congreve was rector of Kilmacow.

Although he had been Mayor previously in 1736/37, it is not apparent why he was not ratified on this occasion. The election took place the previous June when Alderman Congreve defeated Alderman Henry Mason. Alderman Mason held the office of Mayor in 1730. There is a record stating that the town clerk had brought the city books before the Privy Council in Dublin on the petition of Alderman Henry Mason against the election of Mr. Congreve as Mayor and Francis Barker as Sheriff.

This Ambrose Congreve was a great, great, great, great grandfather of Ambrose Congreve who died in 2011 (see entry for May 24th).

The Congreve family were also related to the poet and playwright William Congreve (1670 – 1729). Some of his most famous quotes include *music had charms to soothe a savage breast* and *Hell hath no fury like a woman scorned*.

1740

13 FEBRUARY

Archbishop Michael Kelly

Michael Kelly, the Roman Catholic Archbishop of Sydney from 1911 to 1940, was born in Waterford on the 13th of February 1850.

Ordained in 1872, he spent some time in Wexford before he was appointed Rector of the Irish College in Rome. A staunch Catholic conservative, he became Archbishop of Sydney in 1911. He played a large part in ensuring that proposed legislation by New South Wales making it a criminal offence to promulgate the Roman Catholic Church's Canon Law on Ne Temere decree was lost by one vote. The Ne Temere decree was a declaration of matrimonial law by Pope Pius X that marriages involving a Catholic are invalid unless performed by a parish priest in his own parish.

In 1922 a coadjutor archbishop was appointed to Sydney with the intention of taking over once Archbishop Kelly had died. By coincidence, the coadjutor was also from Waterford. Archbishop Michael Sheehan was born in Newtown in 1870. Having attended St. John's College and St. Patrick's College, Maynooth, he was ordained in 1895. A brilliant scholar, he spent two years teaching at St. John's College and also became Vice-President of St. Patrick's College, Maynooth.

Archbishop Kelly lived to the ripe old age of 90, dying in 1940. Archbishop Sheehan had retired three years earlier.

A bronze statue of Archbishop Michael Kelly stands outside the main entrance to St. Mary's Cathedral in Sydney.

1850

14 FEBRUARY

Demolition of Waterford Jail

A jail had existed on the corner of Ballybricken hill since the early 17th century. In 1861 construction of a new jail began and was completed by 1864. A number of executions took place during the late 19th century while the last one took place in 1900 (see entry for April 10th). The jail was in full use until 1934, when it was converted to a remand centre. Finally in December 1939 Ballybricken Jail was closed. During the Emergency (2nd World War), turf was stored inside the jail complex. This led to the Jail Wall disaster resulting in the death of ten people in 1943 (see entry for March 4th).

Six years later, on the 14th of February 1949, demolition of the jail began. The demolition contractor was James Vaughan Limited. He was paid £2,000 for the job. The first section to be cleared was the Baker Street end, which had been the scene of the disaster six years previously. Tragedy struck two weeks later on the 2nd of March when one of the demolition workers, a man by the name of Patrick O'Connell, was killed in a fall from the roof of the jail. While the height of the fall was not great, some stonework fell on top of him with fatal consequences. Two other workers were also injured in falls that day.

The demolition took about ten months. By November the site was handed over to the Board of Works who intended to build a new Garda Barracks and Employment Exchange. The removal of such a large building from the corner of the hill of Ballybricken had unexpected consequences. The jail had acted as a windbreaker for generations and now some residents complained that *they were frozen*.

Today the Garda Station stands on the site.

1949

15 FEBRUARY

Cardinal Nicholas Wiseman

While Luke Wadding was probably Waterford's most famous clergyman, no Waterford born person was ever elevated to Cardinal.

However, Cardinal Nicholas Wiseman, who was born in Seville in August 1802, was the son of James Wiseman, a Waterford merchant then living in Seville. His mother was Xaviere Strange. Members of her family had served as Mayor of Waterford ten times between 1432 and 1900. When his father died in 1805 the young Wiseman moved back to Waterford until he was sent to boarding school in Durham in 1810. He was ordained in 1826, made Bishop in 1840, and Cardinal in 1850. He was the first Archbishop of Westminster following the re-establishment of the Catholic Hierarchy in England after a lapse of 300 years.

The appointment of Wiseman as Cardinal and Archbishop of Westminster was not universally welcomed in England, as he was considered to be a militant and outspoken Catholic. *The Times* asserted that is was either a *clumsy joke* or else *one of the grossest acts of folly and impertinence which the Court of Rome had ventured to commit since the Crown and the people of England threw off its yoke.*

Wiseman visited Waterford in September 1857 where large crowds came out to greet him. He died on the 15th of February 1865.

Note: Waterford Treasures has on display a small miniature portrait of the Cardinal's mother, Xaviere Strange.

1865

16 FEBRUARY

Coat of Arms

A striking revelation was made by the City Manager at a meeting of Waterford Corporation on Monday the 16th of February 1953. The manager explained that in preparation for the national festival known as the Tostal (see entry for May 25th), he intended embellishing City Hall using the city's coat of arms. He consulted with the Office of the Chief Herald to ensure that he had the correct version, only to be informed that the version used for hundreds of years was incorrect. According to the Office of the Chief Herald, the three lions should not be there at all. A new patent was subsequently issued by the Office of the Chief Herald in 1953 and while it included the three galleys, the three lions are missing.

The city's coat of arms had developed over a number of centuries. At various stages the three lions appear on their own and were symbols of the English monarchy. Similarly the three galleys also appear on their own and are reported to represent the three galleys belonging to the O'Driscolls of Baltimore captured by the Mayor and citizens in 1461 (see entry for February 20th). The motto *Urbs Intacta Manet Waterfordia*, granted by King Henry VII, also appears in most versions. The Charter of Elizabeth I (1574) is the first time that the three royal lions are combined with the three galleys in a coat of arms for the city. Although most Waterford people are familiar with this version (as displayed over the entrance to City Hall and on the side of the Waterford Credit Union building and on the front cover of this book), the correct version as established in 1953 does not include the three lions.

1953

17 FEBRUARY

RAF Plane Crash

During WWII a total of 167 military aircraft of various nationalities crash-landed in Éire (26 counties of Ireland). Four of these occurred in Co. Waterford, two in Tramore in April 1941 and August 1942, one in Bonmahon in April 1941 and another in Whitestown in June 1941.

Another crash occurred close to the city when on the 17th of February 1943 a British Wellington bomber with a crew of five onboard crash-landed in a field at Six Cross Roads in Kilbarry.

The Wellington was returning from a bombing raid on the U-boat pens in Lorient when it was separated from the other eight planes in the squadron. Its instruments failed and the bomber strayed off course. The aircraft circled over Waterford City for a while, but running out of fuel, the pilot put her down in a large field. Having crashed through a ditch at the end of the field, the undercarriage was torn off, but the crew was not injured. Not knowing where they were, the crew activated an explosive device and fire quickly took hold. The rear turret with four machine guns remained undamaged.

Large crowds arrived from Waterford to view the spectacle, many of whom took home scraps of metal as souvenirs. The crew was later interned in the Curragh and were finally returned home in June 1944.

1943

18 FEBRUARY

Waterford Chronicle

The front page of the *Waterford Chronicle* of the 18th of February 1868 displays two very different aspects of Waterford life at that time.

The first article deals with the building of St. John's Church:

> The Exterior of St. John's Church is now complete. The debt of £1,876 is paid. The amount of contracts for building the tower and the side pinnacles, £1,462, is discharged and nearly £300 has been paid on account of the erection of the ornamental railing in front of the church. Only £70 remains due; that is the amount of contracts for the four lamps on the piers and for painting and decorating the railing and gates.
>
> The Rev. P. Nolan deems it his duty to account thus for the application of the large sum of money entrusted to his care, and to thank all those who have so generously contributed towards the beauty of the House of God.

On the same page are five separate advertisements for "self help" books dealing with sexual disorders, including the following reference to some form of electrical device:

> The most marvellous discovery in medical science. Suffer no longer. Cure yourself of Spermatorrhoea, Nervous Weakness, Loss of Sexual and General Strength, Unfitness for Marriage by the new Electro Galvanic Improved Patent Self Adjusting Curative Appliance. This infallible invention surpasses every other means hitherto discovered for curing diseases and restoring an emancipated and debilitated constitution to its original state, stops wasting discharges, removes depression of spirits, indigestion, languor, impotence, eradicates taint impurity and all causes tending to the absence of offspring and bad health.

1868

19 FEBRUARY

Charter

The Great Charter of Charles I was issued in May 1626 and determined how the city was ruled until the Municipal Reform Act of 1840. A number of Waterford histories claim that on the 19th of February 1627 a supplementary Charter was issued, which related to the admiralty of the harbour and fishery rights.

This Charter conferred on the Mayor the new title *Admiral of the Harbour*, with a silver dart as his symbol of office. Tradition required that on Midsummers Day the Mayor would sail down river to the meeting of the waters (where the Suir, Nore and Barrow meet the sea), cast his dart into the sea, driving out King Neptune (Roman God of the Sea) with the words *According to the Charter as Mayor of Waterford and Admiral of the Port, I claim these waters.*

A number of mayors in recent times have continued with this tradition, with the assistance of the naval vessel the *LE Aoife*.

1627

20 FEBRUARY

O'Driscolls of Baltimore

This date in 1538 sees the final clash between the City of Waterford and the O'Driscolls of Baltimore. The O'Driscoll family from Baltimore were one of the premier marine landlords of the southwest in the 15th and 16th century. Because of their tendency for petty warfare, smuggling, piracy and raiding, they became the scourge of the City of Waterford and led to a conflict that lasted from 1365 to 1538 (see entry for December 25th).

The 170-year conflict finally came to an end in 1538. On the 20th of February 1538, four Portuguese ships laden with wine for Waterford merchants were driven by wind towards the west Cork coast. One of these, *La Santa Maria de Soci*, was driven into a bay adjoining Baltimore. As would be expected, the O'Driscolls ransacked the ship and took all the wine. When word of this reached Waterford, an armed expedition was sent under the command of Captain Pierce Dobbyn, arriving in Baltimore on the 4th of March. They retook the *La Santa*, recovered some of the wine and sailed back to Waterford, having fired some guns at the O'Driscoll castle for good measure.

Waterford decided to put an end to this conflict for once and for all. The City Council prepared a small fleet of three ships with 400 men. They arrived at night on the 1st of April and laid siege to Baltimore. After a few days the O'Driscolls were finished, and their castle was burnt and sacked. Other castles and villages surrounding Baltimore suffered a similar fate. The people of Waterford never had to worry about the O'Driscolls again.

1538

21 FEBRUARY

Master McGrath

Just outside Dungarvan there is a monument on the side of the road which is the only public monument to a greyhound in the country. The greyhound was named Master McGrath. He was born in 1866 at Colligan Lodge, Dungarvan, where Lord Lurgan had a shooting lodge. A story goes that as a pup he was not very robust and was to be culled, but a young farmhand named McGrath asked to be allowed take care of him. The young greyhound soon showed its worth in trials, and Lord Lurgan took an interest. After a number of wins in coursing events, he was entered in the Waterloo cup in 1868. The Waterloo Cup was a three-day coursing event held in Lancashire in England. Originally founded in 1836, it ran annually until 2005 when hare coursing was outlawed.

It was on the 21st of February 1868 that Master McGrath first won the Waterloo Cup. What makes him more memorable is that he won it three times: in 1868, 1869 and in 1871. All sort of theories abound as to why he did not win the 1870 event, as he was 3 to 1 on to win. Many claimed he had been drugged. In fact, he nearly drowned having earlier ran onto ice-covered water which broke under his weight. After the third win Master McGrath received much public attention. He was invited to Windsor Castle to see Queen Victoria and Prince Edward was reputed to have fed him biscuits.

Master McGrath died on Christmas Eve 1871. An autopsy was held to make sure he had not been poisoned. While death from natural causes was the result, the autopsy did show that his heart was twice the size of a normal dog's heart. The Master McGrath monument was first erected at Colligan, but was transferred to its present location in the 1930s.

1868

22 FEBRUARY

Freemen

The concept of Freeman goes back to the original King John Charter of 1215. The *Great Parchment Book*, or *Liber Antiquissimus* (now on display in the Medieval Museum), records the annual admissions of Freemen from 1542. At that stage only Freemen were entitled to vote in civic elections, in addition to having various trading and tax concessions. While most Freemen were admitted for hereditary reasons, it was also possible to get Freedom after a number of years in residence. It could be granted as a reward for services rendered.

An example of an admission of Freedom can be seen from the minutes of the meeting of Waterford Corporation held on the 22nd of February 1687:

> *That John Christmas, John Head, Ben Bolton, Sam Hurst, Celeb Wade, Watts Frith, Charles Christmas, John Lapp, John Walker, and Walsingham Calner are admitted free of the city and sworn accordingly.*

Since Freemen had to swear a number of oaths, including *the oaths of allegiance, supremacy and the little oath in the rules against taking arms* this led to a number of candidates refusing Freedom, as the following entry some years previously in 1677 shows:

> *Then Mr Wm Bowles of this city, appeared at this board and being demanded whether he would accept of his freedom of the corporation refused the same, answering that if he should be free some troublesome and chargeable offices would be put upon him, and he loved his peace and quiet and could not swear.*

As he had been trading in the city for a number of years the Corporation fined him twenty pounds.

1687

23 FEBRUARY

Jarvey Cars

Although the first motorcar was only registered in Waterford in 1899, the damage the mechanically propelled vehicles could do to the jarvey car industry was quickly recognised, and a meeting was held on the 23rd of February in 1900 of all jarvey car owners. The purpose of the meeting was to resist "this motor car epidemic".

The following motion was passed:

> *We the car owners, and car drivers of Waterford, respectively call on the members of the town council to oppose the granting to any company, the licence to run cars or any other such vehicles as public conveniences, as same would be detrimental to the interest of car owners, blacksmiths, farriers, saddlers and shopkeepers in the city. We ask you as the Municipal Authority, having the welfare of the citizens at heart, to oppose the granting of such licences, that would deprive the car owner and drivers and a large number of the working class of their livelihood.*

As expected, this threat to the jarvey's livelihood continued for many years to come. In April 1926 by-laws were proposed to regulate the control of motor hackney cars. The Mayor, in opposing their adoption, stated that he did not agree that there was room for two modes of transportation in the city, and the proposal if passed, would be a hard blow to the jarveys of the city. Another Councillor took the view that a motor taxi could do the work of three or four jarvey cars, which would result in a lot more people going up the steps of the Employment Exchange. In 1928 the introduction of buses to the streets of Waterford also raised the hackles of the jarvey car owners who saw them taking their business.

1900

24 FEBRUARY

T. F. Meagher

Thomas Francis Meagher was born in Waterford in 1823 (see entry for August 3rd). A little known fact about one of Waterford's favourite sons is that he had a drink problem. There were accusations of heavy drinking made against him a number of times in his military career during the American Civil War.

It was during the first two years of the Civil War from 1861 to 1863 that Meagher made his reputation with the Irish Brigade. In the midst of the Civil War in May 1863, he resigned his commission following disillusionment after the Battle of Chancellorsville. After 18 months he returned and a new posting was found for him.

However on the 24th of February 1865 he was relieved of duty. An article published in the March 2000 issue of America's Civil War Magazine claimed that three weeks earlier at the beginning of February 1865, Major Robert N. Scott delivered orders to Meagher and found the General so drunk that he could not understand them. Meagher formally resigned from his commission in May 1865, just after the Civil War ended.

1865

25 FEBRUARY

Waterford Dáil Constituency

This date in 2011 saw a major change to the electoral representation of the Waterford constituency. For the first time in over 84 years the constituency failed to return a Fianna Fáil candidate. It was also the first time in 59 years that a woman, Ciara Conway, was elected. The previous female TD was Bridget Redmond who died in 1952. Normally the Waterford constituency has seen at least one change in its representatives at each election. However there have been four TDs who served for over twenty years since the constituency was created in 1923.

The first was Patrick Little (FF). Elected in 1927, he held his seat for 27 years until he retired in 1954. Little was appointed Minister for Posts and Telegraphs in 1939, a ministry he held for nine years until 1948. Following the death of Bridget Redmond in 1952 Fianna Fáil won the subsequent by-election, resulting in the party holding three of the four seats in the constituency. As a result, Little did not contest the 1954 election.

Tom Kyne (Lab) was first elected in 1948 having bridged a long gap since the previous Labour TD was elected in 1923. He held the seat for 21 years until he lost it in 1969, although he regained it again in 1973. He retired in 1977.

Austin Deasy (FG) was first elected in 1977 and held his seat for 25 years until his retirement in 2002. Deasy was Minister for Agriculture from 1982 until 1987.

Finally in June 1989 Brian O'Shea (Lab) was elected. He held the seat for 22 years until he retired in 2011.

2011

26 FEBRUARY

Waterford Giant

It was on this date in 1875 that James Hugh Murphy, known as the Waterford Giant, died. James was born in Waterford in 1842. One of a family of eight, only one other sibling survived to adulthood.

His family emigrated to America when he was six years old and settled in Baltimore. Although both his father and brother were only about six feet tall, James grew to eight feet. He joined a travelling circus called Barnums where he was billed as the Baltimore Giant and described as *one of the great living curiosities of the world*. His hands were reported as being so large that *one of them could cover the head of a large man*.

When the undertaker came to measure the dead giant for his coffin, it was found that he was a full eight feet tall.

1875

27 FEBRUARY

Patrick's Day

On the 27th of February 1903 a letter was issued from the Mayor's office, but signed by a Canon Flynn, which informed all its recipients that St. Patrick's Day was to be a general holiday in Waterford that year and no business would open.

The letter read as follows:

> *At a meeting of Citizens held in the Town Hall, Waterford, on the 18th February, it was unanimously decided to proclaim St. Patrick's Day a General Holiday, and to entirely suspend business on that day. The movement has met with an unqualified success among all classes of traders, including the members of the Licensed Vintners' Association, and it is believed that not one single shop of any importance will be open for business on St. Patrick's Day.*
>
> *The Committee in charge of the advertising of the project desire to have it announced in every district and parish from which the people travel to this city on the 17th March, that Waterford having decided to observe St. Patricks as a National Holiday, no business will be transacted in the city on that day.*

With this letter Waterford became the first city in Ireland to declare St. Patrick's Day a public holiday. Although the feast of St. Patrick's Day was celebrated for centuries, it was not until the mid-seventeenth century that the 17th of March became a holiday of obligation in the Catholic Church. And it was another Waterford man, Luke Wadding, who was responsible for this.

It was later in 1903 that the *Bank Holiday (Ireland) Act* was enacted by the UK Parliament, having been introduced by the Irish MP James O'Mara. This made St. Patrick's Day a national holiday.

1903

28 FEBRUARY

Hal Roach

On the 28th of February 2012 the Waterford born comedian Hal Roach died. Born in Manor Street on the 4th of November 1927, he was brought up at 12 Grange Terrace. When he was about twelve he entered a talent competition as a boy soprano. He won the competition and went on to tour with a magician called the Great Bamboozalem.

At sixteen years old he was elected a full professional member of the exclusive Irish Society of Magicians. In May 1945 he arrived back in Waterford and performed at the Theatre Royal. While he sang the song *Smilin Through* he was reported to have had the audience in stitches with his *extremely funny antics*. He gradually broadened out as a professional variety artist.

The first and only Irish comedian to pack out Carnegie Hall, he also performed in the White House for Presidents Kennedy, Johnson, Nixon, Ford and Carter. In 1998 he was Grand Marshall of the Washington St. Patrick's Day parade. Among other achievements, Roach featured in the Guinness Book of Records for the longest running engagement of a comedian at the same venue – 26 years at Jury's Irish Cabaret, Jury's Ballsbridge Hotel in Dublin.

2012

1 MARCH

Faithlegg

According to a number of sources, this was the date that the Power Family purchased Faithlegg House and Estate in 1816. The Aylward family was originally granted the lands at Faithlegg by Henry II in 1177. They were disposed by Cromwell in 1654 and the lands were granted to William Bolton. It was not until 1783 that the house was built at Faithlegg by Cornelius Bolton. There is no definitive information as to who the builder or architect was. However a number of sources say that John Roberts *was probably the builder of Faithlegg House.*

A few years later Cornelius Bolton suffered financial problems and Nicholas Power bought Faithlegg House on the 1st of March 1816. The Powers originally lived in Ballinakill House. Six years later in 1824, Nicholas Power funded the building of Faithlegg Church on the grounds where Faithlegg Castle originally stood.

Samuel Lewis in *A Topographical Dictionary of Ireland in 1837* includes the following:

> *Faithlegg House, the seat of N. Power, Esq., is spacious and situated in a well-planted and highly improved demesne, commanding a fine view up the river.*

Nicholas Power served as MP for Waterford in the mid 19th century. In 1870 his estate amounted to almost 4700 acres in Co. Waterford as well as lands in Co. Wexford. The house was enlarged in 1873. In 1935 the house was sold to the De La Salle order who used it as a novitiate until 1985. The Tower Hotel Group purchased the property in 1998.

1816

2 MARCH

SS City of Waterford

The Waterford and Bristol Steam Navigation Company was set up in 1826. The first vessel, the paddle-steamer *Nora Creina* was such a success, completing 52 round voyages in that first year, that they expanded the service with a second ship three years later. This ship was called *The City of Waterford* and it was launched on the 2nd of March 1829. As shipbuilding at Waterford was still in its infancy at that stage, the ship was built in Bristol. The Waterford and Bristol Steam Navigation Company added a third ship, *The Water Witch,* in 1833.

Although the company was initially founded by just three businessmen, Nevins, Lapham and Tandy, gradually the number of shareholders increased. In 1833 the names of Strangman, Morris and Malcomsons were added to the list. Finally in 1835, the Malcomsons founded the Waterford Steam Navigation Company taking over the Waterford and Bristol Steam Navigation Company. This was the first major entry of the Malcomsons into the shipping industry. Within a period of twenty-five years they were to become one of the biggest ship owners in the world.

Coincidentally the first wooden built paddle-steamer built by White's shipyard in 1836 was for Malcomsons Waterford Steam Navigation Company, and named the *PS Waterford*.

1829

3 MARCH

Turkish Baths

Turkish Baths were opened on this date in 1861 on the corner of Hardy's Street and Water Street (Hardy's Street later became South Parade). The baths were just opposite the corner of The People's Park. They remained open for 48 years but closed following a severe outbreak of fever in 1909. They fell into a state of disrepair, and for years were an eyesore at that end of the park.

The Turkish Baths were finally demolished in 1935.

1861

4 MARCH

Jail Wall Disaster

The jail at Ballybricken was in full use until 1934, when it was converted to a remand centre. It closed completely in December 1939. During the Emergency (World War II), turf was stored inside in the jail complex. This turf was stacked against one of the external jail walls. At 12.45am on the morning of the 4th of March 1943, the weight of this sodden turf caused the 60ft high jail wall to collapse. It fell onto a row of small single storey houses called King's Terrace, destroying four houses and damaging three others.

By daylight the extent of the tragedy became clear. Nine people died and eighteen were injured. The dead were James Roche (56), Thomas Roche (20), Maureen Roche (16), Seamus Roche (6), James Barrett (13), Kitty Barrett (16), Betty Stewart (2), Joseph Upton (60), and Patrick Upton (15). One of the injured, John Stewart (56), died three weeks later, bringing the total death toll to ten.

The funerals took place on the following Friday. Eight hearses were used, and the city came to a standstill as the cortege made its way from St. Patrick's Hospital to the Cathedral. A military guard of honour was provided, and the Army No. 3 band played the Dead March from Saul. A relief fund was established to help the survivors, as seventy people had to be rehoused. The inquest held on the 25th of March found that the deaths were due to injuries caused accidently by the falling wall, but added a rider to the verdict that the collapse of the wall was due to an excessive quantity of turf stacked against it. In March 1993, 40 years after the disaster, a memorial plaque was erected at Jail Street.

1943

5 MARCH

Corporation Dissolved

During the reign of James I in the early years of the 17th century the non-taking of the Oath of Supremacy became a problem for Waterford. The Oath required that any person taking public office had to swear allegiance to the monarch as supreme governor of the Church of England. This obviously caused a problem for Catholic mayors in Waterford. This first became an issue in 1606. The Lord President of Munster, Sir Henry Brouncher, decided to get tough with any city whose mayors refused to take the oath. In Waterford, four mayors in turn refused to take the oath and were immediately dismissed. Eventually Sir Richard Aylward, who had been Mayor in 1605 and had previously converted to Protestantism, took the oath and was re-elected.

The regime eased somewhat for a few years until 1614. Between that year and 1618 there were 14 separate mayors elected, each of whom refused to take the oath and were thus promptly dismissed. Waterford administration lay in chaos.

Eventually on the 5th of March 1618, the farce came to an end. The Corporation was dissolved, the charters seized and a government appointee ruled the city. This continued until the death of James I in 1625. The new Charter of Charles I in 1626 allowed a fresh start and business life continued as normal (see entry for May 26th).

1618

6 MARCH

Banks

There were many private banks founded in Waterford in the late 18th century. These included Newport's bank which was founded in 1789 (see entry for June 6th). Others included O'Neal's, Haydens and River's, Hunt & Co., Scott, Ivie & Scott, and Atkins & Scottowe. All of these eventually closed. The one exception to this was the Waterford Savings Bank founded in 1816 (see entry for March 28th).

Gradually in the early 1800s national banks began to open offices in Waterford. The Provincial Bank was the first, opening in 1825. The following year on the 6th of March the Bank of Ireland opened a branch in Waterford.

This was then followed by the National Bank in 1835 while the Munster and Leinster Bank did not open until 1889. It was 1902 when the Ulster Bank came to the city. Initially their premises was situated at the corner of the Mall and Lombard Street but in 1922 they opened new premises on the Quay. The location for the new premises was an historic one as it was the site of the former City Exchange which could be considered to be the forerunner of the modern banking system (see entry for August 22nd).

1826

7 MARCH

Tricolour

The tricolour was first flown publicly on the 7th of March 1848. The flag was flown by Thomas Francis Meagher at the Wolfe Tone Confederate Club, which was located at 33 The Mall. This house was originally built as a townhouse for the Carews of Ballinamona, but became the Wolfe Tone Confederate Club in 1848.

It was then presented by Thomas Francis Meagher to the people of Dublin a month later on the 15th of April 1848. A plaque on a wall in Middle Abbey St. states:

> *the unveiling took place at a soiree of 2000 citizens given to the delegation of the Irish Confederation in the Music Hall at this location*

During the Young Ireland rebellion in July that year, the flag was raised in Ballingarry, Co. Tipperary, after which the leaders, including Thomas Francis Meagher, were arrested.

The flag was not used again until it was raised above the GPO in 1916. It was adopted by the Republic during the War of Independence in 1919 and subsequently by the Free State in 1922. It was given constitutional status in 1937.

The raising of the first tricolour is commemorated on the wall of 33 The Mall by a bust of Thomas Francis Meagher alongside a Waterford Civic Trust Blue Plaque.

1848

8 MARCH

Canon Power

The standard reference book for those interested in the detail of the townlands and parishes of Waterford is entitled *The Place Names of the Decies*. It was written by Canon Patrick Power, who is recognised as one of the great Waterford historians. Canon Power was born in Callaghan on the 8th of March 1862.

His early schooling was in Ballygunner, and then the Catholic University School in Waterford. Having studied for the priesthood in St. John's College, he first served in Liverpool. He then moved to Australia for a number of years. On his return to Waterford he served in the Cathedral and Portlaw. Having developed an interest in archaeology while in Australia, it became his passion when he returned home. He became editor of the *Journal of the Waterford and South-East of Ireland Archaeological Society*, a position he held for many years. From 1910 he lectured in archaeology in University College Cork. He became Professor of Archaeology there in 1915, a position he held until 1932.

A prolific writer, he published numerous books as well as countless articles in journals. Some of the more familiar books include *Parochial History of Waterford and Lismore* (1912), *Place Names and Antiquities of Southeast Cork* (1917), and *A Short History of County Waterford* (1937). However it was his *Place Names of the Decies* which was his greatest work. Originally serialised in the *Journal of the Waterford and South-East of Ireland Archaeological Society*, it was first published in 1907 and republished in 1952. The work detailed the meaning and origins of thousands of Gaelic place names as well as the antiquities of every townland in Waterford. Canon Power died in 1951 at the age of 89 and is buried in Ballinaneeshagh.

1862

9 MARCH

Barracks Handover

At 4pm on Thursday the 9th of March 1922, British forces marched out of the Infantry Barracks in Waterford for the last time. Captain Wedgewood, Officer Commanding 1st York and Lancaster Regiment, carried out the formal handover. Captain Hughes, General Headquarters Staff IRA Dublin, accepted it on behalf of the Provisional Government. After the formal handover, the British troops marched out the gate led by their regimental fife and drum band. As they marched down Barrack Street a mixture of cheering and booing met them. Later they were joined by troops who had vacated the Artillery Barracks earlier that afternoon. That evening the troops (some 200 of them) embarked on the *Great Western* to Fishguard. So ended the British presence in Waterford.

The previous Saturday, the 4th of March, the RIC had left the city. The various barracks were each handed over in turn to Captain Hughes representing the Provisional Government. In this case, some 200 RIC from Waterford and another 40 from Dungarvan left Waterford on board two destroyers, *HMS Heather* and *HMS Stenuous*, for demobilisation in Dublin.

1922

10 MARCH

Abraham Lincoln

On the 10th of March 2009, the Smithsonian National Museum of American History announced that they had found a secret message engraved inside President Abraham Lincoln's watch by a watchmaker who was repairing it in 1861.

The American Civil War began on the 13th of April 1861, when confederate artillery opened fire on Fort Sumpter, which was the Federal fort in Charleston Harbour. The watchmaker Jonathan Dillon who was repairing Lincoln's watch, decided to mark that day by engraving the following on the inside:

> *Jonathan Dillon,*
> *April 13-1861 Fort Sumpter was attacked by the rebels on the above date J Dillon*
> *April 13-1861 Washington thank God we have a government Jonth Dillon*

The watchmaker Jonathan Dillon was actually from Waterford and was one of the Dillon family of goldsmiths and watchmakers in the city. (The last Dillon's jewellery shop in the city only closed a few years ago). Indeed Dillon's of Waterford manufactured a claddagh ring for Queen Victoria around 1849. The story of the hidden inscription had been passed down by generations of the Dillon family in America. Following the discovery of an article in the New York Times in 1906 in which Jonathon Dillon, then aged 84, claimed to have written the inscription, the Smithsonian agreed to examine the watch, and so confirmed the link between Waterford and Abraham Lincoln as announced on this date in 2009.

2009

11 MARCH

William Vincent Wallace

William Vincent Wallace was born on this day, the 11th of March 1812, at Colbeck Street in Waterford. His father, also called William, was a bandsman in the British Army. The following year his regiment was transferred to Ballina, and it was there that William lived for the next 12 years. In 1825 the regiment returned to Waterford and the Wallaces lived in Peter Street. By the age of 15 the young Wallace was a competent organist as well as playing a number of other instruments. In 1827 the family moved to Dublin where both father and son joined the Adelphi Theatre Orchestra.

In 1830 William, now aged 18, moved to Thurles where he took up the position as organist in the Cathedral and also as music teacher in the Ursuline Convent School. There he fell in love with one of his pupils, Alicia Kelly, and they were married in 1831. However to satisfy Alicia's father he first had to convert to Catholicism. In addition he took the baptismal name Vincent to show his good intentions, as Alicia's sister who had entered the convent had taken the name Sister Vincent. That same year the couple moved back to Dublin where he became a Professor at the Royal Academy of Music.

In 1835 the family emigrated to Australia. After a short time Wallace parted company with his wife and child who moved back to Ireland. He then spent the next ten years travelling the world before he settled in London. Here he composed his most successful work, the opera Maritana. It was first performed in Drury Lane on the 15th of November 1845. Wallace composed a large body of music, including ten operas. Wallace died on the 12th of October 1865 at the age of 53. Although he died in France, his body was brought back to London and was buried in Kensal Green Cemetery.

1812

12 MARCH

Martin Cullen Senior

On this date in 1962, Waterford Corporation accepted the resignation of Martin Cullen Senior due to illness, and co-opted his son, Tom Cullen, as his replacement (his grandson, also called Martin Cullen became TD for Waterford in 1987).

Martin Cullen Senior was remembered for many things in Waterford, but one of the highlights was that he was suspended from the GAA while serving as Mayor of Waterford in 1953. Martin was a staunch GAA man, having been chairman of the selection committee when Waterford won its first All-Ireland Hurling Final in 1948. In 1953 the Waterford soccer team won the FAI Shield and he was invited to formally present it to them. As Mayor, he considered himself as Mayor of the entire city and not just one section, and although this was the era of the "ban" he accepted the invitation to Kilcohan Park. (The ban was a rule of the GAA banning all its members from participating in any event to do with non Gaelic games). The GAA frowned on this action and they suspended him for six months, after which Martin resigned from the GAA. (The first President of Ireland Douglas Hyde had suffered a similar fate in 1938 when he attended an international soccer match in Dalymount Park).

Martin Cullen Senior, first elected as an independent Councillor in the late 1940s, was elected Mayor in June 1952. His supporters were so excited by his election as Mayor that they had blazing bonfires in tar barrels outside his house in Yellow Road after his election. Martin Cullen Senior died in September 1984. In all, four generations of the family served on the council during the 20th century, three of them holding the office of Mayor.

1962

13 MARCH

De Valera

In early March 1918 John Redmond died. An immediate by-election was called. There were two candidates, Dr. Vincent White for Sinn Féin and Captain Willie Redmond (son of John Redmond). While Sinn Féin dominated nationalist Ireland, they underestimated the strength of the Redmondite tradition in Waterford.

On Wednesday the 13th of March Éamon de Valera arrived in the city and decided he would immediately start canvassing. As he left the election rooms with another canvasser, four volunteers followed them to ensure their safety. A few minutes later an angry de Valera came back to the room remonstrating that he did not need an escort in any town in Ireland and left again without the escort. The four volunteers followed again but kept out of sight. Fifteen minutes later, Dev was rushed back to the election rooms surrounded by the four volunteers, followed by an angry crowd who had attempted to assault him. After that incident Dev decided that perhaps he did need a bodyguard in Waterford after all.

Some 1,000 volunteers were brought into Waterford to ensure protection for the Sinn Féin candidate and his supporters from the Redmondite supporters. The election campaign continued with regular riots between both sets of followers. Dev stayed in the city until the election results were announced on the 23rd of March. Captain Redmond won with 1,242 votes while Dr. White got 754.

Waterford City continued to defy the electoral tide of Sinn Féin in the general election held later that year, when the city was the only constituency outside of Ulster (with the exception of Trinity College) which did not return a Sinn Féin candidate.

1918

14 MARCH

Parish Courts

During the War of Independence an important part of undermining British rule in Ireland was to ignore the official court system. This was achieved by common acceptance of an arbitration court, which was presided over by local Republicans or Catholic clergy. These Sinn Féin Courts or Parish Courts filled a vacuum created by the conflict. In the first year of the fledging new state, these courts continued until the Dáil had time to put a formal judicial structure in place.

One such Parish Court took place in the Waterford Courthouse on the 14th of March 1922. The Rev. Father O'Connor DFM presided. Two men were *charged with burglariously entering the premises of Messrs. George White and Sons, O'Connell Street on the 26th February*. However there were no goods missing from the shop and there was a question of *drink being taken*. The solicitor for the defence stated that his position was that the present courts had no jurisdiction until trials by jury had been formed. The presiding Fr. O'Connor decided to refer the case to the circuit court.

1922

15 MARCH

Ballinaneeshagh Cemetery

In 1847 an order was made to close a number of graveyards within the city (see entry for July 13th). Soon after, £1000 was allocated to purchase *5 acres of ground in the town land of Ballynaneeshagh, in the Barony of Gaultier in the County of Waterford*. The actual purchase cost £500 and another £500 was set aside to build a wall around it. Fairly soon the graveyard was used for burials of inmates of the workhouse. It would appear unlikely that coffins were used for burial as only sixpence was paid for each one. Because of this, there was a reluctance amongst "ordinary people" to use Ballinaneeshagh as it was seen as a pauper's graveyard.

The actual deed for the graveyard is dated the 15th of March 1848. Initially different sections of the graveyard were allocated to different religious denominations. It was not until the 31st of October 1848 that the Roman Catholic section was consecrated and given the name Saint Otteran's. However there was still a reluctance to use the cemetery for the rest of the 19th century. Indeed it was not until the 1950s that it became a popular place for burials.

1848

16 MARCH

Jail

At a meeting of Waterford Corporation held on the 16th of March 1727, a decision was made to build a new jail. The jail was to be located just above St. Patrick's Church adjoining St. Patrick's Gate. Some of the land belonged to Alderman William Thompson and the Corporation agreed to purchase it for the sum of £30. One of the builders was a Mr. Thomas Roberts, a forefather of the architect John Roberts.

Smith in his *History of Waterford* published in 1746 describes the building as follows:

> *The city-gaol, situation on St. Patrick's Gate is a handsome structure of hewn stone, the arch supported by pilasters of the Tuscan order. The first storey is vaulted with stone, to prevent accidents by fire from the prisoners or escapes, the chimneys, shores, windows, and other apertures are double grated; and the whole strongly built, and commodious for this intention.*

A new courthouse (designed by Gannon) was built beside the jail in 1784, however both were knocked down in the mid-19th century to make way for a completely new jail which was built on the site and opened in 1864. This remained until 1949 when it was demolished and replaced by a Garda Barracks and Social Welfare Office.

1727

17 MARCH

St. Patrick's Day

It was mentioned already that Waterford was the first city in Ireland to declare St. Patrick's Day a public holiday in 1903 (see entry for February 28th). There were various religious and civic events on this day down through the years.

In 1913, in addition to the St. Patrick's Day parade, the members of the CYMS (Catholic Young Men's Association) marched from their rooms in Parnell Square to the Cathedral, headed by the Barrack Street Brass and Reed Band. Later that night the CYMS presented their annual Irish concert in the Theatre Royal.

In 1923, the city was in the midst of an industrial dispute at the Gas Works and many industries had closed down due to lack of power. Even the St. Patrick's weekend edition of the Munster Express could not be printed.

In 1933 a large St Patrick's Day procession was planned. Note this was a religious procession and not a parade. The starting point was at the Clock Tower and the procession was to parade all around the city, taking in Thomas Street, Morgan Street, Ballybricken, Lower Yellow Road, Morrisson's Road, John Street, Michael Street and Barronstrand Street, where an altar was erected for benediction. Householders along the route were expected to decorate their houses appropriately. However heavy rain put paid to all that and the procession had to be abandoned. Instead, the large crowd assembled at the altar in Barronstrand Street for a short service, and benediction was held in the Cathedral.

1913, 1923, 1933

18 MARCH

William Crotty

On this day in 1742 the highwayman William Crotty was hanged. Born in 1712, he is reputed to have turned to crime when his family was evicted from their farm. His various hiding places in the Comeragh Mountains allowed him to remain free for many years. However one of his long time companions, a man by the name of David Norris, betrayed him in exchange for a pardon for himself. Crotty was finally captured on the 16th of February 1742. He was tried at the Waterford Assizes (court) on the 17th of March. Having been found guilty he was sentenced to death. His wife is reputed to have stood up and asked the judge for a stay of execution because she was pregnant and wanted him to see the face of his child. The judge refused, and execution was fixed for the following day.

On the 18th of March 1742 William Crotty was hanged. He was then decapitated and his head put on the spike of the County Jail in Ballybricken. There is a story that his hair continued to grow even as the head rotted. His body was taken to the Leper Hospital in Stephen Street for dissection by medical students. This was apparently a common method of acquiring human cadavers for practical instruction in anatomy. Crotty's skeleton was then publicly exhibited at the Leper Hospital for some time.

Crotty's wife is said to have written a caoine or lament at his wake, the words of which are still in existence. She is also reputed to have thrown herself off the top of the cliff in the Comeraghs which is now known as Crotty's rock.

1742

19 MARCH

Lifeboat

While the RNLI was established in 1824, it was not until the early 1880s that consideration was given to establishing a lifeboat station in Dunmore East. In November 1882 the RNLI's Chief Inspector of Lifeboats and the District Inspector for Ireland visited the area and decided that Dunmore East would be the best location for a lifeboat on the Waterford coast. A boathouse and slipway was built at a cost of £613 (close to the current Coastguard boathouse). The first lifeboat was delivered in June 1884 and the station became operational.

Since then, the station has had ten different lifeboats assigned to it. They include the following:

Henry Dodd	1884 – 1911
Fanny Harriet	1911 – 1914
Michael Henry	1914 – 1919
C. and S.	1925 – 1940
Annie Blanche Smith	1940 – 1970
Douglas Hyde	1970 – 1972
Dunleary	1972 – 1973
Euphrosyne Kendal	1973 – 1975

Note the station was closed for a six-year period from 1919 to 1925.

On the 19th of March 1975 the *St. Patrick* arrived in Dunmore East. At 44 feet, she was a Waveney class lifeboat. During her 21 years of service in Dunmore East she was launched 252 times and saved 83 lives. She was replaced on the 7th of October 1996 by the current Trent Class lifeboat the *Elizabeth and Ronald*.

1975

20 MARCH

Henry D. Inglis

There was a number of travel writers who visited Waterford in the 17th and 18th centuries who subsequently described their experiences (see entries for July 14th and October 17th). One of these was Henry D. Inglis who died on the 20th of March 1835. Inglis visited Ireland in 1834 and published his book *A Journey throughout Ireland during the Spring, Summer and Autumn of 1834* soon after. The following are some extracts from his visit to Waterford:

> *The entrance to Waterford is extremely imposing; the river Suir is crossed by a very long wooden bridge; and the first part of the town one enters is the quay, which whether in its extent, or in the breath of the river, or in the beauty of the opposite banks, is unquestionably one of the finest quays I recollect I have ever seen. At full tide, the views are indeed beautiful.*

> *I noticed among the inferior classes in Waterford – I do not mean the mendicant or destitute poor – too many evidence of idle, slovenly habits, – ragged clothes, which might have been mended, uncombed hair, which might have been in order, dirty caps and faces, ragged children, and an untidy and slatternly look about things, not warranted by the circumstances of the inmates.*

> *Before leaving Waterford, I visited some of the worst quarters of the town, and was introduced to scenes of most appalling misery. I found three and four families living in hovels, lying on straw in different corners, and not a bit of furniture visible; the hovels themselves, situated in the midst of the most horrid and disgusting filth.*

> *There are two watering places, or rather sea-bathing places, in the vicinity of Waterford; Tramore and Dunmore. I visited both, though they scarcely repay a visit. The road lies through an uninteresting country, and the places themselves are merely assemblages of indifferent houses.*

1835

21 MARCH

Bishop Foy

Nathaniel Foy was born in early 1648 in the City of York in Britain. Soon after, the family moved to Dublin. The first definite date we have for Nathaniel is the 21st of March 1663 when he entered Trinity College at the age of 15. He was ordained into the Anglican ministry in 1669 and appointed Bishop of Waterford and Lismore in 1691.

Throughout his life he attempted to introduce reform into the Church of Ireland. In 1692 he persuaded the Mayor to introduce strict observance of the keeping of the Sabbath (see entry for June 18th). In 1702 he oversaw the building of the Widows' Apartments in Cathedral Square (this was for housing the widows of clergymen). In 1704 he formulated a plan to set up a new school for the poor Protestants of Waterford, and was granted a plot of land from the Corporation on the east side of Barronstrand Street. When Bishop Foy died in December 1706 his school was in operation. In addition, he left funds in his will to ensure it was sufficiently endowed.

In 1728 an *Act to better perpetuate and better regulate the charitable foundation of Dr. Nathaniel Foy* was passed by the Irish Parliament. This was the first of a number of acts over the years dealing with the school, including one in 1808, another in 1902 and another in 1930. The school in Barronstrand Street soon became too small and moved premises to Grantstown in 1817. In 1902 they moved to a purpose built school on The Mall. In 1920 the Bishop's Palace was purchased as accommodation for boarders. The Bishop Foy School eventually closed in June 1967 having been in existence for 260 years. Soon afterwards the building was demolished and the ESB Office (now Waterford Crystal) was built on the site.

1663

22 MARCH

Airmount

An unusual event occurred on this day in 1952. Airmount Maternity Hospital owed the Corporation £130 in rates. As they had not paid the debt the bailiffs were called in. On Saturday the 22nd of March 1952, the bailiffs arrived at the hospital and attempted to seize the matron's car in lieu of the rates. They were unsuccessful and the following week the matron used her bicycle to get to work.

The Waterford Maternity Hospital had its origins in a facility in Barrack Street, but moved to Parliament Street in 1838. Run as a charitable institution, it delivered over 10,000 babies over the next 100 years. In 1948 Waterford Corporation acquired a two-acre site and in April 1949 the first sod was turned for Airmount Maternity Hospital. Dr. Noel Browne opened the hospital in 1951. However the voluntary committee did not have sufficient funds to run the hospital, and the Department of Health refused to take responsibility for it. Therein lay the problem with the non-payment of rates. Approaches were made to the Medical Missionaries of Mary in Drogheda who took over the hospital in 1952.

Airmount hospital closed in 1995 (see entry for July 25th).

1952

23 MARCH

Count John McCormack

Although only aged twenty-four at the time and still at the beginning of his career, Count John McCormack packed out the Theatre Royal for two performances on this date in 1908.

Organised as a fundraising event for St. John's Church, initially there was only meant to be one evening concert. However tickets sold out so quickly that a matinee was also put on. In addition, special trains ran from Dungarvan, Clonmel and Carrick for the event.

A number of soloists performed including Miss Annie MacCabe, soprano, Miss Lucy Becker, contralto, Mr. Maurice Murray, tenor and Mr. Frank Twigg, baritone. However it was John McCormack that the audience wanted to hear. On the night, he had to sing three encores before the audience would leave the theatre.

As mentioned, McCormack was only twenty-four at the time, and had made his opera debut in Covent Garden the previous year. For the next thirty years he toured the world. In 1928 he received the title of Papal Count from Pope Pius XI. He is best remembered for his performance during the Eucharistic Congress in Dublin in 1932.

Count John McCormack died in September 1945.

1908

24 MARCH

Food Parcels to POWs

Nearly 5,000 men from Waterford joined the British Army and fought in World War I. By the time the war was over, some 700 of these had been killed in action. During the war itself many were taken prisoner and held in Prisoner of War camps. The Germans held over 2,000 Irish POWs in a camp in Limburg in Germany. The Germans had hoped that by concentrating all the Irish in a single camp, Roger Casement would have an opportunity to recruit men for an Irish Brigade. Previously, Casement had approached the German Government with a view to creating an Irish Brigade in return for German help in supplying the Irish Republican cause. However Casement managed to only recruit 55 men.

In early 1915 an appeal from Waterford soldiers who were prisoners of war in Limburg reached the city. A committee was set up, and subscriptions were sought from local firms and individuals. The first parcels, made up of food items, clothing and cigarettes, were sent on the 24th of March 1915. Within weeks postcards were received from the prisoners thanking them for the parcels and asking that they would be continued. A prisoner exchange which occurred in September 1915 included a Waterford man, Private J. Casey from 6 Well Lane. He claimed that prisoners in the camp were living solely on the contents of parcels from home.

In March 1916 there were a total of 80 Waterford men in the Limburg POW camp. A flag day was held in March of that year in order to fund more food parcels.

1915

25 MARCH

Charter

Waterford City Council has in its possession six Charters from the 15th century dating from 1449 to 1488. The fourth of these was issued by Richard III on the 25th of March 1484.

To put this date into context, the Mayor in that year was James Rice who held the office of Mayor eleven times and whose contribution to the city was immense (his cadaver tomb can be seen today in Christ Church Cathedral).

Other matters of interest from around that time and detailed in the Great Parchment Book include:

- The gates of the city were closed at 6pm from Michaelmas to Easter and at 9pm from Easter to Michaelmas. (note Michaelmas, or the feast of Saint Michael the Archangel occurred on the 29th of September). A special licence from the Mayor was needed if the gates were to be opened outside these hours.
- The authority of the Mayor was supreme. Anyone who shed his blood was liable to a fine of £100 or suffer the loss of the right hand.
- Breaking the glass windows of churches or chapels was specifically outlawed, and any man, woman or child that did so could be fined an amount equal to the cost of repair.

1484

26 MARCH

Michael Collins

The Anglo-Irish Treaty was signed on the 6th of December 1921, and approved by the Dáil on the 7th of January 1922. The first Free State election was set for the 16th of June 1922. Prior to the election, both sides in the treaty debate undertook tours of the country explaining their position and seeking support in the election.

On Sunday the 26th of March, Michael Collins addressed a "monster" public meeting which was held on the Mall. Over 15,000 attended the meeting, however a party of about sixty irregulars continuously tried to disrupt the proceedings. In introducing Michael Collins, the Mayor Vincent J. White, stated that he was the man who won the war for Ireland. In his address to the crowd, Collins immediately attacked de Valera's position. He made particular reference to a speech made by him the previous week in Thurles, where de Valera had suggested the possibility of the IRA wading through the blood of the soldiers of the Irish Government to get their freedom. This was the first mention of the possibility of civil war.

Following the meeting Michael Collins made his way to Dungarvan for another meeting. Here the platform used was the back of a lorry but as the Chairman of Dungarvan UDC began to introduce Collins, the lorry began to move. Three men had entered the cab and proceeded to drive the lorry away. Eventually it dawned on the crowd what was happening and they set off in pursuit. It finally came to a halt when one of the party on the back of the lorry drew a revolver and put it through the glass at the back of the cab. Putting the gun to the head of the driver he ordered him to stop. In the confusion the driver and his companions then made their escape.

1922

27 MARCH

French Church

Greyfriars, the ruins of the Franciscan Friary, is also known as the French Church. This results from a decision taken by the City Council on the 27th of March 1693:

> *That the city and liberties do provide habitations for fifty families of the French Protestants, to drive a trade of linen manufacture, they bringing with them a stock of money for their substance till flax can be sown and produced in the lands adjacent, and that the freedom of the city be given gratis and that the Mayor and Recorded are desired to acquaint the Lord Bishop of this diocese therewith.*

The Protestant Bishop at the time was Bishop Nathaniel Foy (see entry for March 21st). He immediately set about finding a suitable place of worship which might be exclusively used by these French Huguenots. He settled on the Chapel of the Franciscan Friary. The Friary was dissolved in 1539, and the Holy Ghost hospital was set up there in 1545 (see entry for April 2nd & October 28th).

The Huguenots held their services in this chapel for over a hundred years which led to the name French Church. Gradually the Huguenots merged with the Irish Protestants and left their church in favour of St. Olaf's. The roof of the French Church collapsed during the early years of the 19th century.

According to tradition, the Huguenots are credited with the introduction of the blaa into Waterford. Originally called *pain blanc* by the French, it was corrupted by Waterfordians to the blaa.

1693

28 MARCH

Savings Bank

In early 1816 a barrister in Waterford by the name of Horace Twiss mooted the idea of a savings bank when he stated at a public meeting:

> The poor it is common to say have the hopeless vice of wasting their earnings in idleness or drink. But it seems to me that their improvidence is owing, not so much to evil inclinations as to want of a secure depositry for savings too slender to be invested in Public Funds.

He went on to suggest:

> the establishment of a Savings Bank among the poor to be managed on their behalf by the higher classes.

A meeting took place on the 28th of March 1816 to establish the savings bank. The bank was to be established on a non-profit basis, and overseen by a board of trustees. This Waterford Savings Bank was the first to be established in the country.

The bank began its activities in the Exchange Building and opened on the 5th of August. That first day attracted seventy-five depositors. The lowest amount which could be deposited was 10d. and the highest was £30 with an interest rate of 4% per annum. A total of £58 3s 9d was deposited on the first week. By the second week deposits had increased to £64 18s 6d. Twenty years later deposits had risen to over £75,000. In 1849 a new building was opened in O'Connell Street.

In 1988 it amalgamated with the Dublin Savings Bank and in 1992 a full amalgamation with the Cork and Limerick banks formed the TSB Bank.

1816

29 MARCH

Wild Man from Borneo

The Waterford horse *The Wild Man from Borneo* won the 1895 Aintree Grand National held on the 29th of March. Owned by John Widger and ridden by Joe Widger, he was returned at 10 to 1.

On the following Sunday the owner John Widger arrived back in Waterford to a hero's welcome. A procession, led by the Wolfe Tone Fife and Drum Band, took place to his house in Mayor's Walk. On the following Tuesday, his rider Joe Widger (John's younger brother) arrived back on the steamship *Reginald* and a similar reception was held for him. It was reported that every man, woman and child had money on the horse and bonfires blazed on Ballybricken for a week after the race.

When the horse died, his head was stuffed and was mounted on a wall inside Aintree. It is still there today.

On a side note, the Grand National was also won by another Waterford horse, *Freebooter*, in 1950.

1895

30 MARCH

Poor Law Union

Until 1838, no government agency was responsible for helping the destitute poor in Ireland. The *Poor Law Act of 1838* divided the country into 130 sections called *Poor Law Unions*, each administered by its own board of guardians. Each Union was responsible for building a workhouse to accommodate the poor and destitute. The cost of poor relief was to be met by the payment of rates.

The Waterford City Union was founded on this date, the 30th of March 1838. It immediately set about building a workhouse in the city and a site on John's Hill was chosen. The Waterford Workhouse opened in March 1841 (the building is the present Saint Patrick's Hospital on John's Hill). The Waterford Workhouse was built to serve the area comprising most of East Waterford and South Kilkenny. Designed to house 900 people, it cost £7,850 to build. Its first inmates were from the Mendicity Institute, which stood off the present Railway Square. The inmates from the House of Industry followed. A small graveyard was opened within the grounds for the burial of inmates. However, the workhouse was soon overwhelmed with the arrival of the famine, and auxiliary houses had to be rented throughout the city. The small graveyard was totally inadequate. Inmates were then buried in Kill St. Lawrence graveyard, and when that was full, Ballinaneeshagh was used. In February 1848 the workhouse was said to be *crowded to suffocation*. Sixty-four had died in the previous fortnight.

The workhouse system remained until the 1920s. Most of them then became known as County Hospitals. The Waterford Workhouse became St. Patrick's Hospital.

1838

31 MARCH

SS Mars

The *SS Mars* was built at the Neptune Yard in 1849. At 184 feet she was the first screw steamer to be used on the Waterford-Liverpool route. However she had a definite list due to the fact that she was originally intended to be a paddle steamer and was in the process of construction when her method of propulsion was changed.

Her list caused her to heel over in June 1859 on leaving Waterford. A large number of cattle on board were killed. While the list was subsequently remedied, it was a while before she gained the confidence of live animal exporters.

On the 31st of March 1862, the *SS Mars* left Waterford for the last time with 50 passengers, 178 cattle, over 300 pigs and 10 horses. The next day she ran aground on Linney Head near Milford in Pembrokeshire. Only four passengers survived, one of whom was a small boy who had climbed into one of the lifeboats to keep warm. He fell asleep and awoke to find himself alone in the boat having floated away from the sinking ship.

1862

1 APRIL

Good Shepherd

On this date in 1858 five Good Shepherd Sisters arrived in Waterford to assist in caring for *women in circumstances of deprivation* at a house of refuge in Barrack Street. This house of refuge was originally opened in 1842 by two priests in the city and was governed by two lay matrons. Soon after the Good Shepherd Sisters arrived, the refuge moved to a house in Hennessy's Road. The Presentation Sisters formerly occupied this building before their move to Slievekeale Road.

During the next thirty-six years approximately 500 women and girls were admitted to the Hennessy's Road Magdalen Asylum. In May 1892, the foundation stone for the new convent, penitentiary and laundry was laid in College Street. This building was occupied in October 1894. In the 1901 census there were 105 women in the institution. By 1928 this had risen to 190.

Canon Power in his *Parochial History of Waterford and Lismore during the 18th and 19th Centuries,* published in 1912, states the following:

> *The convent proper for the use of the Religious is entirely separated from the Magdalene Asylum by courtyard, garden and wall, so that the sisters, excepting those who are appointed to instruct and superintend them, never see or speak to the penitents.*

The Waterford Good Shepherd Asylum finally closed in September 1996 when the building was purchased by Waterford Institute of Technology.

1858

2 APRIL

Franciscan Friary

In 1533 Henry VIII broke with Rome and declared himself Supreme Head of the Church. Thus began a period of intense social upheaval. In 1536 he set his mind to the suppression of religious houses in Ireland. One of the first to go was the entire estate of the Priory of St. John. Sir William Wyse was granted these lands.

On the 2nd of April 1539 the Franciscan Friary was surrendered to the Crown and the friars were ordered to leave the city. The Franciscan Friars originally came to Waterford in the year 1240 (see entry for April 26th). Ryland's *History of Waterford* (1824) states that at the time of surrender, the friary contained:

> *a church and steeple, recently used as the French Church, a cemetery over which a Holy Ghost hospital was built, a hall, six chambers, a kitchen, two stables, a bakehouse and four cellars.*

Being a mendicant order, their land holdings were negligible.

Exactly two years later on the 2nd of April 1541, the Dominican Friary was surrendered to the Crown and their friars were also ordered to leave the city. At that stage the Friary was based at Blackfriars. Its other property at Kingsmeadow (about 25 acres) had already been taken. The Dean and Chapter of Christchurch held these lands. The Blackfriars property was leased by James White, Recorder of Waterford. The property eventually became the County Court House and another part of it became a theatre.

1539

3 APRIL

Irish Chancery Letters

As mentioned in the introduction, an on-going research project in TCD involves reconstructing the Rolls of the Irish Chancery. These rolls were the formal records of decisions reached or orders made on behalf of the King from 1244 to 1509. Unfortunately the originals were destroyed in 1922, but by collating all known transcripts throughout the world, researchers have succeeded in reproducing the records.

The following entry is dated the 3rd of April 1258:

> *To the treasurer and chamberlains of the exchequer:* ORDER *to pay 50m to the citizens of Waterford in part-payment of 280m that the Lord Edward owes for a loan which they made to him.*

Note the amount *50m* was 50 marks. The mark was not a unit of monetary currency but was a unit of account, and was commonly used in the Irish and English Exchequer (although the mark did end up as a unit of currency in Germany). The value of a mark was two thirds of a pound or 13s 4d. Thus the value of the loan of 280m was £186 13s 4d and the amount to be paid was 50m or £33 6s 8d.

To put this date into context, Waterford City burned to the ground in 1252, and the first reference to a Mayor of Waterford was in 1272.

1258

4 APRIL

Manor Street Railway Station

The Waterford - Tramore Railway operated for 107 years from 1853 to 1960. The line was originally planned as part of a Cork - Waterford line with a spur off to Tramore. However this railway company found itself in difficulty and the proposal was abandoned. The people at the Waterford end of the company then took it upon themselves to progress the Tramore line as a separate company. The bill for construction of the line was passed by the British Parliament on the 24th of July 1851. A contractor named William Dargan was appointed and the price was fixed at £41,500.

While the first sod was turned in early February 1853 it was not until the 4th of April 1853 before construction of the Waterford station began. The building was two storied, with the manager's office on the second floor. Two ticket hatches were provided with a third for busy periods. The area in front of the building was redeveloped at the same time (incorporating most of the old Mendicity Lane) and became Railway Square. The terminus itself consisted of a long single platform, 239 yards in length, with about half of it covered. A turntable just over 22 feet in diameter with a small number of spurs was at one end.

The station at Railway Square was demolished in May 1970.

1853

5 APRIL

Clock Tower

In early 1954, a new clock piece was installed in the Clock Tower on the Quay. This led to lots of interest regarding the history of the tower. Some research was done and the results were displayed at an exhibition in the City Library during the week of the 5th of April 1954. At that stage the City Library was in O'Connell Street.

The first proposal to erect a clock tower on the Quay was made during the mayoralty of Councillor John Mackesy in December 1859, specifically for the regulation of boats and ships in the harbour. In 1861 tenders were invited for construction of the tower and spire. In early May 1861 the contract was awarded to John Murphy, John's Hill, for the sum of £200, and work commenced immediately. The clock mechanism itself was built by Dillon and Mosley for the sum of £78 10s. Built on the site of the old fish market, it was completed by 1864. The Corporation paid for the clock itself but Councillor Mackesy arranged for subscriptions to help defray the cost of the tower.

Over time the clock itself ceased to work and the tower became dilapidated. In late 1953, the tower was completely renovated and a new clock installed. The mechanism on the clock was a double three-legged escapement which was the exact same mechanism used on Big Ben in London.

1954

6 APRIL

Bishop Charles Henderson

Charles Henderson was born in Ballybricken in April 1924. Having attended Mount Sion, he entered St. John's College in 1941 and was ordained in 1948. He served in a number of parishes in England before he was made Auxiliary Bishop of Southwalk in 1972.

The following year on the 6th of April 1973 he was made a Freeman of Waterford. He was the seventeenth person to be admitted as a Freeman since the enactment of the *Municipal Privilege Act of 1876*.

The Mayor in his address stated that it was likely that Bishop Henderson could establish his entitlement to be a Hereditary Freeman. Research had shown that in January 1801 an Abraham Henderson became a Freeman of the City. His son also called Abraham became a Freeman in 1830. His sons John and George became Freemen in 1837 and 1843. This George Henderson was the great grandfather of Bishop Henderson.

In his response, the Bishop stated:

> *Waterford City has always been home to me. It is the city of my family for generations. I'm proud to have been born here. It is here that I enjoyed my early years and spent my very few energetic years on the sports field. Most of us can recall the wisdom of our elders, often quickly spoken in very shrewd remarks. And one such remark of my paternal grandfather handed on to me by my father, is this: no matter where you go in the world you can always be proud of your native city. And as I grow older, I realise more fully the great truth of this utterance.*

Bishop Henderson died in April 2006 at the age of 81.

1973

7 APRIL

Waterford Glass Recreation Centre

The Minister for Local Government, Bobby Molloy TD, officially opened the Waterford Glass Recreation Centre on this date in 1972. Also present was The Mayor, Councillor T. Galvin, Mr. P. McGrath, Chairman, and Mr. Noel Griffin, Managing Director. In his address the Minster stated that it was a wonderful example of what could be achieved by effective co-operation between a major company and its workers.

> *It took an enlightened and progressive company to give essential backing to a project of this scale and it takes people with courage, imagination and an admirable sense of values to organise themselves as the Waterford Glass Workers have done to find the time and energy that has obviously been put into this aspect.*

Paddy Holden, chairman of the club, stated:

> *As far back as 1957 unsuccessful attempts were made to establish a social and sport centre. In 1968, however a joint committee drew up recommendation. Management purchased 15 acres of land and allocated £80,000 for capital development. As a result of these joint efforts, the Sport and Social Centre was today being officially opened. This was Stage 1 of the development. Already the swimming pool was being used all through the year. All playing pitches had been laid and seeded and would be playable next summer. The basketball court and children's playground was already in use. They also intended to provide in the future squash courts, a golfers driving range, a new car park area and modern changing rooms for outdoor activities.*

1972

8 APRIL

Brennan on the Moor

Most people have heard of the ballad *Brennan on the Moor*, made famous by the Clancy Brothers.

> *Oh it's of a brave young highway man this story we will tell*
> *His name was Willie Brennan and in Ireland he did dwell*
> *'Twas on the Kilworth Mountains he commenced his wild career*
> *And many a wealthy noble man before him shook with fear.*

While there are various locations given for the birth of Willie Brennan, no less a historian than our own Canon Power (of *Place Names of the Decies* fame) states that Brennan was a Waterford man. In an article for the *Journal of the Waterford and South-East of Ireland Archaeological Society* in 1911, he wrote that Willie Brennan:

> *was born at Raspberry Hill, a frontier townland of Co. Waterford on the north bank of the Blackwater.*

A report by the *Lancaster Gazette* on the 8th of April 1809 stated:

> *Brennan and his associate, the Pedlar, after a short trial, have been capitally convicted at the Clonmel Assize.*

1809

9 APRIL

Death of Elizabeth I

Queen Elizabeth I died in late March 1603 and over two weeks later on the 9th of April, news of her death reached Waterford. There followed a period of rejoicing throughout the city and surroundings as it was assumed that her successor James I, who was a son of the Catholic Mary Stuart, would allow complete freedom to practice the Catholic religion. Within a few days they had cleaned the Cathedral and restored it to its former glory just in time for Holy Week ceremonies. News of the celebrations in Waterford reached far and wide, and churches in other cities and towns also reopened.

However the Lord Deputy, Lord Mountjoy, considered that the population had gotten a little ahead of themselves, and that no direction had come from the new King on any relaxation of laws against Catholics. He immediately ordered that churches be closed again and decided that the City of Waterford needed to be reminded of its place. He marched with his army to Waterford and arrived outside the walls on the 1st of May with the intention of razing it to the ground and putting all its inhabitants to the sword.

While the citizens gave their assurances of their complete loyalty to the King, they were reluctant to admit Lord Mountjoy or his soldiers until the issue had been sorted. The Bishop of Waterford, Dr. James White, played a large part in the discussions. Eventually a compromise was reached that priests could wear clerical garb and say mass in private houses. Mountjoy entered the city on the 3rd of May. He stayed two days and left a garrison of 1200 men. In practice, the expected religious relaxation did not happen during the reign of James I (see entry for March 5th).

1603

10 APRIL

Last Hanging in City

The last hanging to take place in Waterford was on the 10th of April 1900 in Ballybricken Jail. This hanging also had the distinction that the condemned man was the oldest man to be hanged in Britain and Ireland in the 20th century.

The man was Patrick Dunphy, aged 74. Living on the Yellow Road, his second wife died in June 1899 and he was left to care for his eight children. Within a few months two of his sons had died, apparently from epileptic fits: Edward aged ten on the 19th of September, and John aged twelve on the 19th of December. Suspicions were aroused when it became apparent that he had life insurance on the two boys at a cost of a penny a week with the Prudential Insurance Company. The qualifying period had just elapsed when Edward died in September and the company paid out a lump sum of £10.

Patrick Dunphy was arrested and charged with the murder of his two sons. At his trial, evidence was produced to show that he had purchased strychnine, supposedly to use as rat poison. It was also stated that on the 19th of December he purchased a bottle of lemonade from Mary Cooney's pub in Parade Quay, which he said was for the boy outside. John collapsed soon after in Parnell Street and was taken to the Infirmary where he died later that evening. Following John's death, his brother Edward's body was exhumed on the 30th of December and a professor from the Royal College of Surgeons stated that he had enough strychnine poison in his intestine to kill ten people. Dunphy offered no plea in his defence and the jury took only minutes to find him guilty. The judge sentenced him to death. He was hanged inside Waterford Jail at 8am on the morning of the 10th of April 1900.

1900

11 APRIL

Noel Browne

On this day in April 1951 Minister for Health Noel Browne resigned over the Mother & Child Scheme.

Noel Browne was born in Bath Street in Waterford on the 20th of December 1915. He was baptised a Catholic in St. John's Church on the 23rd of December. His father was Joseph Browne, and his mother was Mary Teresa Cooney. In his autobiography, Noel said his father was an unskilled son of a small farmer in Co. Galway. However years later it was discovered that his father Joseph was actually a Sergeant in the Royal Irish Constabulary, and had been stationed in Waterford for thirteen years (he is recorded in the 1911 census as being a member of the Royal Irish Constabulary living in 38 Bath Street). Sergeant Joe Browne abruptly resigned from the force in May 1918 and the family moved to Derry. In 1920 the family moved to Athlone.

Noel Browne was elected to the Dáil in 1948 and was appointed Minister for Health on his first day. However, he soon came into conflict with the Catholic Church. He was the only minister to attend the Church of Ireland funeral of Douglas Hyde, the first President of Ireland (the rest of the Catholic cabinet remained outside the Cathedral grounds while the service took place, and only joined the cortege as the coffin left the Cathedral). His real problems with the church came with the Mother and Child Scheme. This scheme was to provide free state-funded healthcare for all mothers and children under sixteen. But the church, who managed the hospitals, would not accept that a public body could get involved. Noel Browne resigned as Minister for Health on the 11th of April 1951. This subsequently led to the collapse of the government.

1951

12 APRIL

Anna Manahan

On Friday the 12th of April 2002 the Freedom of the City was bestowed on Anna Manahan. Waterford's first lady of theatre was born on the 18th of October 1924. Trained in the Gaiety Theatre in Dublin, she worked with many famous actors including Micheál MacLiammóir and Hilton Edwards. She married Colm O'Kelly in 1955, but sadly ten months later Colm died having contracted polio while on tour in Egypt.

Highlights of her stage career include her performances in John B. Keane's *Big Maggie* and her Tony award for Martin McDonagh's *The Beauty Queen of Leenane* in 1998. Her television career included roles in *The Riordans*, *The Irish R.M.* and *Fair City*. Anna Manahan died on the 8th of March 2009.

Anna Manahan was the first Waterford woman to receive the Freedom of the City. Indeed she was the second woman ever to receive it. The other female recipient was President Mary Robinson in 1994.

2002

13 APRIL

First X-Ray

The first use of X-rays in Ireland took place on this date in De La Salle College when Brother Potamian took an X-ray of a woman's hand to see a metal splinter. Brother Potamian was Michael Francis O'Reilly and was born in Co. Cavan in 1846. In 1848 his family emigrated to America after the famine. After his early education in a De La Salle school he entered the novitiate in Montreal, taking the name Brother Potamian. In 1870 he began teaching physics in St Joseph's, Clapham, London. Having obtained a degree and doctorate from the University of London, he was appointed Professor of Physics in 1893 in the new De La Salle Teacher Training College in Waterford which had been opened two years previously.

In 1895 the German physics professor Wilhelm Roentgen discovered X-rays and reports were published in various journals. Brother Potamian learned of these discoveries, and soon after on the 13th of April 1896, he was able to provide a practical demonstration of their use in the science laboratories of De La Salle College, Waterford. A young woman complained of a sore hand and Brother Potamian was requested by a Doctor Atkins to take a radiograph. This revealed the presence of a steel splinter in the hand of the young woman, which was then removed by the doctor. This X-ray was the first of its kind in Ireland. The photographic plate was preserved until 1956, when unfortunately it was lost while on loan to an exhibition in New York.

In August 1896 Brother Potamian was transferred from Waterford to the De La Salle Manhattan College, New York, where he died in January 1917. The New York Herald described him as *one of the pioneers in radiography*.

1896

14 APRIL

Last Public Hanging

The last hanging took place in Waterford Jail in 1900 (see entry for April 10th). However the last public hanging took place in the city thirty-six years earlier on the 14th of April 1864.

Patrick Hennessy, his wife Biddy, his grandfather Thomas Connolly and Biddy's father Thomas Walsh were living in the same house near Ballymacarberry. There was great animosity between the two elderly men. On the morning of the 29th of September 1863, Walsh murdered Thomas Connolly in the kitchen of the small house. He dragged the body out to the turf house, hacked it to pieces and buried the different parts in various holes in the garden. His daughter Biddy had caught him in the act but was persuaded to stay quiet.

Eventually Patrick Hennessy called in the police when his grandfather could not be found. On the 9th of October the first of the body parts was found. Thomas Walsh and his daughter Biddy were arrested and brought to Waterford Jail. Biddy told the truth and on the 15th of March 1864, Thomas Walsh came before Waterford Court. He was found guilty and sentenced to death by hanging.

It had been twelve years earlier in 1852 that the previous public hanging had taken place in Waterford, so a large crowd of between two and three thousand came to view. The actual gallows was outside the jail in Ballybricken. However all did not go to plan, as when the executioner removed the pin to release the trap door, the door did not open. Eventually a sledgehammer was used to release the door although it took three heavy blows to do so. His body was left hanging in public view for about thirty minutes before it was removed and buried in quicklime within the prison walls.

1864

15 APRIL

Joseph Malcomson

On this date in April 1858 Joseph Malcomson died. He was the eldest of the Malcomson brothers whose company was one of the largest in Ireland at the time. As he was the senior partner and the leading light in the company for many years, his death was a major contributing factor to the decline of the business empire until eventually they were declared bankrupt in January 1877.

The Malcomson family were Quakers who originally came to Waterford from Scotland in the late 17th century. The founder of the Malcomson business empire in Waterford was David Malcomson, who in 1825 established a cotton mill in Portlaw. When the factory was completed it was considered to be the greatest factory of its kind in Europe, employing over fifteen hundred people. In 1835 he founded the Waterford Steam Navigation Company. In 1837 David handed over the running of his business to his seven sons and from that time they were known as Malcomson Brothers. After his father's death, Joseph became head of the firm.

The Neptune Ironworks was founded in 1844, initially as a repair depot for their ships, but they later began to build their own ships. Soon Malcomsons was one of the most powerful companies in Ireland and England with interests in corn, cotton and tea, in addition to shipbuilding, steamship lines, railways and coalmines. Although after Joseph's death in 1858, the Neptune yard continued to build ships over the following years, the decline had begun. The American Civil War meant a shortage of raw cotton for the factory in Portlaw. The business battled on for some years, but in January 1877 the company was declared bankrupt and their enterprises were sold off one by one.

1858

16 APRIL

Steamships

Steamships began to revolutionise shipping in the early 1800s. Initially steamboats were used only on inland waterways on the great lakes and rivers in America. A similar paddle steamer service was in existence on the Suir in 1817.

But it was the development of steam power for use in ocean vessels that really revolutionised the shipping industry. By 1815 commercial steamships were in operation between Liverpool and Glasgow. In Waterford they were first seen as a possible reliable way of getting post across the Irish Sea.

Ryland, in his *History of Waterford* published in 1824, stated that earlier that year on the 16th of April the first regular steam service began from Milford Haven to Dunmore East. He goes on to state:

> *Steam packets sail every day between Waterford and Milford, and afford a cheap and expeditious conveyance: the passage is usually effected in about nine hours. The time occupied in conveying the mail between London and Waterford rarely exceeds eight and forty hours. On the arrival of the packet at Dunmore, in the evening, a well appointed mail coach is to convey the passengers to Waterford; and from thence coaches proceed to Dublin and Cork, where they arrive on the following morning.*

1824

17 APRIL

Theatre Royal

Originally built in 1785, the Theatre Royal was rebuilt in its present form and opened on the 17th of April 1876. The original building (designed by John Roberts) was built as a Playhouse and Assembly Rooms (see entry for May 18th). This later became the Town or City Hall in 1816 (see entry for February 2nd).

In 1874 a group of individuals came together and proposed to the Corporation that a proper theatre should be built on the west wing of the Town Hall. Permission was granted and plans were drawn up. However the proposal was not without its detractors, specifically both Protestant and Catholic Bishops. The Protestant Bishop held that it would lower the tone of the morality and religion of those who attend. The location being so close to his residence and to Christ Church Cathedral was also a cause of concern. The point was made that Catholics would object if it were built close to the Catholic Cathedral. The Catholic Bishop supported the Protestant Bishop. There was a suggestion for a while that the theatre would be positioned at the old fish market (site of the present Bolton Street car park). However the City Hall site won out.

The theatre was designed in a similar style to the Gaiety Theatre in Dublin and was to accommodate between 1,100 and 1,200 in the audience. It opened with great fanfare on Easter Monday April 17th 1876 and the first performance was a Mr. John Royston's *Comedy and Opera Bouffe*.

1876

18 APRIL

FAI Cup

This date is a special day for Waterford soccer as it was on the 18th of April 1937 that the Waterford team won their first FAI Cup. It was to be another forty-three years before they won it for the second time on the 20th of April 1980.

Although the club was only founded in 1930 they won the Shield in that first year, 1930/31, and again in 1936/37. The final of the 1936/37 FAI Cup was held in Dalymount Park on Sunday the 18th of April. Three special trains carrying over 2,500 supporters were laid on, as well as numerous buses. The game was played in ideal weather conditions and the opposition was St. James's Gate. The match was played at a hectic pace and Waterford won out in the end by a score of two goals to one.

When the victorious team arrived back in the train station on Monday night they were met by thousands of supporters. The Barrack Street Brass and Reed Band led them on a triumphant procession through the city, going down the Quay, the Mall, John Street, Michael Street and O'Connell Street to a reception at the Bridge Hotel, where the cup and each member of the team was presented at an upstairs window to the crowds outside.

The 1980 final was again played in Dalymount Park on the 20th of April and their opponents were St. Patrick's Athletic. Captain on the day was Al Finucane and the goal was scored in the 22nd minute by a young defender from Preston named Brian Gardner. The Man of the Match award went to the legendary goalkeeper Peter Thomas. Again thousands packed the streets of Waterford when the victorious team arrived back on the following Monday night.

1937

19 APRIL

Don Pedro Sherlock

In medieval times burial at nightime by torchlight was a prevalent custom. For example Mary Queen of Scots and George II were both buried at nightime. I have no evidence of this happening in Waterford, but in the *Journal of the Waterford and South East of Ireland Archaeological Society 1899* there is a reference to the will of Don Pedro Sherlock, who died in Madrid in the 18th century, asking that he be buried at night.

Don Pedro was a member of one of the oldest Waterford families. Members of this Sherlock family had filled the office of Mayor of Waterford some fourteen times in the 16th and 17th centuries. His will is dated the 19th of April 1742 and states:

> *I order that I may be buried at night without pomp or vanity, and with as little expense as shall seem convenient, …. And that the day after my death the Mass of the Presence, and the Vigils and Responses may be said. … And I likewise order that they give the necessary and accustomed charity to the Holy Places at Jerusalem.*

The same article (written by Canon Power) goes on to state where death occurred by suicide, the coroner was directed to arrange a private interment in the churchyard without religious rites, within twenty-four hours of the inquest, and between the hours of nine and twelve at night.

1742

20 APRIL

SS Olga

Spencer Coal Merchants was founded by Geoffrey Spencer in 1869. The son of a farmer from Killure, he married Catherine Lyons, the only daughter of a coal merchant who had a coal yard at John Street. In 1869 he purchased his first ship, a second-hand brig called the *Oriental*, in poor condition. Following repairs in White's shipyard, he started shipping coal from Cardiff to Waterford. Over the following years he purchased a number of ships, the brig *Caradoc*, the barque *Madcap* and the brig *Olga*.

On the 20th of April 1895 the *Olga* was wrecked off Creadan Head close to the spot where the fully rigged ship the *Alfred D. Snow* was lost seven years earlier in 1888. The *Olga* was built in Prince Edwards islands in 1875, was 115 feet in length, and her Captain was named W. Peenycook. She had a full load of coal on her when she was wrecked.

Geoffrey died in 1917 and his son Joseph took over the business. However the age of sail was gone, being replaced by steam ships. The Spencers could not compete and the firm ceased trading in 1920. In 1928 the *Madcap* and the *Zayda* were broken up after lying idle for several years.

Note: An exhibition of *The Spencer Ships and Waterford 1869 - 1920* was held at Greyfriars Gallery as part of an exhibition called "Ship to Shore" during the 2011 Tall Ships Festival. Many of the descendants of Geoffrey Spencer attended the launch of this exhibition.

1895

21 APRIL

Freedom

In Medieval Waterford the City Council kept a very tight control who could trade in the city. The following excerpt from the *Great Parchment Book of Waterford* is dated the 21st of April 1628. It deals with the situation of how to deal with children of Freemen of the City who were not living in the city:

It is enacted, established and agreed by the said Mayor, Sheriffs and Citizens the day and year above written, that the Child or Children of Freemen of this city not dwelling or cohabiting within the City, the Liberties or franchises thereof, shall not be admitted to serve as an apprentice or apprentices in merchandise to any dwelling within the city, until each of them or their parents shall pay to the use of the corporation ten pounds Irish before their admission to service, except the said parents do and shall from time to time contribute and bear all taxes, talladges, levies, loans, impositions and charges equally and rateable with the rest of the inhabitants of the city, and this law is made for the good and advancement of the children and officers of the ancient families of the city.

1628

22 APRIL

Excessive Drinking

Excessive drinking at wakes obviously exercised the minds of members of Waterford Corporation in the 17th century. At its meeting held on the 22nd of April 1663 the following decision was made, as recorded in the *Council Books of the Corporation of Waterford*:

> *Concluded, that henceforth no funeral shall be served with drinking of wine or any liquor but wear mourning clothes and give to the poor in money or bread as the persons concerned think fit. This conclusion is made to prevent unseemly drinking and expense of poor men's estates who commonly spend more on the funeral of a child that they have left for the maintenance of the living. And if any shall hereafter presume to offend in not conforming to this conclusion of the council they shall if of the council, be fined according to the councils discretion, and others not of the council to be dealt with as contemners of the wholesome laws and policies of this ancient city.*

It is somewhat ironic that at the same meeting the members also decided that since the following day was the King's Coronation, 6s 8d was to be allocated to the water bailiff at Passage to buy wine. The water bailiff was also instructed to build a bonfire in Passage:

> *on the night of the Kings coronation day according to the ancient customs of this city.*

1663

23 APRIL

Civil War Compensation

The band room of the Thomas Francis Meagher Fife and Drum Band on Yellow Road was completely destroyed by fire early on Sunday morning the 23rd of April 1922. As the band was known to be supporters of Captain William Redmond, it was accepted that the fire occurred as a result of differences with Republican forces. The fact that three fires had occurred in the city that night strengthened this suggestion.

In 1923 the Irish Free State Government passed the *Damage to Property (Compensation) Act* to allow for compensation to be paid to individuals where damage was caused as a result of civil strife during the War of Independence and the Civil War. At a court hearing held in Waterford in December 1923, the band was awarded £90 compensation by the courts on the basis that the fire occurred as a result of the civil strife at the time. The list of the items destroyed included six side drums, two bass drums, twenty-one caps, eight pairs of side drumsticks, two pairs of brass drum sticks, eight music stands and eight books of music.

The same sitting of the court awarded the Granville Hotel £1,275 for damage occurred during the siege of Waterford the previous July. Other awards included:
- £250 to the Adelphi Hotel
- £550 to Major Congreve for damage and items stolen from Mount Congreve
- £17 12s 6d to J.J. Barry, a publican from Kilmacow for consignment of stout from Guinness destroyed following the burning of a goods store

1922

24 APRIL

Hallé Orchestra

In 1953, in an attempt to extend the tourist season and attract overseas visitors, a national festival called An Tóstal was formed. This was the original "gathering" concept. During the year cities, towns and villages across the country held events of various forms.

One of the big events in Waterford that year was the visit of Sir John Barbirolli and the famous Hallé Orchestra from Manchester. Along with Our Lady's Choral Society they performed Handel's Messiah in the Cathedral of the Most Holy Trinity on Friday the 24th of April 1953.

The event was one of the biggest musical occasions to take place in the city for many years, with over 1,500 people attending. It was the first time the Cathedral was used for such an event. A special rostrum of twelve tiers was built in front of the high altar by John Hearne and Son Builders. All the seats in the Cathedral were completely booked out and patrons started queuing from 6pm for the 8pm start. The pews in the epistle aisle were reserved for 500 schoolchildren and members of religious communities who were guests of Waterford Music Club.

The soprano on the night was Veronica Dunne who had finished her musical education and was just embarking on her international singing career.

1953

25 APRIL

Oliver Cromwell

We have all heard of the phrase *By Hook or by Crooke* which refers to Cromwell's siege of Waterford City in November 1649. It was on the 25th of April 1599 that Cromwell was born in Huntington in Britain. He died on the 3rd of September 1658 and was buried in Westminster Abbey.

When the Royalists returned to power in 1660 his body was exhumed and he was posthumously executed. This involved hanging his body in chains and beheading it. His head was then stuck on a spike on top of Westminster Hall where it is said to have remained for twenty four years.

The story then goes that during a storm in 1688 the head fell off and was brought home by a soldier who hid it. The head is then reported to have been sold to a travelling circus, after which it came into the possession of a private collector. For the next 250 years various private collectors acquired the head. Eventually it was buried in the grounds of Sidney Sussex College in Cambridge in 1960 where Cromwell was reported to have studied.

1599

26 APRIL

Irish Chancery Letters

The Dominicans came to Ireland in 1224 and arrived in Waterford in 1226. The Franciscans arrived fourteen years later in 1240. The Dominicans were known as the *Friars Preachers* while the Franciscans were known as the *Friars Minors*. The two groups were also distinguished by the colour of their cloaks, the Dominicans being called *Blackfriars* and the Franciscans being called *Greyfriars*.

Some years later there is a reference in the Irish Chancery Letters dated the 26th of April 1292 as follows:

> ORDER *to pay Friars Preachers of Dublin, Cork, Waterford, Limerick and Drogheda 35m from Michaelmas 19 Edward until Michaelmas 20 Edward which the King grants to them annually of his alms at the Exchequer, Dublin: unless that sum has already been paid to them already by another writ.*

The reference to 19 Edward to 20 Edward refers to the 19th and 20th year of Edward's reign (1290-1292). Note the amount "35m" was 35 marks. We saw earlier (see entry for April 3rd) that the value of a mark was two thirds of a pound or 13s 4d. Thus the value of the grant paid to the Friars was £23 6s 8d.

A week later on the 2nd of May 1292 a similar order was made to pay the Franciscans the same amount:

> ORDER *to pay Friars Minor of Dublin, Cork, Waterford, Limerick and Drogheda 35m from Michaelmas 19 Edward until Michaelmas 20 Edward which the King grants to them annually of his alms: unless that sum has already been paid to them already by another writ.*

1292

27 APRIL

Marquess of Waterford

Curraghmore, the home of the Marquess of Waterford, can be traced back to the arrival of the de la Poer family in 1167. The first Marquess of Waterford was George de la Poer Beresford, born in 1735. Down through the years many holders of the title Lord Waterford have died tragically. There is a story that back in the penal days, a young peasant was dragged in chains into Curraghmore one day and flogged. His widowed mother pleaded for mercy to no avail. In her grief she prophesied that not one of the heads of the Beresford clan would die in their beds.

This was certainly the case for the fourth Lord Waterford born on the 27th of April 1814. In his younger days he was a Protestant clergyman and when he came into the title he spent much of his time roaming the grounds of Curraghmore. One day in 1866 he went missing, and a few days later was found dead in a remote part of the estate. Although the mystery of his death was never solved, it was assumed he died as a result of accidental poisoning having eaten some raw mushrooms.

His father, the third Lord Waterford also died accidently having broken his neck in a riding accident in 1826. His son, the fifth Lord Waterford died in 1895 of gunshot wounds following a riding accident which left him crippled.

The misfortune continued into the 20th century when both the sixth and seventh Lord Waterford died in tragic circumstances (see entry for December 2nd).

1814

28 APRIL

SS Pomona

While the biggest shipwreck off the Waterford coast was the *Seahorse* in Tramore Bay on the 31st of December 1816, with the loss of 336 lives, a bigger tragedy was to strike the Wexford coast on the 28th of April 1859 when the emigrant ship *Pomona* was wrecked on a sandbank off Ballyconigar. This time 388 lives were lost.

The *Pomona* had left Liverpool the previous day, sailing for New York. However the Captain lost his bearings during a gale, and the ship ran aground on a sandbank about seven miles off the Wexford coast. Some hours later she slipped off the sandbank and sank in deeper water. Only twenty-three survived. All the survivors were ordinary crewmen. One of these, a cook by the name of Philip Mulcahy, was from Waterford. In his deposition to the inquiry afterwards he stated that the crew had made no attempt to save the passenger's lives. One of those who drowned was the father of the artist Sir John Lavery.

While most of the bodies were washed ashore on the Wexford coast, a number made their way around to the Waterford coast, as well as two bodies which were found in Youghal Bay two months later.

Note: This ship should not be confused with another ship also named the *Pomona* owned by the Malcomson Brothers and built in 1859 in Jarrow in England.

1859

29 APRIL

Mercy Convent

An indication of the state of Catholicism in Waterford in 1928 can be gained from the following report of a ceremony in the Mercy Convent on Sunday the 29th of April 1928 attended by twenty-two priests. Five young women were received into the Mercy Order, another four made their first profession and another five made their final vows. Similar ceremonies took place on the same day in the Mercy convents in both Wexford and Carrick on Suir.

The Mercy Sisters first came to Waterford in 1876 to take charge of the hospital at the workhouse. In August 1900 they opened their first school in Philip Street. On the first day 210 pupils enrolled. In 1906 the present convent in Military Road opened. A Montessori school was opened in 1920. In 1927 W.B. Yeats visited the school and it is said that his poem *Among School Children* was inspired by his visit. The first verse reads as follows:

> *I walk through the long schoolroom questioning;*
> *A kind old nun in a white hood replies;*
> *The children learn to cipher and to sing,*
> *To study reading-books and histories,*
> *To cut and sew, be neat in everything*
> *In the best modern way — the children's eyes*
> *In momentary wonder stare upon*
> *A sixty-year-old smiling public man.*

Although a "Secondary Top" had opened in 1935 it was not until the advent of free secondary education in 1967 that the secondary school was established. A new secondary school was built in Ozanam Street in 1977.

1928

30 APRIL

Cap of Maintenance

The Silken Thomas Rebellion against Henry VII took place in 1534. At the time William Wyse was Mayor of Waterford and he played a significant part in helping to suppress the rebellion. Wyse had previously served in the court of Henry and he received many rewards for his royal service. Waterford City was also the recipient of many favours by Henry, who granted the city three Charters.

In 1535 Wyse was no longer Mayor but was the Emissary of the City to the Royal Court. In early 1536, the King presented Wyse with a gift for the city. This consisted of a bearing sword *to be borne before the Mayor from time to time within our said city*. This sword was ceremoniously carried in front of the Mayor from 1536 until 1922. It is still in the possession of Waterford Corporation and is on display in the medieval museum. The sword is one of the finest 16th century swords still in existence.

Soon after on the 30th of April 1536, Wyse was sent back to Waterford with another letter and gift. This time the gift was a Cap of Maintenance. The significance of this cap to be worn by the Mayor was that the wearer did not need to doff his cap to anyone. The cap was made of red velvet and decorated with gold embroidered tudor roses. It was the first time that a subject of the British monarch was presented with such a gift. Again this cap is on display in the medieval museum. It is one of the oldest such caps in Europe and is the only piece of Henry VII's wardrobe to survive to the present day.

1536

1 MAY

Snowcream

On the 1st of May 1948 two brothers, Johnny and Jimmy Aylward, started the firm of Southern Ice Cream and Dairy Products at Thomas Hill. Initially they called their ice cream Snow White but after an intervention by representatives of Walt Disney, they changed the name to Snowcream. Due to the lack of ice cream sales during the winter, they decided to branch out into the pasteurised milk business.

In October 1952 a new pasteurisation plant was installed at the back of the ice cream plants at Thomas Hill. On the 2nd of December, the first bottles of pasteurised milk were produced. Waterford was the second city in the country after Dublin to so. A distinctive red top on the glass bottle was used to identify the pasteurised milk.

Over the next few years Snowcream expanded. In 1955 a plant opened in Wexford and in 1958 a plant opened in Moate, Co. Westmeath. It soon became apparent that the Thomas Hill premises was insufficient to meet their needs, so in 1959 Glenville House and 22 acres around it were purchased for £3,000 (Glenville House, the Goff family home, had been destroyed by fire in 1957). The house was demolished and a new dairy plant was built. It opened in March 1960.

In 1973 Snowcream became a subsidiary of Waterford Co-op (later Waterford Foods), and in 1997 Avonmore Foods and Waterford Foods merged, rebranding as Glanbia in 1999.

The Glenville plant finally closed in March 2010.

1948

2 MAY

Visit of King Edward VII

The last visit by an English monarch to Waterford took place on the 2nd of May 1904. King Edward VII, accompanied by Queen Alexandra, paid a brief visit to the city. Arriving by train at Waterford North Station at 12.50pm, they processed down the Quay for lunch in the Large Room of the City Hall. At 2.30 they visited the Waterford Agricultural Show at Newtown, after which they departed the city from the Waterford South Station in Bilberry, heading to Lismore Castle for the night.

The visit did not attract universal approval, with thirteen of the City Councillors absenting themselves from the reception at City Hall. However the Mayor, James Power, was there and was in fact knighted by the King at the train station in Bilberry just before he left. He was the tenth and last knighted Mayor of Waterford in its 1,100 year history.

In April 1920 a photograph of the King's visit, which had been on display on the wall of the Mayor's office, was taken down on the direction of the then Mayor Dr. V. J. White, and replaced by a picture of Eamonn de Valera (at the same time a marble bust of John Redmond was also moved to a less conspicuous part of the office).

Coincidentally 109 years later to the day (May 2nd 2013), King Edward's great grandson, the Duke of Kent, was in Waterford in his role as President of the RNLI.

1904

3 MAY

Quartering of Soldiers

The upkeep and supervision of soldiers quartered in the city was a frequent source of annoyance and expense for the Corporation and for businesses in Waterford. Public houses, butchers, bakers and innkeepers were expected to billet soldiers as a matter of course. An unusual request was made by the Corporation on the 3rd of May 1672 that:

> *The High Constable be requested to quarter the soldiers of the Garrison more contiguous and not to quarter fewer than two in any public house*

Two years earlier in July 1670 the Corporation had:

> *Ordered that William Wickham, High Constable do cause his petty Constables to bring in an account of the names of all persons in their respective Parishes capable of Quartering soldiers and that he prepares billets for Quarters of four companies of foot containing two hundred and forty men besides officers expected in Town to-morrow.*

Quartering of soldiers was just one duty of Waterford Corporation in the 1600s. Administration of their property which comprised most of the city and surroundings, including property as far away as Rosbercon and Thomastown, was one of their main functions. The Corporation also had to look after and regulate the entire business of the port including collection of customs and various dues. Trade in the city also had to be regulated. The city walls, courthouse, jail and all public buildings had to be maintained. The city water supply from various springs also had to be conserved. In addition to these duties, the Corporation also had to administer the finances of the churches.

1672

4 MAY

Corporation Dissolved

On the 4th of May 1937 the Minister for Local Government and Public Health, Sean T. O'Kelly, made an order dissolving Waterford Corporation to take effect the following day. This order was made following a public sworn inquiry, held in September and October of the previous year. The property, powers and duties of the Council were transferred to Commissioner Mr. P. J. Megan, who had previously acted in a similar capacity in South Tipperary and Kilkenny. The newly appointed commissioner held his first meeting in City Hall on Friday the 14th of October and began his new duties. However some confusion arose around the office of Mayor, as the then Mayor James Aylward refused to accept that the dissolution order also suspended the office of Mayor.

The dissolving of a council was not completely out of the ordinary as several local authorities had been dissolved in the first years of the new Free State and replaced initially by a commissioner and later by a council – manager system. This happened first in Cork in 1929, in Dublin in 1930 and in Limerick in 1934. This new system of administration came to Waterford with the passing of *The Waterford City Managers Act* in 1939, setting up the City Council consisting of fifteen elected Councillors.

The first meeting of the new City Council took place in the first week of November 1939, and Alderman James Aylward was re-elected Mayor.

1937

5 MAY

Catholic Cathedral

In 1693 the Catholics of Waterford petitioned the Protestant Corporation to allow a large chapel at the back of the houses in Bailey's Lane, and if permitted *it should be hid from view of the Corporation so as not to be offensive to them.* This petition was successful and the *big chapel* was built on the site of the present Cathedral but at right angles to it, and hidden behind a row of houses in Barronstrand Street. However after one hundred years, the building decayed and repairs were needed.

In 1792, they again petitioned the Corporation who bestowed on them on the 5th of May *all the ground from Bailey's Lane to Mr. Charles Clark's house for 999 years at 2s 6d per annum.* The old chapel which had stood for nearly one hundred years was taken down and the new building commenced in 1793. The cost was £20,000. The work was completed in 1796. The architect was John Roberts who had also designed Christ Church Cathedral seventeen years previously.

There is a story that Roberts (who was then in his eighties) regularly rose early in the morning to supervise the workmen. However, on one occasion he got up too early, and in waiting for the workmen he fell asleep and caught a chill from which he died at the age of eighty-four.

In Ryland's *History of Waterford* published in 1824, he states that the Cathedral, *in Barronstrand Street, supposed to be one of the largest buildings in Ireland, is capable of accommodating 11,000 people.* The assumption here is that everyone would be standing up as no seats were provided.

1792

6 MAY

SS Indiana

The largest ship ever built in Waterford, the *SS Indiana,* was launched on this day in 1867. She was built at the Neptune Yard, weighed 1572 tons and measured 325 feet in length. Owned by the Malcomsons, she was built for the London - Le Harve - New York Line. Bill Irish in his book *Shipbuilding in Waterford* states that that due to its size there was a window of only fifteen minutes each side of high water in which they could achieve a successful launch. She had three decks, the lowest of which was intended to carry 900 third class passengers.

Malcomsons realised that they had overestimated the need for a liner of this size on the transatlantic route so she was sold a few months later in August 1867 to a French company and renamed *Pointou*. She made her maiden voyage to Brazil in September 1867.

The *Indiana* was the last ocean liner to be built at the Neptune Yard.

To get an appreciation of the size of this ship, the largest ship to visit Waterford during the Tall Ships races in 2011 was the Russian ship *Mir* which is 358 feet, while the second largest was the Norwegian tall ship the *Christian Radich* at 240 feet. Another tall ship which visited Waterford in 2011, the *USS Coast Guard Eagle*, is 295 feet.

1867

7 MAY

City Charter

By definition, the City Charter gave authority to the Corporation to govern the city. When Waterford Corporation was dissolved in 1618 (see entry for March 5th) the charters were seized and a Government appointee ruled the city. Following the accession of Charles I in 1626 a new Charter was issued to Waterford.

By the 1670s the Corporation was seeking improvements to the charter. To that end, the existing Charter was sent to the Lord Lieutenant in late 1671 in order that it might be renewed in some way. However things did not go quite according to plan, and without possession of the charter, the Corporation's authority was on shaky ground. At its meeting on the 7th of May 1672, the City Council decided that:

> Mr. Recorder and Alderman Watts, city agents, shall prepare a petition to the Lord Lieutenant to get our old Charter returned.

The Charter was obviously returned, as at a meeting in early January 1674 the Corporation approved the appointment of Alderman Watts *to act as agent of the Corporation in prosecution of a new charter*. Then at a further meeting later that month, it decided that the *city duties would be raised for two years*, and the money raised for gaining a new Charter was to be lodged with Alderman Watts.

It was to be another fourteen years before a new Catholic Charter was issued to Waterford in 1688 by James II. However this was a short-lived one, as soon after the Battle of the Boyne it was withdrawn. The 1626 Charter of Charles remained the basis for municipal authority until 1840.

1672

8 MAY

Staple of Waterford

The following entry in the Irish Chancery Letters, dated the 8th of May 1406, makes reference to the staple of Waterford:

> *Acceptance and ratification of the election of William Lyncoll as mayor and Henry Lane and John Rykyll as constables of the staple at the City of Waterford.*

The concept of the staple was initially established in the 13th century and used to regulate the trade of basic or "staple" goods such as wool and hides. These goods could only be sold to foreign merchants in designated "staple" towns, which included Waterford, Dublin, Cork and Drogheda. The merchants of the staple elected a mayor and two constables. There is a distinction therefore between the mayor of the staple and the mayor of the town.

Reference has been made elsewhere to the close trade links between Waterford and Bristol. In a publication titled *The Staple Court Books of Bristol* (Ed E.E. Rich., 1934) the following appears:

> *There is a suggestive similarity between this institution in Bristol and that in Waterford, her faithful imitator in so many things. In Waterford also there was a close connection between the town and the Staple, the Mayor of the town being ex-officio Mayor of the Staple, and there also it was recognised by the town that the Staple jurisdiction was an exception to the otherwise complete competence of the municipal authorities.*

This was certainly the case in 1406 as the Mayor of Waterford in the year was the same William Lincoln mentioned above as *Mayor of the staple at the City of Waterford.*

1406

9 MAY

Bowling Green

Although a bowling green was opened on the site of the present Tower Hotel in 1735 (see entry for December 19th), an earlier bowling green also existed in the city. This was situated close to Castle Street where the current Closegate housing estate is built. Indeed the original name for a portion of the existing Manor Street was Bowling Green Lane.

As mentioned earlier (see entry for May 3rd), one of the main functions of the Corporation was to administer their property which comprised most of the city and surroundings. The property was leased on a regular basis, either at a council meeting itself or at the dernhundred. The dernhundred was a county or city court convened by the mayor and city officials which was legally empowered to administer justice. A hundred was a division of part of a county originally thought to have contained a hundred families or Freemen.

A record for the 9th of May 1693 from The Council Books for Waterford states:

> *At Dernhundred held publically in the Tholsell for setting leases in revision of the corporation lands etc. …..*
>
> *John Hickes bowling green and gardens let to said Hickes at ten shillings yearly rent, and the term to cease if he neglect to keep the green on order for the recreation of citizens, etc.*

Interestingly, the same meeting also agreed to lease: *Barronstrands mill and house and garden, lime kiln above highwater mark* to Mr. Sheriff Austin.

1693

10 MAY

Richard Mulcahy

Richard Mulcahy was born in Manor Street on the 10th of May 1886. Educated at Mount Sion, the family later moved to Thurles where his father was postmaster. Mulcahy joined the Irish Volunteers in 1913 and was second in command to Thomas Ashe during the Easter Rising. Following release from internment he became Commandant of the Dublin Brigade of the Volunteers. He was elected to the first Dáil in 1918 for the Dublin Clontarf area. In March 1919 he became IRA Chief of Staff during the War of Independence. He was commander of the pro-treaty forces during the Civil War and became Commander-in-Chief following the death of Michael Collins in August 1922.

He served as Defence Minister and Minister for Local Government in the 1920s. For much of the 1930s he served in the backbenches but became leader of Fine Gael in 1944 following the resignation of W.T. Cosgrave. At the 1948 general election, he stepped aside in order that the interparty government could come together under John A. Costello as Taoiseach (see entry for January 25th). He spent two terms as Minister for Education in the 1950s. He resigned from leadership of Fine Gael in 1959 and from the Dáil in 1961. He died in Dublin on the 6th of December 1971.

1886

11 MAY

Passage to America

The *Waterford Chronicle* of the 11th of May 1816 includes the following advertisements for ships offering passage to America:

> *First Ship for America. Now in port and expected to sail in fourteen days from Waterford. The beautiful fast sailing ship San Doming. Captain: Fitzgerald. For freight or passage apply to John Allen and Son.*

> *Passengers for the United States of America. The remarkably fast brigantine Queen now lying at the port of Ross is intended to be dispatched to New York in the early part of next month.*

Another issue of the *Chronicle* that same week included:

> *Mr. P. and M. Farrell hourly expect the arrival of the new fast sailing brig the Shamrock, burden 200 tons. Thomas Walsh, Master. This vessel will immediately take on cargo for New York and proceed about the 20th May. For freight or passage apply to Mr P. and M. Farrell, Ship Agents or the Master on board.*

> *For St. John's Newfoundland, the fast sailing brig Sisters of London. 180 tons register. William Dyer, Master. For freight of passage apply to Mr. Richard Pope, Quay, Waterford.*

> *Passengers to British America. The brig Saltom bound for Canada, an excellent vessel, burden 250 tons will take fifty passengers to Quebec. As this vessel will be ready for sea in June, persons wishing to go out must engage their passage before the 5th of that month. Application to Thomas Nevins.*
> *NB Mechanics are allowed by Government to proceed to Canada where considerable encouragement is given to settlers.*

1816

12 MAY

SS Gipsy

The *Gipsy* was a steamer built by the Malcomsons at the Neptune Yard in 1857 and launched in January the following year. She was introduced on the Waterford-Liverpool-Bristol route by the Waterford Steam Navigation Company. Although only 200 feet, her passenger capacity was 330 in summer and 229 in winter.

After nineteen years of service she ran aground on the Avon River soon after leaving Bristol on the 12th of May 1878. Later the tide carried her across the channel where she sank. Unfortunately salvage efforts were unsuccessful and she was wrecked. The wreck completely blocked the channel and it required army explosives to clear it for shipping again.

In the years following the launch of the *Gipsy* in 1859, the Neptune Yard and the Malcomson empire were at their height. Between 1859 and 1869 nineteen ships were built, eleven of which were built for the Waterford Steam Navigation Company.

1878

13 MAY

King Richard II

According to Smith's *History of Waterford* (1746), it was on this date in 1399 that King Richard II landed in Waterford for the second and last time. His first visit had occurred five years earlier in 1394 (see entry for October 2nd).

Richard was reputed to have an armada of two hundred ships. Ryland in his *History of Waterford* (1824), states:

> *the monarch was welcomed with every demonstration of joy, and spent six days in receiving the deceitful homage of his people.*

Ryland goes on to state:

> *at this time the citizens were mean and slovenly, in their appearance, and exhibited in this respect, as well as in their dwellings, a degree of poverty and wretchedness which we should not have expected to find in so considerable a city.*

Richard's second visit to Ireland was to prove his downfall. While he was here his cousin Henry, whom Richard had banished to France, returned to England and claimed the Crown. By the time Richard left Ireland in July 1399, he had lost his power. Henry IV was crowned in October of that year.

1399

14 MAY

Irish Chancery Letters

As mentioned in the introduction and in earlier dates, the Rolls of the Irish Chancery (1244 to 1509) have been reproduced by an ongoing research project in TCD.

One of the earliest documents referring to Waterford deals with the issue of difficulties with the port of New Ross as follows:

> *14 May 1275*
> *To the Sheriff of Dublin.*
> *The King is informed that although in Gascony, England, Ireland and elsewhere, he had forbidden any ship intended for the port of Waterford to go to New Ross unless it belonged to the land and liberty of Leinster, but should go instead to Waterford as was customary in times past, nevertheless, ships go to New Ross in breach of the said prohibition and to the grave damage of the said city. ORDER, notwithstanding the liberty of Carlow, to go to New Ross in person and seize into the King's hand such ships which by inquiry are found to be in breach of the said order, together with all the merchandise in them, and keep them in safe custody until further order, and to arrest all the masters and their men and keep them in prison until further order.*
>
> *Geoffrey Geneville, Justiciar*

1275

15 MAY

Freedom of City

The ninth Freeman of Waterford was the Papal Nuncio Monsignor Paschal Robinson. Born in Dublin in 1870, he emigrated to the United States in his youth. He joined the Franciscan order in 1896. In January 1930 he was appointed the first Papal Nuncio accredited to Ireland since the 17th century. On the 15th of May 1930 he was conferred with the Freedom of Waterford City.

Although the Monsignor had asked for less elaborate arrangements, a procession started from the "borough boundary" in Newrath, where he was welcomed by the Mayor and members of the Corporation. The procession then proceeded to the bridge where the Bishop of Waterford and Lismore Dr. Hackett awaited the Nuncio at the entrance to his diocese. The whole Quay was decked with bunting, business houses decorated their premises and papal flags were in abundance. The lengthy procession took place from the bridge along the Quay to the Cathedral for benediction. After these ceremonies were concluded the procession carried on to City Hall where a large crowd had gathered. A platform was erected on the Mall, and after a number of speeches, the formal ceremony took place in the Large Room.

In his address the Nuncio referred to the fact that as he was a member of the Franciscan order, he had to pay homage to a previous member of that order, specifically Fr. Luke Wadding, and his description of Waterford as *Parva Roma* (or Little Rome).

1930

16 MAY

Air Show

An air show was held at Kilcohan on Thursday the 16th of May 1935. The show was performed by Sir Alan Cobham's squadron.

Alan Cobham was an English WWI fighter pilot who became famous as a pioneer of long distance aviation. In 1932 he formed what was known as Cobham's Flying Circus. Using a team of different aircraft from single seaters to passenger planes, he toured the world performing aerobatic displays in addition to giving people their first flying experience.

His show came to Waterford in May 1935 and included eight aircraft. Six of these were used for aerobatic displays while the other two were used to carry passengers (one could hold twenty-two passengers while the other could hold ten). The first flight included Mayor Alderman E. Dawson in addition to a number of other civic officials. Both planes were busy all day taking members of the public on flights.

A number of aerobatic displays were also carried out, including low level flying with the aircraft upside down. Parachute drops also took place.

1935

17 MAY

Food Riots

The end of the Napoleonic Wars in 1815 brought a recession to Waterford. The number of ships using the port dropped dramatically. In addition bad potato harvests over a number of years led to distress throughout the south of the country. In 1817 a number of food riots took place in Tralee and Kilkenny. In Waterford the emphasis seemed to be on stopping food being exported rather than plunder.

However on the 17th of May 1819, one major food riot took place in the city. A crowd carrying a banner *Bread or Work* marched along O'Connell St. until they reached White's bakery. They broke in, grabbed as much bread as they could, and distributed it to the masses. The cash box was also rifled. The crowd then moved to Bridge Street where they attacked the house of a merchant named Thomas Jacob. However the arrival of the police soon dispersed the crowd.

Tensions remained high during the following days, and following a tip off regarding future protests the Corporation initiated a form of martial law by banning any grouping of more than three persons *to meet or assemble in this City or Liberties; and we direct and order all persons to remain in their houses, or at their lawful occupations, as they shall answer the contrary at their peril.*

1819

18 MAY

Assembly Rooms

The history of the Theatre Royal has already been explored in the entry for the 17th of April, as it was on that date in 1876 that the modern Theatre Royal was opened. However the original playhouse, which stood on the same site, was built in 1787.

In 1783, a group of Waterford's leading merchants came together to build Assembly Rooms on the Mall. The building was designed by John Roberts and was also to include a playhouse. Although the backers for the project were the merchants, the Corporation minutes show that on the 18th of May 1784, the City Council *resolved that the sum of £200 be granted by the Corporation for the purpose of carrying out the building of the new Playhouse and Assembly Rooms.*

The building was done in piecemeal fashion with the Assembly Rooms opening in 1785, the Playhouse in 1787 and the Great Ball Room (Large Room) in 1788. As mentioned earlier, a number of different authors give conflicting dates for these.

This building was later to become City Hall in 1816 (see entry for February 2nd).

1784

19 MAY

Seven Years War

The Seven Years War officially began when England declared war on France on the 15th of May 1756, although fighting and skirmishes between the two countries had been ongoing in North America for years previously. The link with Waterford occurred a few days later when a French vessel was impounded.

A letter dated the 19th of May 1756, published in a Bristol newspaper, gave details of a French vessel, the *Brilliant*, sailing from St. Domingo to Bordeaux when she was blown off course. She met a fishing boat off the Waterford coast, and unaware of hostilities being declared, she asked to be brought to the nearest port. On arriving in Waterford she was boarded by British officers and seized. She had a crew of twenty-eight and five passengers. Her cargo was valued at £11,000 and included sugar, coffee, indigo and cotton.

1756

20 MAY

Emigrant Ships

Potato blight, which had originally appeared on the eastern coast of America in 1843, spread to Europe early in 1845. It appeared in Ireland in September 1845. However, its late arrival limited the impact that year. The following year, there was total failure of the potato crop and the famine began in earnest. Emigration began on a vast scale. Approximately five thousand ships sailed across the Atlantic from Irish ports with emigrants over the next few years. These ships sailed from ports large and small, some making the journey direct, others going to Liverpool first for onward sailing to America.

As a major port, Waterford was no exception to this mass emigration. In 1845, seventeen emigrant ships left Waterford. In 1846 this dropped to fifteen. But in 1847 at the height of the famine this number grew to forty-three. This is just counting the ships which sailed directly to America. Many other emigrants left Waterford for Bristol and Liverpool to continue their onward journey.

The largest number of emigrant ships to leave on a single day occurred on the 20th of May 1847. Five left for Quebec and one for New York.

1847

21 MAY

First Railway Link

It was on this date in 1845 that the first railway reached Waterford. This was the line from Kilkenny to Waterford. In practice the Waterford line finished at Dunkitt, and passengers and their luggage were transported to and from the city by horse and car.

Eight years later the Waterford to Limerick line opened, in August 1853, but it was September 1854 before the line from Dunkitt to Waterford City was completed and a new station opened at Sallypark. This Sallypark station was on the site of the present CIE freight depot. Ten years later in August 1864, the line was brought closer again when a new Waterford station (known as Waterford North Station) was opened at the other side of the bridge (its present location).

In 1868, a line from Kilkenny to Portlaoise was completed, but it was to be 1900 before direct train service between Waterford and Dublin was introduced.

The Waterford, Dungarvan and Lismore line was opened in August 1878 with the terminus at the Waterford South Station in Bilberry.

In 1906 the Waterford-Rosslare line was opened.

1845

22 MAY

Great Escape

There were a number of escapes from the Waterford jail in Ballybricken down through the years. The *Great Escape* took place on Sunday the 22nd of May 1836 when fourteen convicts managed to set themselves free.

The escape was led by the two famous Connery brothers from west Waterford (see entry for July 22nd). The escape began when the two brothers overpowered a prison guard by the name of James McLaughlin. They took a key from him, and opened a number of other cells. While some prisoners declined to join in, twelve did, seven of whom were in jail awaiting transportation. The lock to the yard was smashed using a heavy treadmill. The Governor, James Bruce, attempted to keep the door closed, however he was overpowered and the prisoners made their escape.

When they made their way out of the jail they were applauded by the people of Ballybricken. While some of the escapees were captured within a short time, the two Connery brothers remained at large for another two years.

Major Woodward, Inspector General of Prisons in Ireland, held an inquiry into the escape. The Governor James Bruce was found not guilty of neglect but was dismissed as Governor. The prison guard James McLaughlin was found guilty of negligence and sentenced to seven years transportation. Evidence was produced to show that he had been somewhat complicit in the escape.

1836

23 MAY

County and City Infirmary

The origin of the Infirmary goes back over eight hundred years when King John founded a leper hospital in Stephen Street in 1210. In 1785 the leper hospital was transferred to John's Hill. In the late 19th century concern was expressed that there was no hospital in the city to deal with normal injuries and illnesses, not to mention any possible outbreak of contagious disease. Both the city and county authorities came together with various private benefactors until eventually a proposal was made to take over the leper hospital and convert it into a modern hospital.

The Waterford Infirmary Act was passed by Westminster in 1896. Plans were drawn up and the local building firm of John Hearne and Son began work in March 1897. The Infirmary opened on the 23rd of May 1898. From the start it was made clear that the hospital was not for the destitute poor (who should attend the Union or County Hospital), but for the working classes. A little over three months later in September 1898, a report by the Resident House Surgeon stated that 102 patients had been hospitalised and over four hundred were treated as outpatients.

The hospital closed eighty-nine years later at the end of October 1987.

1898

24 MAY

Ambrose Congreve

Mount Congreve was built by the Waterford architect John Roberts around 1760. Rev. John Congreve was the first of the Congreve family to settle in Waterford in the 17th century. His son Ambrose Congreve was Mayor of Waterford in 1736/37 (see entry for February 12th). The line continued over the next two hundred years with each descendent named either John or Ambrose.

The last of the line, Ambrose, was born in 1907. Having worked in England and China he took up residence in Mount Congreve in 1968 and devoted all his time to the continuing development of the gardens. The gardens are reputed to have the largest collection of plants grown outdoors in Europe. At a party celebrating his one hundredth birthday, he quoted what he described as an old proverb:

> *To be happy for an hour, have a glass of wine. To be happy for a day, read a book. To be happy for a week, take a wife. To be happy forever, make a garden.*

Ambrose Congreve died in London while attending the Chelsea Flower Show on the 24th of May 2011, aged 104.

In July 2012 a two-day auction of the contents of Mount Congreve began. Some of the items auctioned fetched very high prices.
- Chandelier €44,000
- Rolls Royce €46,000
- Chinese Vase €50,000
- Collection of delph €55,000
- Desk €82,000

2011

25 MAY

Adelphi Hotel

It was on this date in 1970 that the Adelphi Hotel was demolished. Standing on the corner of the Mall and Adelphi Quay (the site of the bar in the present Tower Hotel), it had closed three years earlier. In 1967 developers purchased the hotel and the adjoining Steamship Offices and Country Club building, with the intention of erecting a new luxury eighteen-story hotel on the site, at an estimated cost of £300,00.

Note the Country Club had been used as the Garda Station from 1940 to 1968 (see entry for October 23rd).

However, demolition did not begin until May 1970 and the planned development of the eighteen-story hotel did not go ahead. The site was then used as a car park for a number of years. In 1984, it was planned to build a £3 million office block on the site. These plans included a curved wall on the corner to blend in with Reginald's Tower. Again this development did not go ahead.

The Tower Hotel group eventually purchased the site in the late 1980s. However, Tower Lane, a public roadway, divided the site from the adjoining Tower Hotel. At a meeting of the City Council held in July 1989, agreement was reached on the closure of Tower Lane and its sale to the Tower Hotel for a sum of £14,000. Building worked started quickly and the new extended Tower Hotel opened in April 1991. Aptly enough the new bar was called the Adelphi Bar.

1970

26 MAY

Great Charter

As mentioned in the entry for March 5th, the ascent of King James I to the throne in 1603 saw the beginning of a much less tolerant regime. James insisted that mayors take the Oath of Supremacy accepting him as head of the Church. The refusal by the elected mayors to do this led to the charters being seized and the dissolution of the Corporation for the next seven years. James died in 1625, and was replaced by his son Charles I. Waterford citizens immediately applied for a new charter. Charles granted this Charter on the 26th of May 1626. Known as the Great Charter it incorporated all the previous charters and set out in detail the rights and responsibilities of Waterford Corporation. It was under the terms of this Charter that the city was governed for the next 214 years until the *Municipal Reform Act of 1840*.

A supplement to this Charter was issued the following year in relation to the admiralty of the harbour and fishery rights (see entry for February 19th).

1626

27 MAY

King's Birthday

In 1649 Cromwell came to Ireland. Although he failed to capture Waterford (see entry for August 10th), the city fell to his General Ireton in August 1650. There followed a decade of tyranny. By the time Cromwell died in 1658, only 950 people lived within the walls of Waterford, of which about 540 were foreign adventurers.

In 1660 the monarchy was restored and the merchants of Waterford began to thrive again. They lost no opportunity in displaying their loyalty to the crown.

At its meeting held on the 27th of May 1663, Waterford Corporation decided that the King's birthday (Charles II), two days later on the 29th of May, should be celebrated. Not only that, but twenty shillings was to be given to schoolboys to make decorations as the following excerpts from the minutes show.

> *It is ordered that the day of solemnity of the King's birth be with all solemnity carried on, and that the sum of 20s be given to those schoolboys that make decorations, and the sum to be disposed of at the discretion of the Mayor.*

1663

28 MAY

Tower Hotel

The Tower Hotel first opened its doors on Monday the 28th of May 1962. Built on the site of the old Imperial Hotel, it was the first purpose built hotel in Waterford for a long number of years. Built by Sisk Ltd. it cost £150,000. The formal opening was performed by the Minister for Transport and Power Mr. Erskine Childers TD.

A description of the Tower Hotel showed that it had 58 bedrooms ranging from single rooms to a family suite of three rooms with bunk beds (complete with ladder). There were two 2-bedroom executive suites on each of the three floors. Each bedroom had its own bathroom or shower. The bedrooms themselves were fitted with *Odearest beds*. The B&B rate at the time was 25/- to 45/- in summer while winter rates were 25/- to 35/-. Lunch cost 8/- and dinner 15/-. Staff accommodation was provided on the premises of Merry's on the other side of the Mall (backing onto Bailey's New Street).

As mentioned, the Tower Hotel was built on the site of the old Imperial Hotel. The Imperial Hotel was in some ways a Waterford institution, and many historical events had taken place inside and outside its doors. It had a number of different proprietors, but the Holy Ghost Hospital Board also had an interest in the freehold of the site. As the Holy Ghost was a charitable institution, the consent of the High Court was required for its sale. When the company building the Tower Hotel purchased the freehold, a last minute difficulty occurred with a sub tenant of the former Imperial Hotel. Building operations were suspended for a while until the matter was resolved.

1962

29 MAY

Handwriting

An unusual advertisement appeared on the front page of the *Waterford Chronicle* on Saturday the 29th of May 1830:

> *For a short time only.*
> *The Royal Lewisian System of Writing.*
> *Teaching Rooms at Mr. McLean's, Henrietta Street.*
> *Terms for the whole course – one guinea.*

Mr. Lloyd respectfully announces that he has opened an institution in Waterford for a short time, where he will give instruction in the new mathematical system of converting bad writers into good ones in six short and easy lessons.

The Royal Lewisian System for reforming the style of bad writers is the most efficient ever invented. Its peculiar advantage is, that it is not confined to one particular method – for how inelegant and absurd would it be for a Lady to write a bold masculine mercantile hand, or for a Gentleman to be confined to a fine, high effeminate one, adapted only to epistolary correspondence, complimentary cards, invitation, etc. It is applicable to all purposes and to persons of all ages; and however bad the pupil may write, or what ever may be his capacity, it will positively qualify him for any situation whatsoever, so far as regards his hand writing.

Attendance will be from nine o'clock in the morning till ten at night.

N.B. From six till ten in the evening is appropriate to the instruction of those persons whose engagements in business preclude their attendance in the day time.

Separate apartments for Ladies.

Pupils are delayed only one hour each lesson and may attend at any time (within the above hours) that suits their convenience.

Lloyds fine and broad nib pens from 4s to 10s per hundred, may be had at the rooms.

1830

30 MAY

Meeting of Unionists

Waterford always had an eclectic mix of aristocrats and wealthy local merchants, all of whom normally got along. An interesting exchange took place on this day in 1912 between two of the major figures of the day. On one side was Sir W.G.D. Goff, from Glenville House, a Protestant unionist, and one of the largest employers in the city. On the other side was Mayor Michael Kirwan, proprietor of Queen's Hotel in Mall Lane, elected Mayor in January 1912.

The 3rd Home Rule Bill was introduced into the House of Commons in early April with support from John Redmond, MP for Waterford and leader of the Irish Parliamentary Party. The bill did not go down well with many of the old aristocracy including W. Goff. On the 30th of May 1912 Goff looked for permission to use City Hall for a meeting of unionists. The following day Mayor Kirwan refused and told him he could use it for *any purpose except that of holding an anti Home Rule meeting.*

1912

31 MAY

Battle of Jutland

The outbreak of World War I in 1914 led many Irish men to join the British forces. Nearly 5,000 men from Waterford joined up. By the end of the year, some 700 were dead. There were many battles in which large numbers died, such as the Battle of LE Pilly on the 19th of October 1914. Of the 228 Irish men killed, thirty-eight were from Waterford.

Waterford men also joined the British Navy. The biggest naval battle of the war, the Battle of Jutland, was fought on the 31st of May 1916. A total of fourteen British ships and eleven German ships were sunk with a total loss of life of 8,645. One hundred and forty-one of these were Irish, of which twelve were from Waterford.

Of the 1,015 men lost aboard *HMS Indefatigable*, five were from Waterford; Joseph Coghlan, James Daley, Daniel Doyle, James Founds, and Michael Mulcahy.

Of the 903 men lost aboard *HMS Defence*, five were again from Waterford; Thomas Carlton, Joseph Hogan, Stephen Power, William Ryan and Edward Wallace.

Of the 185 men lost aboard *HMS Tipperary*, one sailor, Albert Randel, was from Waterford.

HMS Tiger was badly damaged in the battle resulting in the death of Albert Poole, also from Waterford.

1916

1 JUNE

Milford Haven

Up to the early 1820s the mail service from Waterford to London was unreliable, depending on the vagaries of sail. However. the introduction of steam ships changed all that. We saw on the 16th of April 1825 that the first regular steam service began from Milford Haven to Dunmore East. This developed over the years and by 1835 there were four vessels on the route, which was now extended to Waterford City. In 1837 the Admiralty took over the service from the Post Office. However very few passengers used it, mainly due to the inadequate rail service at the Milford Haven end.

The Admiralty closed the mail route in 1848 and for a while there was no regular passenger sailings between Waterford and Wales. A proper rail connection opened in Milford in 1856, and soon again a Waterford-Milford service reopened. A substantial growth in traffic occurred especially in the export of cattle which necessitated a daily sailing.

The daily service began on the 1st of June 1858. The steamer left Adelphi Quay at 3pm (after the arrival of the Limerick train), and arrived in Milford Haven in time for the 2.45am express train to London, arriving in Paddington at 11.10am.

1858

2 JUNE

Barronstrand Street

Smith's *History of Waterford*, first published in 1746, includes a map of the city. What is very apparent from the map is the narrowness of the streets and the lack of any public squares or open spaces. Smith himself states: *several of the streets and lanes are for the most part exceedingly narrow and the houses crowded very thick together.*

During the mid-19th century the Wide Street Commission was formed and set about widening some of the streets. One of its projects was Barronstrand Street. Here a number of lanes such as Royal Oak Lane, Garter Lane and Little Barronstrand Street were demolished and cleared to form the open area which was previously known as Barronstrand Street and now known as John Roberts Square. In addition Barronstrand Street itself was widened from its junction at the Quay.

According to *A Calendar for the year 1900* by M. J. Hurley, the new Barronstrand Street opened on the 2nd of June 1857.

Other projects by the Wide Street Commission included:
- The opening up of the Applemarket by the removal of a large building block which was situated in the centre
- The removal of buildings which formed an island at the junction of Patrick Street and Stephen Street
- Extending Arundel Square by the removal of Arundel Lane

1857

3 JUNE

Dredger Urbs Intacta

When the Harbour Commissioners were first set up in 1816, one of their first schemes was the deepening of the Ford or Queen's Channel. By 1839 the commissioners saw the need to have their own dredger. The Neptune Foundry was tasked with building the vessel, however problems arose and the *dredge boat was completed by the Royal Phoenix Iron Works in Dublin*. This dredger does not appear to have been very successful, and in the late 1850s, the commissioners sought a *dredge boat more suitable for the Waterford river*. This was built at the Water Street Dockyard in Cork and it arrived in Waterford on the 3rd of June 1861.

The dredger was aptly named *Urbs Intacta* and was of bucket design. Its captain was Peter Lawlor, and the engineer, Thomas Schlanders. *Urbs Intacta* worked on the river for the next 46 years until it was replaced by the hopper design *Portlairge* in 1907. It is reputed that after she was disposed of she ended up in China where she eventually sank.

1861

4 JUNE

Cherry's Brewery

On this day in 1806, the *Waterford Mirror* announced that William and Richard Cherry had commenced brewing of the *Best Table Beer* in their premises at Peter Street. Another brewery followed soon after in King Street (O'Connell Street). In 1818 William took over the whole business and eventually the Peter Street brewery closed down. The site in Peter Street later became the Arundel Ballroom and later again an amusement arcade (see entry for October 7th).

In 1828 William purchased the Creywell Brewery in New Ross and transferred the whole operation there. The brewery remained in the Cherry family until 1953 when they sold the business to Guinness (who continued to operate the business under the Cherry name). Cherry's returned to Waterford in 1954 when they took over the Strangman's brewery in Mary Street (this had closed in 1950, see entry for January 4th). Initially Phoenix was brewed here followed later by Hoffmans, and then Smithwicks. In 1990 a ceremony was held to mark the occasion of the brewing of the 20 millionth pint.

Brewing ceased in Cherry's in 2002 and following a major investment into the premises, Guinness commenced production in 2004 of the *essence of Guinness* which was then exported to 50 countries where the final product was brewed. In April 2013, Guinness announced that the plant would close by the end of the year.

1806

5 JUNE

Court Case

A rather unusual case was held in the Dublin courts on this date in 1916. It involved a Waterford lady by the name of Hilda Brabazon who brought a case of breach of promise against a William Bernard, a Dublin bank clerk, as he would not marry her.

Counsel for Ms. Brabazon stated that on the 1st of August 1914, the defendant had proposed marriage to the plaintiff while they were at the Imperial Hotel in Dublin, which she accepted. The defendant subsequently *took advantage of her* while staying in his mother's house and a child was born in May 1915. Mr. Bernard denied having ever promised to marry the plaintiff, but admitted the *misconduct had taken place*. He said he was fairly fond of the plaintiff at the start of their acquaintance, but he had never intended to marry her, as he had not means enough. The Justice asked him if he still refused to marry her and he replied, *I do*.

While the Judge was very sympathetic to Miss Brabazon, he pointed out that there was no corroboratory evidence that the promise of marriage was actually made so he reluctantly directed the jury to find the defendant innocent.

1916

6 JUNE

Newport's Bank

The Newport family was already been mentioned on the 9th of February, when Sir John Newport MP for Waterford died in 1843. Sir John was the son of Simon Newport, the founder of Newport Bank, which was for a time the largest bank in Waterford. Founded around 1760, the Newport name carried immense confidence and at one stage had £150,000 of its own notes in circulation. Although a number of the Newport family were involved in running the bank, the senior partner in 1820 was William Newport of Belmount.

Following the Napoleonic wars there was a sharp recession in Ireland, leading to the collapse of many private banks. In May 1820, Roche's Bank in Cork failed. This financial contagion quickly spread throughout Munster and on the 6th of June 1820, Newport's bank collapsed. A story goes that a doctor was called to the house of William Newport in Belmount. Having spent a small amount of time there he left and went to Newport's Bank on the Quay where he withdrew all his savings in gold. On the way out he told the staff that William, the senior partner, was dead having committed suicide. The bank collapsed within a few hours.

The repercussions of the collapse spread throughout Waterford where, according to Reverend W. P. Burke, *strong men lost their reason and steady men drank themselves to death and ladies living on a slender income were reduced to absolute beggary*. There is a report that Thomas Francis Meagher Senior (later Mayor of Waterford) bought some of the assets of Newport's Bank including the building now known as the Granville Hotel. That is how Thomas Francis Meagher came to be born in the Granville in 1823.

1820

7 JUNE

Major Willie Redmond

Willie Redmond was brother of John Redmond (Waterford City MP from 1891 to 1918 and leader of the Irish Parliamentary Party). The Redmond family was originally from Wexford where their father William Redmond was MP. Willie himself was elected MP for Wexford on his father's death. He served briefly as MP for Fermanagh before taking the East Clare seat in 1892. He continued to serve for East Clare until his death in 1917. His brother John held the Waterford seat for a similar length of time from 1891 until 1918.

Like John Redmond, Willie fully supported Irishmen joining the British Army at the start of World War I. He took it one step further in that at the age of 53 he joined himself. He is reputed to have said *Boys! I will not ask you to go, but I may ask you to come.* Major Willie Redmond died at the Battle of Messines on the 7th of June 1917.

There is an interesting connection between the Redmond family and Eamonn de Valera. When Major Willie Redmond was killed in 1917, he was succeeded in the Clare seat by de Valera. In his campaign, de Valera concentrated on attacking John Redmond. A campaign leaflet stated: *East Clare must keep the flag flying and defy John Redmond and the English Government.* De Valera won the seat with 71% of the vote. When John Redmond himself died in 1918, de Valera assumed he could achieve a similar result in Waterford and spent a week in Waterford campaigning for the Sinn Féin candidate Dr. Vincent White. However de Valera underestimated the strength of the Redmondite tradition in Waterford, and Captain Willie Redmond, (son of John Redmond) won the by-election, achieving 62% of the vote (see entry for March 13th).

1917

8 JUNE

Food Riots

When we think of famine in Ireland, we automatically think of the mid-1840s. However there were many other occasions when there were major food shortages. A bad potato harvest in 1816 led to severe unrest in the early months of 1817. News of food riots across Munster reached Waterford on Sunday the 8th of June. The following day, a large crowd gathered on the Quay as a ship laden with oatmeal departed. The military were needed to keep order. On the Tuesday, the crowd succeeded in boarding one of the food ships and removed her sails. The disturbances continued for the rest of the week. Eventually the Mayor organised some food relief after £1,650 had been raised in donations.

Another occasion was in November 1792, when large crowds marched to the Mayor's office to complain about the high price of food. On not getting any satisfaction, they then went to Cheekpoint to stop any outward bound ships which might have a cargo with food. Having boarded some ships to search they returned to the city empty handed. The Mayor at the time was Sir Simon Newport, and he managed to reduce tensions somewhat by securing an agreement with the corn merchants to stop shipping corn.

Some seventeen years earlier in 1775 there had also been food riots in the city. On that occasion the Mayor had to obtain the assistance of Major William Murray with the 42nd Regiment of Foot and also Captain Richard Rodney Bligh of his Majesty's Sloop of War, *The Wasp,* lying in the harbour. Both Major Murray and Captain Bligh were given the Freedom of the City in thanks for their assistance. Captain Richard Rodney Bligh (later Admiral) was actually a cousin of Captain William Bligh of *HMS Bounty* fame.

1817

9 JUNE

Conscription

Conscription was first introduced in Britain in January 1916, but following nationalist opposition, Ireland was not included in the Act. However as the war progressed the need for more troops became greater. On the 16th of April 1918, Westminster passed a bill empowering the government to extend conscription to Ireland. This provoked an immediate backlash. It actually had the effect of uniting many opposing Irish groups. Two days later on the 18th of April an anti-conscription committee was formed in Dublin with representatives from the Irish Parliamentary Party, Sinn Féin, the All Ireland Party, Labour and trade unions. A national day of protest occurred on the 23rd of April. In Waterford about ten thousand participated in the rally that day.

Another protest held in Waterford was on the 9th of June when Cumann na mBan organised an anti-conscription march. About 1,500 women marched behind a banner declaring: *The women of Waterford will not have conscription.*

The campaign against conscription continued right up to Armistice Day on the 11th of November 1918.

1918

10 JUNE

Presentation Convent

In 1798 Presentation nuns first arrived in Waterford. Initially they lived in Jenkins Lane in the vacant parochial house attached to St. Patrick's Church. In 1880 they moved into their new convent in Hennessy's Road. This site was quite small being just over a quarter of an acre. In the 1840s a decision was made to move to a new larger convent in Lisduggan.

On the 10th of June 1842 the foundation stone was laid for the new convent. The architect was Augustus Pugin, one of the most celebrated architects of his day. Of note was that while most of the city clergy attended the event, none of the nuns themselves attended due to the rule of enclosure. Building took quite some time and when the nuns moved from Hennessy's Road on the 3rd of May 1848, the new convent was only half built. Indeed it was to be another 15 years before the chapel was finished and consecrated in 1863.

Pugin is best remembered for his interior design of the Palace of Westminster following a fire in 1834. In Ireland, he also designed the Presentation Convent in Lismore, St. Mary's Cathedral in Killarney, St. Aidan's Cathedral in Enniscorthy and the Dominican Church in Tralee. His other link to Waterford was that he designed the interior of Lismore Castle when it was restored in the 1840s.

The building was sold by the Presentation Order in 2006 and following renovations opened as Waterford Health Park in 2009. A Blue Plaque dedicated to the memory of Pugin was erected by Waterford Civic Trust on the building in May 2013.

1842

11 JUNE

Millennium Plaza

The William Vincent Wallace Plaza was opened by Minster Séamus Brennan, Chairman of the National Millennium Committee on Monday the 11th of June 2001. Also in attendance was the Minister of State Martin Cullen and Mayor Davy Daniels. Costing £1.2 million, it was grant aided by the Millennium Committee to the tune of £850,000. Built on the site of a large semi derelict concrete shed at the Clyde Wharf, it was named after William Vincent Wallace.

The Mayor, Cllr. Davy Daniels stated that the plaza was situated on the very spot where the Vikings landed so many centuries ago. He explained the three elements of the plaza. Firstly, the outdoor performance space is protected by a tensile tent structure backed by strongly coloured elements that simulate Viking shields and maritime flags. Secondly, the large timber area provides a dry viewing area and the long curved steel tubes simulate wooden boats. Finally, the tall sculpture element provides a counterpoint to Reginald's Tower, and mirrors the vertical elements of a yacht mast.

Interestingly, both Minister Cullen, who was responsible for the Office of Public Works, and the OPW Chairman Barry Murphy were of the opinion that the plaza should be extended the length of the Quay.

2001

12 JUNE

St. John's Priory

John's Street, John's Bridge, John's River and St. John's Gate were all named after St. John's Priory which was founded circa 1191 by King John on his first visit to Ireland. At the beginning of the 13th century it was the only religious house in Waterford. The original charter for the Priory was quite clear that all its brothers and property were under the protection of the King. In addition they had entitlement to trade without paying any taxes. Over the next three hundred years the Priory operated without fear.

However the arrival of Henry VIII and the Reformation led to its downfall. Saint John's Priory was the first religious house to be closed in Waterford. *The Great Parchment Book of Waterford* has the original decree of suppression dated the 12th of June 1536. The decree is quite specific and legalistic as the following excerpts show:

> *The house and monastery, priory, convent, hospital or cell of Saint John the Evangelist close by Waterford in the County of Waterford in the diocese of Waterford in Ireland, be absolutely suppressed and the title of the same to be abolished and also the convent or hospital guardians or boonworkets in the same to be abolished and also the convent or hospital or the monks and brother and sisters there to be forever dissolved diminished and banished accordingly.*

In November 1537 William Wyse and his heirs were granted the monastery and all its lands.

1536

13 JUNE

Water Supply

The issue of a suitable water supply for the inhabitants of the city was always a matter of concern for Waterford Corporation. In 1685 the Corporation official who looked after the water supply was Bartholomew Butler.

In 1861 there is a reference in the Corporation records as follows:

> *That Bartholomew Butlers salary of eight pounds per annum for maintaining the waterworks and conduits shall be continued and paid by Mr Mayors rent and Moccully, and that the six pounds arrears be paid to him the first money.*

He was still employed thirty years later at the same salary as a reference in 1699 states:

> *That Barth Butlers have eight pounds paid him by the receiver for a years salary of the looking after the waterworks ended last Michaelmas.*

Part of his duties involved digging wells in various locations. In May of 1688 there is a reference that he should finish his diggings in Dr. Madden's garden within two months. He was obviously successful in finding water, as on the 10th of June certain members of the Corporation were ordered to view the new spring discovered by him.

On the 13th of June 1685 the Sheriff Receiver was instructed to pay him forty shillings *towards the work of finding out the summer spring*.

See also the entry for October 5th for more on the city's water supply.

1685

14 JUNE

Rebellion

In October 1641 a rebellion began in Ulster and gradually communal uprisings spread to the rest of the country. Very quickly events spiralled out of control with many sectarian attacks on Protestant settlers, which in turn led to reprisals.

Although the unrest continued for many years, swift action was taken in Waterford to quell the uprising and on the 3rd of December 1641 Sir William Saintleger, Lord President of Munster, on his way from Clonmel to Waterford with some three hundred soldiers, killed two hundred of the rebels. Another forty of the ringleaders were hanged in Waterford three days later on the 6th of December.

Although the Civil War broke out in England the following year between the Parliamentarians and the Royalists, a commission was set up to investigate and bring to justice all those who participated in the uprising. Statements were taken from any Protestant settler who wished to give his story. The problem was that it gave an opportunity to all and sundry to claim all sorts of loss and settle old scores. Copies of these depositions remain in Trinity College Library and were the subject of a book published in 1912 entitled *Waterford during the Civil War 1641-1653* by Thomas Fitzpatrick.

In a deposition dated the 14th of June 1642 John Orton of the parish of Clashmore and county of Waterford swore that:

> *He was stripped of his wearing apparel, and as by the report of his neighbours, was robbed by John Butler and his brother, and one John Mcsline and Edward his brother both of Ardsala in the barony of Decies and one Francis Gough of the same.*

1642

15 JUNE

Piracy

An article in the *Journal of the Waterford and South-East of Ireland Archaeological Society, 1911* refers to a collection of manuscripts which at that time were held in Dublin Castle. The author, Philip Herbert Hore, states that they appeared to be copies of orders of the Lord Deputy and Council. A number of these refer to piracy off the south east coast.

The following is the text of an order dated the 15th of June 1652 at Kinsale:

> *To the Captain of the Hector.*
> *It is this day ordered that you with ye first opportunity of wind and weather serving do forthwith repair to the Port of Wexford, and thence you do use all Diligence to clear the Coast of Pirates and other enemies between Dublin and Waterford, or where you understand the Pirates shall be between the Welsh and Irish Coasts, and to ply to and again in ye Irish seas, as may be of most encouragement to the merchants and traders between England and Ireland, and for so doing this shall be your Warrant.*

Another order dated two weeks earlier at Crooke states:

> *Whereas the Commissioners are informed that there are several Pirates lying upon ye. Coast between Kinsale and Wexford to ye great hindrance of trade and prejudice of Merchants. It is therefore ordered that such of ye states Shipps as are now in ye river of Waterford and at liberty do, with the first opportunity of wind, or other, put to sea, to the end the coast may be cleared of ye Pirates aforesaid, provided the same be not inconsistent with the orders given them, by the Council of State or the Generals at sea, and to certify their proceedings with the condition of the Court forthwith to the said Commissioners of Parliament.*

1652

16 JUNE

Charter

The earliest Charter in the possession of Waterford Corporation is that of Henry VI from 1449. However there are transcripts of earlier Charters in the Great Charter Roll. One of these is the first Charter granted by Henry III. According to Egan's *History of Waterford* (1894) this Charter was granted on the 16th of June 1237, although recent publications by Eamonn McEneaney and Julian Walton state that the Charter was issued in 1232.

This Charter is important in that it gave the power to the Corporation to raise its own taxes for the first time. In practice it allowed the Corporation to collect all the rents due to the King in the city. However, the King himself only required a fixed sum. Thus the Corporation could retain any rents collected above the fixed sum. At the time the fixed amount due to the King was 100 marks (recall: a mark was a unit of account equivalent to two thirds of a pound – see entry for April 3rd), which was the second highest amount in the country. This implies that Waterford was the second most populated city in the country, behind Dublin.

Another interesting fact from this Charter was that it allowed the Corporation to keep half the tax levied on wine imports. Since at that time Waterford was the main port in the country for importing wine, this was a major source of finance for the Corporation.

1237

17 JUNE

Reginald's Tower

Reginald's Tower has served many purposes down through the years. During the last two hundred years it has been a prison (1819-1861), a residence of the High Constable (1861- 1954) and a museum.

It was on the 17th of June 1955 that Mayor Patrick Browne formally opened Reginald's Tower as a civic museum. At the opening, the Mayor referred to the fact that one of the few things in Waterford older than the Corporation was Reginald's Tower. Bord Fáilte mainly funded the conversion of the tower with a £2,600 grant. Unfortunately in keeping with the ethos of the time, the conversion of the tower was more of a modernisation and rebuild. All of the internal walls were plastered, covering up most of the original features. A new balcony was also built.

In 1993 a restoration project began. The plaster was removed, uncovering many features that had been hidden since the 18th and 19th centuries. Detailed examination showed first and second floors dated from around 1200, while the top two floors dated from the 15th century. The balcony erected at the third floor in 1950 was removed. In 1995, Dúchas, the Heritage Service, took over the guardianship of the tower and completed the restoration. It was reopened in 1999. Today Reginald's Tower is home to the Waterford Viking Museum.

1955

18 JUNE

Observance of Lord's Day

As mentioned earlier (see entry for March 21st), Bishop Nathaniel Foy attempted to introduce strict observance of the keeping of the Sabbath. He obviously had great success, as at a meeting of Waterford Corporation held on the 18th of June 1692, the following order was made:

Whereas the due and pious observance of the Lord's day is not only of Divine institution but also strictly enjoined by the laws of this land, and the profanity thereof both highly dishonorable to Almighty God and also of evil and dangerous consequence to all nations and societies permitting the same: These are to require all and every inhabitants and residents within this city and liberties thereof, both young and old, with all pious diligence to apply themselves and intend the due observation of the Lords day, forbearing all manner of manual labours, gamings, plays, revelling, swearing, cursing, unnecessary walkings abroad or to public places except the Church, and all other undue and profane practices on said day. And all high and petty constables within this county are strictly required within their respective limits to see to the due observance of the said day, and to return to Mr. Mayor every Monday the names of all delinquents, upon pain of being prosecuted and punished themselves with the greatest severity for neglect of their duty.

1692

19 JUNE

Christ Church Burials

The disruption caused by indiscriminate burials both inside and outside Christ Church caused the following order to be made by Waterford Corporation at its meeting on the 19th of June 1683:

> *Ordered that the sexton of Christ Church do take care that none shall be suffered to break ground to bury their dead in any part of the cathedral church or outstalls or Lady's chapel belonging to the Corporation, but shall at their own cost and charges provide paving stones and mortar to make the ground even with other payment and also pay for the ground according to the order of the council.*

The issue of burials at Christ Church had also been discussed the previous January:

> *Ordered that the sexton shall not break ground in the body or outstalls or choir of Christ Church belonging to the city, or Lady's chapel, without order from Mr. Mayor and sheriffs for the time being; and that every foreigner pay fifty shillings, every freeman and inhabitant thirteen shillings and four pence, for burying a man, woman, or child in the body, outstalls, or chapel and in the choir, double.*

Four years later in 1687, the Corporation decided that:

> *The Mayor, alderman and council for time past and to come, and their wives and children, shall be free to be buried there without paying anything.*

1683

20 JUNE

King John

There are a number of dates given for King John's second visit to Waterford. The most recently published *History of Waterford* by Power (1990) gives it as the 20th of June 1210, as does Downey (1914). However Smith (1746) says it was the 8th of June 1211 while both Ryland (1824) and Hansard (1879) say it was the 6th of June 1211.

Irrespective of the date, we do know this was John's second visit to Waterford. He had first come in May 1185 on the instruction of his father King Henry II. It was on that first visit that Prince John was reputed to have become ill and fearing he had contracted leprosy, he endowed a leper hospital on Stephen Street, the precursor to the Infirmary on John's Hill (see entry for May 23rd).

When John returned in 1210, his palace was situated where the Widows' Apartments now stand (directly opposite the front door of Christ Church). He arranged the affairs of Ireland from Waterford and also visited many parts of the country. He also arranged a major addition to the city, nearly doubling its size while adding new city walls and towers. Many of these still exist today.

1210

21 JUNE

Undercroft

One of the highlights of the new Waterford Medieval Museum is the incorporation of the undercroft into the new museum building. There are in fact two adjoining undercrofts, both located under the late 18th century deanery building. The oldest undercroft dates from around 1270 while the second upper undercroft is smaller and dates from the early 15th century (see entry for July 6th).

Although the undercrofts have a long history, they remained hidden for hundreds of years until 1871. On the 21st of June 1871, the Dean of Waterford issued a statement confirming their existence and that he had explored them and reopened "the crypt". He states:

It was always known that a large vault existed beneath the Deanery House at Waterford, but it was never explored, nor was it known how far it extended. On coming to reside there, I found this an object of interest to the antiquary, and proceeded to explore and re-open the crypt.

The whole length is 60 feet and breadth 19 feet. The ceiling is supported and divided by two equal aisles, by massive arches sprung from ponderous columns. The interior is filled to a depth of about five feet with rubble; evidently the remains of buildings that were previously on the site. In the rubbish I found a coin, having on one side a ship and on the reverse, three "fleur de lis". I also found several tobacco pipes of a particular design and with small bowls. These are believed to have been left by some of Cromwell's soldiers who occupied the Deanery.

1871

22 JUNE

Freeman

Controlling trade in the city was an important element of the Corporation's responsibilities. This was achieved by limiting the practice of trade to Freemen. Freedom of the City could be achieved in a number of ways, the most common of which was its purchase. Freedom could also be gained by marriage or by apprenticehood. In addition, the son of a Freeman was automatically entitled to the position. Being a Freeman confirmed certain diverse privileges; it also tied the Freeman to the wellbeing of the city, as he had to take an oath of allegiance (see entry for February 22nd).

In June 1674, it was ordered that all persons inhabiting the city who kept shops or were engaged in any craft or trade were required to purchase their Freedom forthwith. Since many did not comply with this order, on the 22nd of June 1674, the Council ordered:

> *That the Sheriffs of this city shall shut down the shops of all persons driving trade in the city and not free of the same, unless such as make application for their admission to the city freedom by Friday next.*

Seven days later, the Corporation took action:

> *Resolved that the Sheriffs shall shut down the shop windows of Mr Benjamin Powell for refusing his freedom of the city now tendered to him by the council, and that he be not permitted to trade or keep shop until he purchase his freedom.*

1674

23 JUNE

Garda Stations

In 1922 the Civic Guards inherited the old RIC organisation and the various police barracks around the city. These included stations in Manor Street, Mary Street, Poleberry, Lady Lane and Ferrybank. On the 23rd of June 1930 all these garda stations except Ferrybank were closed and moved to a sole station located in the Infantry Barracks in Barrack Street.

The large space available at the new location led to many community events taking place there. Many organisations held their meetings there and "whist drives" were also held. At other times however, the barracks was in lock-down mode and persons seeking admission had to produce identification.

The Garda Station remained at the barracks for the next ten years until 1940 when, during the Emergency, army troops moved back into the barracks. Under the Emergency Powers Act, the County Club premises at Adelphi Quay was commandeered and the Garda Station moved there in July 1940.

1930

24 JUNE

Ferry Disaster

The *On This Day* slot by Julian Walton on WLRFM introduced local history to many Waterford people down through the years. On many an occasion Julian managed to surprise people with new historical facts. One such item was the Waterford ferry disaster of 1621, an account of which has only appeared in the journal of the 17th century historian Sir James Ware.

Up to the end of the 18th century, crossing the River Suir could only be done by ferry (Timbertoes opened in 1794). There were two ferries, one from Grannagh to Gracedieu, and another from the city quayside to Ferrybank.

Sir James Ware records that on the 24th of June 1621 the ferry was loaded with some 140 passengers. However, as it made its way across the river to Ferrybank it gradually began to take on water. It sank completely within yards of the opposite shore. It is believed that most of the 140 passengers drowned.

As mentioned, there is no other account of this disaster. The journal of Sir James Ware remains unpublished.

1621

25 JUNE

Karel Bacik

Karel Bacik, co-founder of the modern Waterford Glass industry, later Waterford Crystal, was born in Nova Rise, near Prague, Czechoslovakia, on the 25th of June 1910. The Bacik family had a number of crystal factories in Czechoslovakia. However, after WW2, the new Communist Government began to nationalise industries and Bacik felt the need to move.

In 1946 Bacik arrived in Ireland having made contact with a Dublin jeweller by the name of J. B. Fitzpatrick. He learned of the history of glass making in Waterford and decided to base a new glass-making factory here. He leased three acres of land in Ballytruckle from the Corporation and set about building a factory. On the 29th of March 1947 the sod was turned on the enterprise by the Mayor Cllr. M. Coffey.

Its first employee arrived in July 1947. His name was Miroslav Havel. Havel had previously interned at a glass factory in Bohemia owned by Bacik and was invited by him to assist in rebuilding Waterford's crystal industry. Havel became chief designer. The rest is history.

1910

26 JUNE

Irish Chancery Letters

An interesting series of entries occur in the Chancery Letters dealing with the granting of a job for life for a Thomas Holhirst, culminating in this entry dated the 26th of June 1374:

26 Jun. 1374
On 4 July 1371, the King granted for life to Thomas Holhirst the office of collector of the customs from wools and hides and all other merchandise in the ports of Cork, Waterford and Limerick, to have £20 annually. ORDER *now that he is to have the said office for life with £20 annually.*

The original order was made in July 1371:

4 Jul. 1371
GRANT, *for life, to Thomas Holhirst of the office of collector of customs, great and small, in the ports of Cork, Waterford and Limerick, with the custody of one part of the cocket seal in those ports, on condition that he answer yearly at the Irish exchequer for the issues, taking £20 p.a. for his fee out of the issues of the said customs, to be allowed in his account.*

It was confirmed in November 1373:

12 Nov. 1373
INSPEXIMUS *of letters patent of 4 July 1371 granting to Thomas Holhirst the office of collector of customs, great and small, in the ports of Cork, Waterford and Limerick with one half of the cocket seal receiving for life out of the issues thereof his fee of £20 p.a.*

1374

27 JUNE

Corporation Meetings

Local elections today have become hard fought battles with each candidate vying to get the upper hand. This was not always the case as the following two examples from the *Council Books of Waterford* of the 27th of June 1673 show:

Resolved that Captain Jasper Grant, a member of this council having being formally elected to the office of Sheriff, and refused to take the same upon him and hath removed himself and his family from these parts and absented himself a long time from this board, shall be and is hereby removed and displaced from being any longer a member of this council.

That Mr. Humphrey Adams was elected to be a member of the Corporation who appearing and alleging several things by way of excuse, it is thereupon ordered by this board that the said Humphrey Adams do appear here on Monday morning next by eight o clock and comply with the said election and become a member of this council, on pain of twenty pounds sterling to be levied on his goods and chattels to the use of the Corporation of which he is a freeman.

1673

28 JUNE

Christ Church

This is the date of a licence granted to the Dean and Chapter of Waterford to purchase lands to the value of 100 marks. This licence was granted by King Edward IV. We mentioned earlier (see entry for April 3rd) that the value of a mark was 2/3 of a pound or 13s 4d. Thus the value of 100 marks was £66 13s 4d.

In the early 13th century King John had endowed Christ Church with possessions to support twelve canons and twelve vicars. However, in the 1463 petition to King Edward by the Dean and the Chapter, it was claimed that that the possessions had been so destroyed by Irish enemies, that the four principal dignitaries (Dean, Chantor, Chancellor and Treasurer) had not enough to support them with decency. Following this petition the licence was granted by King Edward IV and is dated the 28th of June 1463.

Note it was in that same year that the Parliament met in Waterford and passed an act establishing a mint in Reginald's Tower.

1463

29 JUNE

Earliest Painting

On the 29th of June 1763 Waterford Corporation commissioned the Flemish painter William Van der Hagen to paint a view of the city. The resulting panoramic view of Waterford is oil on canvas measuring 128 by 214 cm. He was paid £20 by the Corporation for the painting. For years the painting hung on the wall of the Council Chamber in City Hall, but is now on display at Treasures of Georgian Waterford at the Bishop's Palace.

A great deal of information about the city in the late 18th century can be gleaned from the painting. What stands out immediately is the absence of a bridge, as it was not until thirty-one years later in 1794 that Timbertoes Bridge was built. While the city walls at the west of the city can be seen, the walls which had existed along the Quay forty years earlier are gone. Instead, lines of new buildings dominate the Quay, including the Custom House and the Exchange. Also of interest are the rows of narrow three, four and five storey gable-front houses on the "newer" western end of the Quay (in the Dutch style). These allowed the largest houses possible in a small space.

This painting by der Hagen in 1763 is the earliest landscape view of any Irish city. Coincidentally, the earliest image of an Irish city is also of Waterford, and that is the view of Waterford displayed on the Great Charter Roll from 1373. In 2004 the painting underwent a three-month restoration to ensure its preservation into the future.

1763

30 JUNE

Mayor's Name Drawn Out of Hat

The first time that the Mayor of Waterford was chosen by drawing names out of a hat occurred on Tuesday the 30th of June 1942. A change had occurred in the system of voting following the *Local Government Act of 1941* which meant that the candidates proposed were now entitled to vote. Although there were fifteen Councillors in Waterford, one FF member was absent on the night.

The meeting itself was full of surprises. Firstly, the outgoing Mayor (Cllr. Dunne) was proposed for re-election by Cllr. O'Connor, but he did not get a seconder. Secondly, the FF front runner, Ald. Jones, who had been Mayor on two previous occasions declined to accept a nomination, stating that Fianna Fáil, as the Government party, did not intend to put forward any official candidate and would let the issue lie between Labour and Fine Gael.

Two candidates were then proposed, Cllr. Paul Caulfield (FG) and Cllr. Jas O'Connor (Labour). However they each received seven votes. The outgoing Mayor stated that the issue would have to be decided by drawing lots, either by tossing a coin or drawing names from a hat. The meeting decided on the latter. The law advisor put the two names into a hat and the City Manager drew one of them. Cllr. Paul Caulfield was thus chosen as Mayor of Waterford.

A similar occurrence happened in 1979 when Ald. Stephen Rogers' name was also pulled from a hat after a tie had occurred between himself and Ald. Joe Cummins. Twenty years previously in 1959, a three-way tie occurred and a name was pulled out of a hat for the purpose of elimination. A vote was then held between the remaining two candidates. On that occasion Ald. Dick Jones was elected Mayor.

1942

1 JULY

First Battle of the Somme

The Battle of the Somme began on the 1st of July 1916 and continued for five months. Over one million men were either wounded or killed. On that first day, the 1st of July, the British Army suffered some 60,000 casualties, which was approximately 20% of its forces. Of these, thirteen men were from Waterford. They ranged in age from 16 to 33. All were enlisted men.

The location of the graves for seven of the thirteen are known. Of these, five were from the city, James Breen, Jeremiah Horan, Hugh Murdoch, Frank Phelan and Robert Power. James Culleton was from Ferrybank and Thomas O'Brien from Stradbally.

The other six have no known graves. John Conners, Maurice Grant, Henry McLoughlin and James Murphy were all from the city. Joseph Butler was from Portlaw and John Guiry was from Stradbally.

An interesting fact concerning Waterford men who were killed in action in WWI is that fifty-two of them were named Power, of which twenty-three served in the Royal Irish Regiment and eleven served in the Royal Navy.

1916

2 JULY

Cholera Outbreak

In 1832 a cholera epidemic reached London, claiming over six thousand lives. It was only a matter of time before it arrived in Ireland. In early June the epidemic reached Dungarvan. Power, in his *History of Waterford* (1990) states that the reason it spread so rapidly was that when a woman by the name of Cashman died of cholera in her own home, her husband insisted on having a wake in the house. All of the subsequent cholera victims had either attended the wake or had come into contact with somebody who had. By the 30th of June twenty-one people had died. On the 2nd of July 1832 the first case hit Waterford City.

Over the next nineteen days, 250 people were stricken, 128 of which died. It took six months for the outbreak to clear, during which time some 560 cases had been recorded in the city with 290 deaths. The leper hospital in John's Hill (precursor to the Infirmary) admitted some 438 cholera patients, of which only 32 died.

The races on Tramore Strand, which had been held on a yearly basis since 1785, were cancelled in 1832 due to the cholera outbreak.

A further outbreak occurred in 1849 during which over 500 died.

1832

3 JULY

First Charter

This is an important date in Waterford's history, as on the 3rd of July 1215, the first Charter for the city was granted by King John. Unfortunately the original Charter has not survived. However it is mentioned in many of the succeeding charters and in the Great Charter Roll, which was compiled circa 1373. In fact each time it is mentioned, the number of clauses in it increases.

Despite not having a copy of the original Charter, what is clear is that it gave the provost (the equivalent of the Mayor) the power to act as Chief Justice within the city. He could, along with representatives of the citizens, make laws and settle legal disputes. In one of the earliest versions of this Charter there were thirty provisions, dealing with the rights of citizens, ownership of property, right to trade, taxes etc. Waterford thus became a distinct civic administrative unit, having a special relationship with the King.

1215

4 JULY

Letizia Bonaparte Wyse

Sir Thomas Wyse was born in 1791 (see entry for December 1ˢᵗ). In 1815 while in Rome, he met the family of Prince Lucien Bonaparte (brother of Napoleon). A few years later in March 1821, Thomas married Lucien's daughter Letizia. He was aged 30, she was 16. Their first son Napoleon was born in January 1822. Very soon their incompatibility became apparent. Following a domestic disturbance in the autumn of 1824 Letizia was forced to enter a convent, where she remained for seven months. Finally after a fulsome apology to her husband, she was allowed out.

In August 1825, Thomas and his family came back to live in Waterford and settled in a house on The Mall. Their second child William was born in February 1826. While initially Letizia was content with the social scene in Waterford, their marriage difficulties continued. Finally in January 1828, Letizia left her husband and two sons and departed from Waterford.

Letizia went on to have three more children, and although she had not seen her husband since 1828, in each case she claimed Thomas as the father. In 1849 Thomas read a report of the marriage of *Martie Letitia Bonaparte Wyse, daughter of Mr. Wyse of the Manor of St John, Waterford*. On further investigation he found out that a man at the wedding had claimed to be the father of the bride and had signed the register *Thomas Wyse*. On foot of these reports Thomas decided to take legal action. Such a court case would have caused great scandal throughout France, so on the 4ᵗʰ of July 1849 the British Ambassador to France wrote to Wyse pleading with him to drop the case. Wyse refused, but when Louis Napoleon (first cousin of Letizia) became President of France in 1852 he succeeded in quashing the case.

1849

5 JULY

Tramore Motor Races

The third annual motorcar races were held on the strand in Tramore on this date in 1931. The event had begun three years earlier when on the 22nd of September 1929 large crowds of between 15,000 and 20,000 gathered in Tramore to see motor and bike races on the strand. The event was such a success that it was held again on the 15th of June 1930 and again on the 5th of July 1931. The list of events in the 1931 meeting included:

Motor Cycle handicap race for machines up to 350 cc, distance 15 miles.
Motor Cycle handicap race for machines up to 500 cc, distance 20 miles.
Motor Cycle handicap race for machines unlimited cc, distance 25 miles.
Motor Car handicap race for cars up to 12 hp, distance 12 miles.
Motor Car handicap race for cars unlimited hp, distance 20 miles.

Each of the races had a handicap system with different vehicles attracting different time handicaps. One of the entrants for the motor cycle race under 500 cc was the well known TT rider G.D. Manders, who covered the twenty miles in a time of eighteen minutes and sixteen seconds, although due to his handicap of six minutes and fifteen seconds he came in third position in the race.

Not only was the prom full of spectators but the sloping green area of the Doneraile was also packed.

The races were held for a few more years before eventually discontinuing.

1931

6 JULY

Undercroft

As mentioned already on the 21st of June, the Dean of Waterford in 1871 issued a statement confirming the existence of the undercroft. It was actually many centuries earlier that the undercroft came into the church's possession. This occurred on the 6th of July 1468. A register of property records confirms that a number of properties were given to the Dean for the purpose of the upkeep of an almshouse, known as the Good Mens' House.

There are in fact two adjoining undercrofts. The original larger undercroft dates from the thirteenth century, and was built by Stephen Fulbourne, Governor of Ireland and Bishop of Waterford in about 1281. It is believed that the first purpose of the undercroft was a mint. An elaborate stone built structure, it has an architectural style common to the period.

The upper smaller undercroft was built in the early fifteenth century and was the property of James Rice. James Rice was Mayor of Waterford eleven times between 1467 and 1486 (his cadaver tomb can be seen in Christ Church today). What is spectacular about this undercroft is the almost perfect example of a wicker imprint in its stone roof (the outline of the timber supports used in construction of the roof is still embedded in the mortar). Rice used this undercroft as a wine store. Indeed the door of the undercroft faces out towards the river where Rice had his own private dock.

On handing over to the Dean, the undercroft and the building above it were incorporated into the deanery building.

1468

7 JULY

First edition of Munster Express

The Munster Express was founded by a man named Joseph Fisher in 1860. Fisher already owned the *Waterford Mail* which was founded in 1823. Various reports state that the *Waterford Mail and Daily Express* was a daily paper while the *Waterford Mail and South of Ireland Advertiser* was a tri-weekly, published on Mondays, Wednesdays and Fridays.

In 1859, the then MP for the city and former Mayor, John A. Blake, founded *The Citizen*, which was published weekly on a Friday. This proved to be a major success so Fisher decided to publish his own weekly newspaper *The Munster Express* in opposition. The first edition was published on the 7th of July 1860. Both the *Munster* and the *Citizen* flourished. In 1898 James McGrath, who was Blake's partner in *The Citizen,* was so confident of the paper's future that he set about building new offices at the corner of Hanover Street.

At the turn of the century Edward Walsh bought both papers; *The Munster Express* from Fisher and *The Citizen* from McGrath. In addition he bought the *Waterford Daily Mail*, as well as the *Kilkenny* and *Wexford Express*. In 1908 he amalgamated all the titles together into one weekly paper. The last edition of the *Waterford Daily Mail* was on the 19th of September 1908. The title of the new paper was *The Munster Express and the Celt with which is incorporated The Waterford Citizen*. Its price was one penny.

The long title was dropped on the 22nd of August 1930 and the paper became simply *The Munster Express*.

1860

8 JULY

Sir Neal O'Neill

Sir Neal O'Neill was the oldest son of Sir Hugh O'Neill of Shane's Castle in Antrim. Born in 1658, he was commissioned into King James' army shortly before the Williamite War. He was with James at the Battle of the Boyne in 1690, where he was wounded. After their defeat he made his way to Waterford with James, intending to accompany him in exile to France. However his wounds were so severe that he died while in Waterford on the 8th of July. He was 32 years old.

He was buried in the ruins of the Franciscan Friary (or Greyfriars), which at the time was an almshouse known as the Holy Ghost Hospital. O'Neill's monument now stands against the wall on the left-hand side of the chancel. The inscription reads:

> *Here lyes the Body of S. Neale O'Neille Barronet of Killilag(h) in the County of Antrim who dyed ye 8 of July in the year 1690 at the age of 32 years and 6 months. He married the second Daughter of the Lord Viscount Molyneux of Sefto(n) in Lancashire in England. Requiescant in Pace*

Note the Battle of the Boyne is commonly celebrated on the 12th of July, yet Sir Neal O'Neill's tombstone in Greyfriars states he died on the 8th of July. This can be explained by the fact that the Gregorian calendar was not adopted in Britain until the middle of the 18th century. In the old style Julian calendar, the Battle of the Boyne actually took place on the 1st of July.

1690

9 JULY

Daniel O'Connell

It is not generally well known that Daniel O'Connell was MP for Waterford for a two year period from 1830 to 1832. He was first elected an MP in Clare in 1828. As a Catholic he refused to take the oath of allegiance to the British Crown. The English Government, fearing an uprising, finally gave in to Catholic Emancipation in 1829. In February 1830 he became the first Catholic in modern times to sit in the House of Commons. In the general election of August 1930 O'Connell stood for the Co. Waterford seat. As there were only two candidates for the two seats he was deemed elected (along with Lord Beresford). He held this seat until the general election of May 1832 when he was elected MP for Kerry. Over the next decade he set about campaigning for repeal of the Act of Union. One of the tactics used was "monster meetings" that attracted hundreds of thousands.

On Sunday the 9th of July 1843 O'Connell held a monster meeting in Waterford. It was reputed to be the biggest gathering ever held in the city. Crowds of people came to Waterford from all over the south east. 5,000 were reputed to have come from Castlecomer alone. Early that morning a massive procession left Waterford to meet O'Connell who was travelling from Kilmacthomas. When the two groups met up, the procession with over thirty bands then paraded back into the city. Because of the huge crowds the procession was over three miles long, and O'Connell did not actually reach the platform in Ballybricken until 5pm. It is reputed that over 300,000 people attended this meeting (over a million people attended the monster meeting held at Tara on August 15th).

1843

10 JULY

SS William Penn

The *SS William Penn* was the largest ship built at the Neptune Yard in terms of tonnage. At 1799 tons she measured 318 feet in length. Another ship, the *SS Indiana*, launched two years later, was seven feet longer although she was only 1572 tons. Both ships were built for the London-Le Havre-New York route.

Owing to her immense weight she was always going to be difficult to launch. The first attempt was made on the 24th of June 1865. This was not successful and a second attempt was made on the 26th of June. Again this was not successful. Finally, on the third attempt, on the 10th of July 1865, a successful launch was achieved with the assistance of hydraulic jacks.

On one of her voyages across the Atlantic she carried 680 passengers. The passenger list for her Atlantic voyage in April 1868 (available on the internet) shows an interesting spread of countries. Of the 229 passengers, twenty-three were first class and had cabins. Nineteen of these were from England and the other four were from the USA. The rest of the passengers were in steerage; 235 from Germany and Holland, 72 from England, and two from Ireland (Michael Hyde, age thirty-two, a cooper, and his son age four).

The *William Penn* was acquired by the Allan Line in 1869 and renamed the *European*. For the next five years she was used on the Liverpool-Quebec route. She had a number of different owners until she was eventually scrapped in 1897. An interesting fact is that in the early 1890s she was the first steamer to carry live cattle from Argentina to Europe.

1865

11 JULY

Tramore Railway Station

On Tuesday the 11th of July 1911 a fire broke out at about 1pm in the Railway Station in Tramore. It initially started in the lamp room but quickly spread to the whole building. Unfortunately there was no fire hose and when one was eventually found it was not long enough. Another length of hose was brought from Pipers "merry-go-round" and joined to the first hose, except then the fire hydrant could not be turned on, as the key was at the Carrigavantry waterworks over a mile away. Eventually an employee of Pipers managed to turn on the water at the hydrant using a spanner and work began in fighting the fire. However as a result of low water pressure very slow progress was made. A number of men were sent onto the roof to make a breach to prevent the fire spreading.

In addition there was a delay in the fire brigade from Waterford arriving. As they were responsible for Waterford City they were not allowed to leave the city limits without the permission of the Mayor (and of course the Mayor could not be found). Some years previously, the fire brigade had attended a fire in Tramore. When they returned they were asked why they had left the city in an unprotected state and what would have happened if a fire broke out in Waterford while the men and appliances were in Tramore. After that incident it was decided that the brigade should never leave the city limits without the permission of the Mayor.

The fire was brought under control by 5pm but by then half the station was destroyed.

1911

12 JULY

Courthouse

The present courthouse adjacent to the park was opened on this date in 1849.

The site on which the courthouse is built is reputed to be one of the oldest monastic sites in Ireland as it had been the site of St. Catherine's Abbey. Egan in his *History of Waterford* (1894) states that St. Catherine's Abbey was probably founded about 950 when the Ostmen embraced Christianity. It was endowed by Elias FitzNorman in 1210, and in 1211 Pope Innocent III confirmed all its possessions to the prior and canons, and mentions an island on which the abbey was founded. This would have been in the middle of Lombard's Marsh, which was later filled in to become the People's Park. Elizabeth dissolved the abbey in 1552 and it eventually fell into ruin.

In 1820 some of the ruins were knocked to clear the way for a bridge over John's river. Eventually the ruins were cleared completely to make way for the new courthouse. In the *Journal for the Archaeological Society* published in 1858, reference is made to a remarkable find during the excavation as follows:

> *The workmen having uncovered a small vault, or grave of masonry, discovered the remains of an ecclesiastic in full vestments. The figure when first uncovered, seemed quite perfect, but shortly after being exposed to the action of the air, it had fallen into dust. On the finger a ring had been found. It is extremely rude in its workmanship; the device was a shield, bearing a saltier between four indistinctly marked charges three of which appeared to be fleur-de-lis.*

1849

13 JULY

Burial Grounds

At the beginning of the 19th century there were a number of small graveyards scattered throughout the city. These included Christ Church, St. John's, St. Olaf's, Greyfriars, St. Peter's and St. Michael's. On the outskirts, there was Kilbarry and Kill St. Lawrence. Many of these became health hazards due to overuse. It was reported that a grave could not be dug without exposing decomposed corpses. A number of attempts were made to close these graveyards without success.

On the 13th of July 1847 an order was made by the Bishop that the ancient burial grounds of the city be closed. The following day, an area of ground was purchased in Ballinaneeshagh (see entry for March 15th).

People ignored this order and continued using these cemeteries. In July 1849 a resolution of the Waterford Sanitary Association stated that *the interment of bodies in those churchyards must be highly injurious to health*. Two months later in September 1849, the Commissioners of Health made an order *prohibiting for the present any further interment in the graveyards mentioned*. Again this order was ignored and people continued to bury their dead in the traditional graveyards.

Another attempt was made in 1852 and again in 1860. However, concern was expressed that if some of these graveyards were closed, Ballybricken graveyard would be closed next. Finally, in an order made by the Lord Lieutenant in 1860 closing the old graveyards, exceptions were made for Ballybricken and the French Church.

1847

14 JULY

Christ Church

On the 14th of July 1773 the decision was taken to demolish the old Christ Church Cathedral and build a new one in its place. The original Christ Church was built in the 11th century although various additions were made over the years. Smith's *History of Waterford*, (1746) gives a very detailed description of the cathedral. It consisted of a large nave, a choir, two lateral isles, and at the back was Trinity Parish Church. In addition to Rice's Chapel (added 1482), there was the Bishop's consistory court, or St. Stephen's Chapel, and the vestry or chapel of St. Nicholas. Hansard's *History of Waterford* (1824), stated that the original Cathedral was *a confused mass of buildings, attached to the original pile without regard to simplicity of unity of appearance.*

In the 1770s the old cathedral was reputed to have become so decayed that it was judged unsafe for public worship. This was questioned however when the workman charged with its demolition had difficulty actually knocking it down. The architect for the new cathedral was John Roberts, who twenty years later was the architect for the Catholic Cathedral. It was 1779 before the building was fit for service, but it was not finally completed until 1792.

Of note is that during the demolition of the old cathedral, a collection of pre-reformation vestments was found. These dated from the 15th century, and had been hidden when Cromwell's soldiers sacked the cathedral. They were so well hidden that those who knew of their existence died before they could be removed to safety. On their discovery, the Church of Ireland Bishop presented them to his Roman Catholic counterpart. The only complete set of pre-reformation vestments to survive in Britain or Ireland, they are now on display in the medieval museum.

1773

15 JULY

Wimbledon Finalist

It is not generally well known but in the late 1890s and early 20th century, Irish tennis players won four men's single titles and one ladies' singles title at Wimbledon. It was on the 15th of July 1879 that Waterford born Vere St. Leger Goold reached the final. He was beaten 2-6, 4-6 and 2-6. What makes this Wimbledon final so unique is that his opponent was the Rev. John Hartley, who was the only clergyman to have won a grand slam title. But even more unique is that Goold was the only Wimbledon player to have later been convicted of murder.

Vere St. Leger Goold was born on the 2nd of October 1853 in Waterford. A talented sportsman, he became Irish tennis champion in June 1879 and tried his luck at Wimbledon the following month where he reached the final. His tennis career was short and he retired from the game in 1883. In 1891 he married a French woman named Marie Giraudin. Unfortunately she had expensive tastes and very soon they descended into debt.

In 1907 they moved to Monte Carlo, where their debts mounted further. One person to whom they were in debt was a wealthy Danish woman by the name of Emma Leven. Following a row, Leven was murdered by the couple. They put her body into a large trunk and left it at a railway station in Marseille for transfer to London. However when blood seeped out of the trunk, they were apprehended. Following a trial, they were both sentenced to life imprisonment, Marie to Montpellier jail and Vere to Devil's Island. Within a year the Waterford born Wimbledon finalist Vere St. Leger Goold committed suicide.

1879

16 JULY

Removal of Soldiers

There were two barracks in Waterford in the 19th century. The artillery barracks accommodated 5 officers, 121 men and 62 horses. The infantry barracks accommodated 16 officers, 417 men and 8 horses. The presence of so many troops in Waterford was bound to cause resentment, especially when these troops were rotated regularly to ensure that no attachments to the local population could occur. Violent clashes between Waterford men and soldiers were therefore frequent in the streets and pubs in the Ballybricken area.

In 1885 a number of brawls occurred which led to the stoning of the troops and the death of a local man. The culprits were identified as members of the 24th Regiment (the South Wales Borderers) and the magistrate recommended that this regiment be moved out of Waterford.

The matter was brought up in the House of Commons and on the 16th of July 1885, the Secretary of State for War confirmed that the 24th Regiment would be transferred out of the city.

1885

17 JULY

Harbour Commissioners

Although Waterford Harbour has been a major force for growth of the city for centuries, the first reference to its governance is in the Charter of Henry V (1413-1422), which added to the role of Mayor the title Admiral of the Port of Waterford. A previous charter had already confirmed the limits of the port in 1356 as a line linking Hook Head to Red Head (just west of the present day Dunmore East). The Great Charter of Charles 1 of 1626 confirmed all these previous rights and duties.

In 1815 the Chamber of Commerce was incorporated. It immediately set about seeking a bill to constitute a separate harbour authority. This bill was adopted in June 1816. The first meeting of the Harbour Commissioners took place a few weeks later on the 17th of July 1816. The meeting took place in the Chamber of Commerce building in Gladstone St. This building was used for the next 188 years.

The composition of the commissioners shows an interesting spread. Of the 24 commissioners, 12 were appointed by the Chamber of Commerce, 7 by Waterford Corporation and 5 from Clonmel interests. The attendance shows a spread of well-known Waterford families including Mayor Cornelius Bolton and James Wallace representing the Corporation. Josiah Strangman, Robert Jacob, John Strangman, Francis Davis, George Penrose, Richard Davis, John Harris, and John Leonard represented the Chamber of Commerce. Robert Grub, David Malcomson, James Morton and Arthur Rial represented Clonmel interests. There were eleven absentees from that first meeting.

1816

18 JULY

William Thackeray

The English novelist William Makepeace Thackeray (author of *Vanity Fair*) was born on the 18th of July 1811. He travelled throughout Ireland in 1842 and wrote a book called *The Irish Sketch Book* on his travels.

In July 1842 he reached Waterford. His description of the city is less than flattering, some of which is reproduced here:

> *The view of the town from the bridge and the heights above it is very imposing; as is the river both ways. Very large vessels sail up almost to the doors of the houses.*
>
> *But as you get into the place, not a soul is there to greet you except the usual society of beggars, and a sailor or two or a green-coated policeman sauntering down the broad pavement.*
>
> *The quays stretch for a considerable distance along the river, poor patched-window mouldy-looking shops forming the basement-story of most of the houses.*
>
> *In one of the streets leading from the quay is a large dingy Catholic chapel, of some pretensions within; but, as usual, there has been a failure for want of money, and the front of the chapel was unfinished, presenting the butt-end of a portico, and walls on which stone coating was to be laid.*
>
> *All the street was lined with wretched hucksters and their merchandise of gooseberries, green apples, children's dirty cakes, cheap crockeries, brushes and tinware; among which objects the people were swarming about busily.*

1811

19 JULY

Catholic Burial

The fact that a Sir Nicholas Walsh was given a Catholic burial in Waterford led to this missive by an Arthur Chichester to the Lord President of Munster. Dated the 19th of July 1615 the following is quoted from the *Council Books of Munster*:

> *After my very hearty commendations to your Lordships I have received your advertisement of the late bold fact in Waterford or rather scornful affront done unto us all and this whole state at the burial of Sir Nicholas Walsh there with such popish rites and ceremonies openly and by dare as if it were purposely intended for disrespect and scandal. I do perceive by now that you shall retain the impression and sense of it sufficiently and I hope you will make the punishment of the magistrates there the more exemplary by how much the presence of your Lordships in those parties at the time of the enormity committed shall have made them to abstain from that which they had been otherwise inclined to be in their blind zeal towards the dead though no doubt he deserved very well of them during life.*

1615

20 JULY

Ballybricken Ladies

On display in Waterford Museum of Treasures is an embroidered address dated 20th of July 1892 as follows:

To John G. Redmond, Esq., M. P.

Honoured Sir

We on behalf of the LADIES OF BALLYBRICKEN, beg that you, our trusted Representative, will accept the Accompanying Small Souvenir as a token of the Feelings we entertain towards you.

We have noted with pleasure and admiration the noble stand you have taken in defence of the Principles of Independence, and the unflinching support you ever rendered to our lost, but not forgotten Leader, CHARLES STEWART PARNELL.

We the Ladies of Historic Ballybricken, have been brought up to love and cherish the undying Cause of True Irish Independence; and we can assure you that we shall never cease to be the advocates of the Ideas which you and the Gallant Band who have fought with you, will, we trust, in the near future, make a reality, with the wish that you may long continue as the Representatives of our City, and that your life may be ever happy and prosperous.

Yours very sincerely,

SIGNED: Minnie Caulfield, Mary Ellen McGrath, Norah Grant, Annie Henneberry, Mary Catherine Heylin.

Mary Bridget Caulfield, Kattie Arnold, Secs.

WATERFORD, JULY 20th, 1892

1892

21 JULY

Siege of Waterford

The Treaty was passed in the Dáil on the 7th of January 1922. On the 28th of June, the Free State Army took action against the anti-treaty forces that had taken over the Four Courts in Dublin.

In Waterford the vast majority of the IRA took the anti-treaty side, and so led by Pax Whelan they quickly occupied the main buildings in the city, including the GPO, the jail and the military barracks. On the 18th of July 1922 the Free State Army, led by General John Prout with Paddy Paul, former brigadier of East Waterford IRA, arrived at the Kilkenny side of the city and set up artillery on Mount Misery. The attack began on the morning of the 19th of July and the barracks and jail were bombarded with shells. Over the following two days fighting continued with shots being exchanged across the Suir.

On the night of the 20th of July, some one hundred free state troops, commandeered some boats and rowed across, approaching the city from the east. They managed to gain access to the Country Club (on Adelphi Quay) through the back door and secured the garrison without firing a single shot. From there, they quickly took over the Imperial Hotel next door and now had command of both the Mall and the end of the Quay.

Early on the morning of the 21st of July, the Free State troops gradually moved up the Quay. A battle ensued for the GPO, which required the firing of more artillery shells from Ferrybank before the anti-treaty forces retreated up the Quay to the Granville Hotel. Another firefight occurred until the anti-treaty forces had to abandon this position also. The final stand took place at the jail and by lunchtime the siege of Waterford was over.

1922

22 JULY

John Connery

The three Connery brothers, John, James & Patrick, born in the early 1800s, were farmers' sons from Bohadoon near Dungarvan. In their youth they were involved in faction fights between a group called the Poleens (Na Póil) and the Gows (Na Gaibhne). As a result of one of these skirmishes, John Connery was arrested but was found not guilty. He was soon arrested again following another skirmish, this time for murder. Once again he was found not guilty.

In 1835, a landlord agent was attacked and badly beaten. This time the three Connery brothers were arrested. John and Patrick were found innocent but James was found guilty and sentenced to transportation for life. The other two brothers, continued to defy the law and were soon rearrested, found guilty and sentenced to seven years' transportation. On their way to Cobh to be put on board a ship, the two brothers escaped. They remained at large for a number of months but in March 1836 they were arrested again and ended up back in Ballybricken jail. Two months later they, along with twelve others, took part in the Great Escape (see entry for May 22nd).

They then remained at large for another two years, before they were captured near Dungarvan. In a speech from the dock at Waterford Courthouse on the 22nd of July 1838, John Connery stated that as far as he was concerned they had done nothing wrong. He stated that the major cause of turmoil within Irish society was in fact the robbery of the poor by the rich. In this he was not far off the mark as the Connerys had received much public support while on the run. Again the two brothers were sentenced to transportation. In September of that year they left Ireland for the last time onboard a convict ship.

1838

23 JULY

Passage East Car Ferry

Prior to 1982 the villages of Passage East and Ballyhack were connected by a small ferryboat which could carry passengers and bicycles only. In October 1978, an announcement was made of the formation of a company called Passage East Car Ferry with planning at an advanced stage. Over the next few years, with the cooperation of both Waterford and Wexford County Councils, major work was carried out on both sides of the river in building suitable jetties. A flat-bottomed car ferry was procured in Hamburg in Germany and was towed by tug to Passage East for fitting out.

Although the first crossing was held on the 22nd of July, the first full day of service was on Friday the 23rd of July 1982. Taking ten minutes for the crossing, it could carry twelve cars. The initial charge was £2.50 single and £4 return for a car with up to four passengers. The ferry proved very popular in the first few weeks and over 1,300 cars and 5,000 pedestrians used it.

Three different vessels have been used through the years, the *FBD Dunbrody* (twelve cars), the *Edmund D* (twenty-seven) and the current vessel the *FBD Tintern* (twenty-eight cars). By 2012, thirty years later, over 23 million passengers had been carried and the equivalent of over 18 circumnavigations of the globe had been completed. About 400,000 cars use the service annually.

1982

24 JULY

District Court

In the 1930s there were regular reports of prosecutions in the District Court of individuals who were apprehended playing ball on the street or having no lights on their bicycles.

At a court sitting on the 24th of July 1931, the following were each fined 2/6 for ball playing on the street: Maurice Wolfson - Manor Street, John Goff - Alexander Street, Christopher Power - New Street, John Murray - John's Place and Laurence Molloy - Ballybricken.

At the same court, James Quinn - Aglish, John Quinn and Michael Quinn, both from Portnascully were each fined 6d for cycling without a lamp. John Walsh from Dournane, who did not appear, was fined 5/-.

Other District Court reports from around that time were:
Three boys were charged for causing nuisance by ringing the bell at Denny's Bacon Cellar at 9.30pm.
Four boys were summoned for playing pitch and toss. The judge dismissed the case, as the boys were not aware it was an offence.
A messenger boy was charged for *cycling with his arms folded*. He was fined 5s out of his 15s weekly wage.
Thomas Flynn from Stephen St. was fined 2/0 for allowing his donkey to wander.

To put these amounts into context, 2/6 was 2 shillings & 6 pence. In 1931 the daily adult wage was about 10 shillings.

1931

25 JULY

Airmount Hospital

Airmount Maternity Hospital was built as a dedicated maternity hospital in 1949 (see entry for March 22nd). It replaced the old Waterford Maternity Hospital which was originally in Barrack Street, but moved to Parliament Street in 1839. Although planned as a voluntary hospital it was taken over by the Medical Missionaries of Mary in 1952. In 1966 the Report of the Consultation Council on the General Hospital Service recommended that Airmount, the Infirmary and Ardkeen be amalgamated, however it took a further 29 years for it to occur (the Infirmary had already closed in 1987).

Airmount finally closed on Tuesday the 25th of July 1995 and sixteen patients with fifteen babies were transferred to the Regional Hospital. Another five patients were discharged home. There were three births on that Tuesday, one was born in Airmount, another in the new maternity ward in WRH, while a third did not make it to either hospital but was born in a car on the way from Kilmacthomas.

A photograph taken on the last day showed that there were eighty-nine staff working in Airmount at the time of its closure.

1995

26 JULY

Theatre Royal

The Theatre Royal was rebuilt in its present form in 1876 (see entry for April 17th). However the original theatre was part of the Assembly Rooms and Theatre and was designed by John Roberts in 1783 at the behest of a group of Waterford's leading merchants. This building took a number of years to finish, with the Assembly Rooms opening in 1785, and the Great Ball Room (Large Room) not opening until 1788. However the Playhouse was the first element to be finished and was opened on the 26th of July 1784.

According to an article in *Decies* written by Lynn Cahill, the main play of the evening was a shortened version of Shakespeare's *As You Like it*, followed by a presentation of Arthur's popular two act farce *The Citizen*.

Over the following years the theatre relied on touring companies for performances. The first known local involvement was in 1792, when a new opera by a local doctor, James St. John, was produced. It was called *The Siege of Waterford or The Marriage of Earl Srongbow to the Princess Eva*.

1784

27 JULY

Waterford Chronicle

The *Waterford Chronicle* devoted much of its four pages to reports from London, however the advertisements from its issue of the 27th of July 1816 gives a further snapshot of Waterford life at that time.

> *Thomas McCreery, Coachmaker, William Street Waterford has for sale several new and second hand gigs, jaunting cars, Barough and Tilbury gigs. Carriages and cars repaired, painted and varnished in the neatest manner and on the most reasonable terms.*
> *N.B. He is now building some of the newest London fashioned Tilburies, which he is determined to furnish in the best manner.*
>
> *Rope Manufactory. Wm. White and Co. having commenced work on their new Rope-Walk now offer for sale Hawsers, Tow-lines, Ropes, Cordage and twines of every description, which they shall be careful to have well manufactured and made of the best material. Cables laid, according to order, at short notice.*
>
> *A. Dudley, Tobacco, Snuff, Soap and Candle Manufactory, Barronstrand Street, Waterford.*
>
> *A box containing some wearing apparel was left at the Bristol Packet House about two years ago and upon which some trifling expense was incurred; it is requested that the owner may call for it, in one month from the date hereof, paying the above expense as well as that of this advertisement, otherwise it will then be sold to defray the same.*

1816

28 JULY

Ballybricken Fire

There are many recorded instances of fires raging throughout Waterford down through the centuries. Between 1031 and 1280 the city was burned to the ground on three occasions. There is also a reference that in the 13th century, a person whose house went on fire, endangering the city was punished by being thrown into the fire.

However in modern times, the last big fire was on Friday the 28th of July 1809, when over sixty houses were burned in Ballybricken. A full report of the fire was given in the *Waterford Mirror* on the following day.

The fire started at about 3pm close to the county jail. The wind was blowing from the west, thus the fire spread along Ballybricken. Most of the houses were thatched, so the fire spread rapidly. Despite the best attempts of the onlookers the fire spread to about sixty houses. Soldiers from the artillery barracks also helped in fighting the fire. It only stopped when it reached the gable end of a slated house.

Despite the devastation, there was only one fatality, a boy of four. The cause of the fire was assumed to be accidental. *The Mirror* reported that some attributed it to *sparks from a pipe, others to children carelessly amusing themselves with burning faggots.*

1809

29 JULY

Church of St. Olaf

The rebuilding of the Church of St. Olaf by Bishop Thomas Milles began in 1734. Believed to be on the site of an old Viking church, the original gothic door was incorporated into the building. It was consecrated on the 29th of July 1734.

A Latin inscription over the main entrance, when translated, reads:

> *This Temple dedicated to St. Olaf, King and Martyr. Thomas Miles, S.T.P. Bishop of Waterford. Re-built A.D. 1733.*

The inscription concludes with:

> *Accepi Lateritiam, reliqui marmoream.*

which translated means:

> *I have chosen bricks; I have abandoned marble.*

The church was renovated in 1911.

Egan in his *History of Waterford* (1894) states:

> *As Christ Church was not founded until 1050, it appears likely that the Danes founded some church before that time, which would be probably St. Olaves. It is therefore asserted that Sitric, having completed the fortifications of Waterford built this church which he dedicated to his great ancestor, St. Aulaf or St. Olave. It was rebuilt by the Normans after they arrived here.*

1734

30 JULY

William Hobson

On the 30th of July 1839 the appointment of William Hobson as the first Governor of New Zealand was ratified. William Hobson was born in September 1792 in Lombard Street in Waterford. He joined the Royal Navy as a cabin boy at the age of nine. He served in the Napoleonic Wars in 1809 and in the war with the United States from 1812 to 1814. His ship, the *Peruvian*, took Napoleon to exile on the island of St. Helena in 1815. Involved as a skipper in the suppression of piracy in the West Indies, he found himself captured twice by pirates, endured ill treatment and survived two daring escapes.

Hobson was promoted to Commander in 1824. In 1836 he commanded the frigate *Rattlesnake* in Port Phillip (Melbourne) where he surveyed the harbour. He was then sent to the Bay of Islands to help reduce tensions between warring Maori tribes. He was appointed Lieutenant-Governor of New Zealand in 1839.

One of his first tasks involved drafting the Treaty of Waitangi, which was signed on the 6th of February 1840. This treaty is known as New Zealand's founding document and takes its name from the Bay of Islands where it was first signed by more that forty Maori chiefs. February 6th is now a public holiday in New Zealand. New Zealand became a crown colony in May 1842 when Hobson took the oath as Governor and Commander in Chief.

William Hobson died in Auckland in September 1842 and is buried in the Symonds Street Cemetery in Auckland.

1839

31 JULY

Plane Crash

During the summer of 1932, Irish Air Lines Ltd. used the beach in Tramore to provide short pleasure flights and also aerobatic displays. On Sunday morning the 31st of July 1932, a two-seater plane piloted by a young 19-year-old man by the name of Woods, took off from the beach at about 11am. A large crowd of spectators had gathered to view the anticipated display. However just after takeoff, the plane seemed to rise up vertically, and on reaching about sixty feet, turned over on its back and nose-dived into the beach.

The injured pilot was taken from the wreck and brought to the infirmary. His injuries turned out to be superficial. However the plane was a compete wreck.

The crash did not deter further pleasure flights which continued for the rest of the summer. However another plane crashed three weeks later on Sunday the 21st of August. This time there were two passengers (both priests) and the pilot on board. As the plane was taking off, the engine stopped and it nose-dived into the mud on the strand. While the plane was badly damaged, the pilot and passengers escaped unhurt.

1932

1 AUGUST

Newtown School

In October 1797 the Wyse family residence at Newtown was put up for sale. The architect John Roberts built this house about twelve years earlier. Sir Thomas Wyse was born here in 1791 (see entry for December 1st). The Wyse family did not live in this house for long as it was rented to the Penrose family before it was sold.

The property was purchased by the Quakers for £1,530 and the sale included the house and eighteen acres. A number of renovations were made to simplify the house, in keeping with Quaker ideas. These included the removal of any forms of ornamentation. It opened as Newtown School on the 1st of August 1798 with thirty-one boys and seven girls, all boarding pupils. It served to educate Quaker children throughout Ireland. It admitted its first non-Quakers in 1858. Although both boys and girls started on its opening day, it became a boys only school for approximately fifty years at the end of the 19th century. Girls were again gradually admitted from 1900 and it became fully co-educational in 1924.

In January 1966 a fire broke out in one of the dormitories. It quickly spread to the roof of the building. All forty pupils in the dorm managed to escape without injury. The fire was believed to have been caused by an electrical fault.

Newtown School celebrated its bicentenary in 1998.

1798

2 AUGUST

Corporation

The issue of traders storing commodities on the quayside was obviously a cause for concern in 17th century Waterford, as on the 2nd of August 1675, an order was made by the Corporation:

> *That the persons that have piles of deal boards on the quay of the city shall pay to the sheriff for the use of the Corporation six shillings and eight pence sterling for each pile, or forthwith remove them, and that henceforth no more deal shall be piled upon the quay without leave of the Mayor and council.*

A similar order made in December 1681 shows the range of goods which were traded at the time:

- *For every punchion or hogshead of tallow lying above forty eight hours on any part of the quay, belonging to a freeman or foreigner, sixpence sterling;*
- *for every barrel of tallow, three pence; for every cask of butter, three halfpence; for every barrel of beef, pork, and mutton, which may require time for rebaling, hoping and pickleing which shall be on the quay above four days and four nights, to pay three pence per barrel;*
- *for every tierce of salmon that shall be on the quay above four days and four nights, four pence sterling;*
- *for every tierce of herring that shall be on the quay above four days and four nights, three pence sterling;*
- *for every pack of frize, leather, or skins lying above four and twenty hours, two pence sterling;*
- *for every thousand of pype, hogshead, or barrel staves lying above two days, to pay twelve pence sterling;*
- *for every thousand of hoopes, lathes, and slates lying above three days, eight pence sterling.*

1675

3 AUGUST

Thomas Francis Meagher

Thomas Francis Meagher was born on the 3rd of August 1823 in the building now occupied by the Granville Hotel. His father Thomas Meagher, born in Newfoundland, moved to Waterford in 1819 and later became the first Catholic Meagher in 1843. Thomas Francis only lived for two years on the Quay as his father sold the building to Charles Bianconi where it became the terminus for Bianconi coaches. The family then lived in Derrynane House on the Mall. Educated at Clongowes Wood College and Stoneyhurst College in England, Meagher then studied for the Bar in Dublin.

Meagher joined the Young Ireland movement in 1842 and advocated radical political change and physical force. This approach caused tensions with Daniel O'Connell especially after Meagher's speech in July 1846 where he likened the sword to a sacred weapon. This led to the title *Meagher of the Sword*. In February 1848 he offered himself as a candidate for a by-election in Waterford, however he failed to secure the support of his father due to their political differences. He was beaten into third place gaining only 20% of the vote. A few weeks later he unveiled the Irish Tricolour for the first time (see entry for March 7th). The same year he participated in the abortive Young Ireland rising. Following his arrest he was sentenced to death, but this was commuted to transportation to Van Diemen's Land. In 1852 he escaped to the US where he practiced at the Bar for a number of years, and also helped found *The Citizen Newspaper*. When the American Civil War started, he supported the North and founded the Irish Brigade, with whom he fought a number of battles. After the war he became Secretary and Acting Governor General of Montana. He died on the night of the 1st of July 1867 when he drowned off a riverboat at Fort Benton. His body was never recovered.

1823

4 AUGUST

German Submarine

On this date in 1917 a German submarine, the UC44, was wrecked off the coast of Dunmore East.

The German submarine UC44 was launched on the 10th of October 1916 in Hamburg. Over the next ten months she undertook six patrols and sunk a total of twenty-eight ships. In early August 1917 she was engaged in mine-laying operations outside Waterford Harbour. On the night of the 4th of August she ran into one of her own mines off Dunmore East and blew up. The only survivor was her Captain, Kurt Tebbenjohanns. He was picked up by a small rowing boat which came out from Dunmore to investigate the explosion.

The following month the Royal Navy attempted to raise the wreck to gather intelligence. It took nine days to gradually tow the wreck to Dunmore East. Using an ingenious method of cables attached to floating barges, the incoming tide allowed the wreck to be towed just above the sea floor during each high tide. On the 25th of September the submarine was safely beached. After any useful intelligence was taken from the wreck, UC44 was taken back out to sea and sunk, although there are suggestions she was used as the foundation for a sea wall at Duncannon.

1917

5 AUGUST

World Record

On the 5th of August 1901 the Waterford solicitor Peter O'Connor set a new world long jump record. This record was to remain unbeaten for the next twenty years. His jump was 24 feet 11 ¾ inches. The record jump occurred at the RIC Sports which were held in Ballsbridge in Dublin.

While his family came from Co. Wicklow, Peter O'Connor was actually born in Millom in Cumberland on the 24th of October 1872, where his father, a shipwright, was working in a new shipyard. The family returned to Wicklow soon after. Although he never attended secondary school, his first job was as a clerk in a small solicitor's office in Clifden, Co. Galway in 1894. In 1898 he moved to Waterford where he took on the job of managing clerk at Dunford's solicitors practice. In 1912 he sat his final law exams and became a qualified solicitor. In 1921 he bought out the practice and the firm Peter O'Connor and Son was born.

Although he was over twenty before he took a serious interest in athletics, he was to be at the top of his sport until he retired in 1906. In that year he took part in the interim Olympic Games held in Athens. He won the triple jump and came second in the long jump. In protest at being put on the British team, O'Connor scaled the flagpole and hoisted a large green Irish flag with the words *Erin go Bragh* on it. This was probably the first overt political act in the modern Olympics. Peter O'Connor died on the 5th of November 1957. In August 2001, one hundred years after his record long jump, a plaque was unveiled at the jumping pit in the Regional Sports Centre marking his achievement.

1901

6 AUGUST

Ursuline Convent

On the 6th of August 1816 four Ursuline nuns arrived in Waterford from the convent in Thurles and set up a house in Waterpark. The following month they received the first children into their school. A year later they moved to a different house at New Grove. In 1824 the order purchased a house at Elysium. In 1844 St. Anne's Day School was opened, and the boarding school was built in 1868.

Canon Power, in his *Parochial History of Waterford and Lismore* published in 1912 states:

> *The proper institute or work of the Ursuline Order is the education of young girls, rich and poor. This is carried on in St. Mary's in four separate schools*
> *1. St John's National school for the children of the laboring and artisan classes. The number of children in attendance is usually from three hundred to four hundred and ten.*
> *2. St Anne's day school for the children of the professional and mercantile classes. The pupils number from eighty to one hundred.*
> *3 The boarding school or St. Joseph's House, where seventy to eighty young ladies receive their education.*
> *4. The college for training of secondary teachers and instruction of young ladies in domestic economy.*

An advertisement for the domestic economy school in 1932 states:

> *The course includes Cookery, Dressmaking, Practical Gardening, etc., everything that enables a girl to take efficient care of a home*

The private fee-paying St. Anne's day school merged with the national school in 1967 and became St. Ursula's school.

1816

7 AUGUST

Tramore Bank Robbery

On the morning of Tuesday the 7th of August 1979, a gang of five armed men entered the AIB bank in Tramore. At least two shots were fired before the raiders grabbed between £2,000 and £5,000. As the gang left the bank, three Gardaí confronted them. The Gardaí were forced to lie on the ground while shots were fired into the tyres of the squad car. Four of the raiders escaped in a stolen Cortina while the fifth escaped on foot. The car was later found abandoned two miles away. Shortly afterwards a car broke though a Garda checkpoint in Dungarvan.

During the raid an innocent bystander, a thirty-two year old civil servant by the name of Eamonn Ryan, was shot dead. Mr. Ryan, from Dublin, was on holiday in Tramore with his wife and three children. His two-year old son was with him at the time of his death.

Two IRA men were given life sentences for the murder, while another was given nine years for his role as getaway driver.

1979

8 AUGUST

Collision on the River

A rather unusual accident occurred on the afternoon of the 8th of August 1882 when a ship was sunk while tied up at the Quay.

The *SS Reginald*, a vessel belonging to the Waterford Steamship Company, was setting off on her twice-weekly sailing to Bristol. Captain Burns started up his engines and moved his ship out into the channel. However, for some reason, the engines failed to stop and he continued across the river bearing down on the collier *Silkstone* which was tied up on the other side. The stern of the *Reginald* struck the *Silkstone* amidships. While the *Reginald* escaped with very little damage, the *Silkstone* was not so lucky. She was badly holed and began to sink immediately. Within fifteen minutes she had disappeared beneath the water. While most of the crew escaped unhurt, one fireman died a few days later from shock and exposure.

The wreck of the *Silkstone* caused a problem for shipping. Naval divers were brought in and planted explosives on the wreck. On Sunday the 13th of December of the same year, the explosives were set off. However, while the wreck was broken up, the strength of the explosion was so great that windows on the Quay were shattered. The shock was felt as far away as the Yellow Road where delph rattled on kitchen dressers.

1882

9 AUGUST

Waterford Chronicle

The issue of the *Waterford Chronicle* on the 9th of August 1870 includes the following advertisements:

Pianoforte, Harmonium and Music Warehouse 120 Parade Quay. The cheapest house in the Kingdom. Fresh arrival of First Class Pianofortes and Harmoniums. Pianofortes expressly for extreme climates packed in tin-lined cases to order. First class pianoforte and harmonium tuners sent to all parts of the country quarterly. Parcels of new music received daily.

The right thing in the right place. Beecham's Pills for females of all ages, these pills are invaluable as a few doses of them will carry off all gross humour, open all obstruction, and bring about all that is required. No female should be without them.

The Lion Hotel, 21 Bailey's New Street Waterford. Marianne Shout, proprietress. Visitors may rely on the utmost attention and cleanliness with moderate charges. Bed and Breakfast 2s. 6d.

Income Tax Refunded or Reduced. Parties seeking the above on insurance of otherwise can still have speedily arranged on moderate terms. Please address Mr. Dowling 31, William Street.

Royal Hairdressing Rooms 131 Quay, near the tower. William Cullen begs to announce to the Nobility, gentry and Inhabitants of Waterford that he has opened first-class hair dressing rooms. Prices as follows:
    Gentlemen's hair cut and brushed by machinery 6d.
        Shampooed 6d. Singed 6d. Curled 6d.
    Ladies hair cut and arranged 1s. 0d.
        Cut 6d. Cut, singed and shampooed 2s 6d.

1870

10 AUGUST

City Surrender

The city motto *Urbs Intacta Manet Waterfordia* or *Waterford remains the untaken city* was granted by Henry VII in 1497. Waterford still remained an untaken city in 1649 when Cromwell set siege.

In August 1649 Cromwell set sail for Ireland, landing at Ringsend in Dublin. Having massacred the inhabitants of Drogheda he then moved south to Wexford where the townspeople fared no better. By the 24th of November Cromwell was outside the gates of Waterford. For the next nine days he laid siege to the city, however the absence of artillery, the bad weather and an outbreak of dysentery among his troops led Cromwell to call off the siege. On the 2nd of December Cromwell marched away from Waterford.

Although the city had been saved, it was not for long. When Cromwell returned to England in May the following year, he left General Ireton in charge. Waterford finally surrendered to General Ireton on the 10th of August 1650.

1650

11 AUGUST

Remains of John Moore exhumed

During the 1798 rebellion some one thousand French soldiers landed at Killala in Co. Mayo under General Humbert. Having met initial success at the Battle of Castlebar, General Humbert declared Connacht a republic and installed local man John Moore as its president. Moore was one of the local gentry who had supported Humbert. A convert to Catholicism, he had also studied at the Bar. However, a few short weeks later, the force was defeated at the Battle of Ballinamuck.

President John Moore was captured and following a trial was sentenced to transportation. He was sent under military escort to Duncannon Fort to await a transportation vessel. However he fell ill during the journey and died when he reached Waterford. He died in a lodging house in George's Street called the Royal Oak Tavern. He was buried in Ballygunner Temple cemetery.

For years his grave lay undisturbed and hidden until it was discovered by accident in 1959. On the 11th of August 1961 his remains were exhumed and brought to the Cathedral. On the following day the funeral cortege brought the remains to Castlebar. On the 13th of August after funeral mass his remains were reinterred at The Mall, Castlebar at a state military funeral attended by President Éamon de Valera and Taoiseach Sean Lemass.

1961

12 AUGUST

Printing

Printing is believed to have begun in Waterford sometime in the 16th century. However it is the middle of the 17th century before we have an exact reference. Downey in his *Story of Waterford* (published in 1914) gives a specific date of the 12th of August 1652 when he states:

> In 1652 an act of parliament was printed at Waterford, entitled "An Act for the Settling of Ireland, Thursday, 12th August, 1652" ordered by the Parliament to be printed and published

Another reference to early printing was in an article in the *Journal of the Waterford and South-East of Ireland Archaeological Society, July 1897*. This article gave an account of an old Waterford almanack which was printed six years earlier in 1646. Its title was:

> *A Manapian's Almanack 1646.*
> *A new Almanack for the Year of Our Lord 1646, being second after Bissextile, or Leap-Year, and since the Creation of the World 5595, calculated for the Longitude and Laitude of the City of Waterford, and may serve generally for all Ireland.*

Some of the claims in its chronological table make interesting reading:
- *From the Creation of the World to this present year's end - 5092 years*
- *From the Creation to Noah's Flood - 1060 years*
- *Since Bartholemus entered this island of Ireland - 4235 years*
- *Since the Building of the City of Waterford by Sitaricus - 1491 years*
- *Since Ireland received the Catholic Faith by the preaching of the glorious Saint Patrick - 1221 years*

1652

13 AUGUST

Factory Fire

Many Waterford people will remember the Hearne and Cahill boot factory which existed in Broad Street / Arundel Square. This was founded in 1878 and closed in 1954. There was a great tradition of shoe and boot making in the city around this era. In the 1901 census 190 people in Waterford listed their occupation as shoemaker. In 1911 this had decreased to 107.

Five years after the Hearne and Cahill Boot Factory opened in 1878, another factory called the Waterford Boot and Shoe factory in Bridge Street burned down. This occurred on the 13th of August 1883. A newspaper report from the time states:

> *So quickly did the devouring element do its work that before an hour had passed the whole building was one mass of flame and all hope of saving it had been abandoned. It was greatly feared that the flames would spread to the Dominican Church, which adjoins the factory, and a hose was brought through the convent, where the Dominicans reside, in order to pour water into the affected building. The fire was also prevented from spreading to Miss Doherty's barm factory, which at one time, it was thought, could hardly be saved. Grave fears were also entertained for Messrs. Denny and Sons' bacon concerns. A regrettable feature is that over one hundred workers engaged at the factory have been thrown out of employment. Messrs. Denny sustained a loss of about a thousand pounds.*

1883

14 AUGUST

Tramore Train Derailed

On the night of Thursday the 14th of August 1947, the last train from Waterford was approaching the station in Tramore at about 11.30pm. For some unknown reason the train failed to stop at the terminus, ran over the turntable and went straight through the station wall out onto the public road. Luckily no one was injured.

The couplings to the carriages had broken, so the carriages themselves remained on the track and were not damaged in any way. A relief engine was sent out from Waterford and the waiting passengers were transported back to Waterford. However it took most of the following day to lift the engine back onto the track. The 15th of August was in the middle of race week in Tramore so the presence of a railway engine squatting in the Strand Road proved a great spectacle for the crowds.

This was the third occasion that the Waterford-Tramore railway suffered a serious derailment. The first derailment occurred on the 9th of August 1858, five years after the line officially opened in 1853. When the 6.20pm train from Tramore entered the Waterford terminus, towed by both its Fairbairn tank engines, it failed to stop. The heavy train went out onto the public street. It smashed through a large gate and damaged the *Pill* wall. One girl on the street was killed and another injured, however none of the passengers were hurt.

The other derailment occurred in 1936 (see entry for August 24th).

1947

15 AUGUST

Civil War Shooting

After Waterford City was taken over by the Free State Army in a siege in July 1922, intermittent hostilities still occurred with Irregulars. A few weeks later on Tuesday the 15th of August a report was received by army troops stationed at the jail that a fire had broken out at Peter's Lane (Shortcourse) police barracks which was empty at the time. Commandant Ned O'Brien and another soldier went to investigate. When they got to the barracks, they attempted to enter. However a shot rang out from the direction of the military barracks. Commandant O'Brien began to return to the jail to seek assistance. Although there was a large number of people on the street, a sniper party lay in wait and Commandant O'Brien was shot. The soldier who was with him carried him to the nearest house in Barrack Street where he died thirty minutes later. During this time, intermittent shooting continued in the Barrack Street area.

An inquest the following day found that Commandant O'Brien had been shot in the back with a single *bullet of a highly destructive type*. That Wednesday night his body was removed from the Jail with full military honours, the procession going from Ballybricken to the Glen, Bridge St., along the full length of the Quay and by the Mall to St. John's Church. A guard of honour of six soldiers remained in the church overnight. His burial took place on Thursday in Ballygunner, again with full military honours.

A native of the city, he had taken part in the War of Independence. He joined the National Army in January 1922 and was promoted following the siege of the city in July just weeks before his death. He was twenty-one when he was shot.

1922

16 AUGUST

Last Race on Backstrand

In 1911 the last race meeting was held on the backstrand from the 14th to the 16th of August. The following December a storm breached the embankment and the entire area was flooded (see entry for December 13th).

In Egan's *History of Waterford* (1894) he describes the course in Tramore as follows:

> Tramore is now distinguished for having one of the neatest and best fitted race-courses in this country, while the annual meets are among the most enjoyable. An enclosed course is a rarity and here the experiment is made a brilliant success...
>
> The appointments here are far above the usual style. The County Stand House is a new and elegant structure of pine wood and iron having large plate glass panelling at both ends....There is also the Grand Stand being enclosed at the ends; and for the multitude bent on economy there is the most extensive and graded Open Stand.
>
> Two features tend to enhance the Tramore course over most of its compeers in this country. One for the visitors is the most delightful pleasure of viewing with ease the race from start to finish; the other for the owners of horses, which is, that owing to the nature of the ground it must be always up to elastic tension. The sandy ocean strata prevents anything like a slimy or soft bottom, while if too hard, a flux from the back strand will soon bring it to consistency suited to going.

1911

17 AUGUST

Mail Coach

The postal service in 18th century Ireland was a haphazard one. Towards the end of the century a system of mail coaches was introduced. This had the added benefit of also being used as a public transport system. The first such mail service between Waterford and Clonmel began on the 17th of August 1789. On that first trip the coach carried two passengers outside and two inside. This service lasted until 1796 when it was abandoned owing to lack of demand.

In 1803 a new service from Waterford to Clonmel, through Kilkenny, was initiated. It too died an early death. Again in April 1809, a third attempt was made to link the two centres by mail coach.

A separate mail coach was initiated between Waterford and Cork in 1791. This daily service went through Carrick on Suir. The coach left Waterford at 4am and reached Cork at about 8pm. The first run on this line was on the 8th of June that year.

It was to be another twenty-five years before Bianconi introduced his coaches (see entry for September 24th).

1789

18 AUGUST

Waterford Boat Club

The first regatta by Waterford Boat Club was held on this date in 1879. The club, reputed to be the oldest club in Waterford, was founded at a meeting held in the Mayor's chambers the previous year in May 1878.

A *racing-four* had been purchased by private subscription, so its first regatta was held on the Suir on the 18th of August 1879. Boats from Limerick, Cappoquin and Shannon rowing clubs took part. The new Waterford club won the inaugural Waterford Challenge Cup.

Initially the boathouse was on Ballast Lane in Newtown, but due to difficulties with the title of the property, the club was forced to move a few years later. In 1887 the boathouse was built at Abbey Lane on the Ferrybank side of the river. For the next ninety years the boathouse was a part of the vista from the Quay with its position directly across the river from Reginald's Tower. Many of the trophies from this period are now on display on the top floor of the Bishop's Palace.

Following negotiations with the Harbour Board and Bell Ferry in 1979, the clubhouse moved from Ferrybank across the river to Scotch Quay and Canada Street. This clubhouse was opened in June 1983. It was demolished again in 1996 and a new clubhouse was built with apartments overhead.

1879

19 AUGUST

People's Park

The first recorded mention of a public park in the city can be traced to an extraordinary Presentation Session held in the City Court in October 1846 when £700 was allocated for creating a public park at Lombard's Marsh or elsewhere. The original idea seems to have belonged to Sir Henry Winston Barron MP for Waterford. However it was March 1855 before the newly elected Mayor John Blake took the lead and a Corporation proposal that the *Mayor be empowered to memorial the Lord Lieutenant on the subject of a Park* was adopted. The Mayor instructed a Mr. Nevin from Dublin, an eminent landscape gardener, to prepare plans.

At a public meeting held at the Town Hall the following March, the Mayor outlined that the estimated cost would be £1,200. It was explained that a number of demolitions which were being carried out around the city would benefit the park. The rubble from old houses in Barronstrand Street would be used to fill in low-lying parts of the marsh, and rock from the road realignment at Bilberry would be used for the park wall. In addition, the Harbour Commissioners would also be able to deposit a vast quantity of mud from the quays to fill in the marsh.

On Wednesday the 19th of August 1857 Lord Carlisle, the Lord Lieutenant, formally opened the park. The bandstand was added in 1869 during the mayoralty of Cornelius Redmond. The fountain was added in 1883 and the cycle track was built in 1891.

The term *People's Park* was actually coined by the *Waterford Chronicle* in 1855. Officially it had always been referred to as the *Public Park*.

1857

20 AUGUST

Cathal Brugha

Although Cathal Brugha was born in Dublin in 1874, he was elected TD for Waterford in December 1918. In the absence of the imprisoned Éamon de Valera and Arthur Griffith, he was elected Acting President of the first Dáil when it met in January 1919. He resigned the presidency in favour of de Valera in April and was appointed Minister for Defence.

He succeeded in remaining at large during the War of Independence. As Minister for Defence he strongly disapproved of independent actions by IRA volunteers without Dáil approval. However due to the decentralised nature of the IRA and the influence of other officers, including Michael Collins, his control of the army was always problematic. In an attempt to keep central control, on the 20th of August 1919 he proposed to the Dáil that all volunteers including Dáil deputies take an oath of allegiance to the Irish Republic and its government. Following a debate, the proposal was carried. However the IRA never formally approved the proposal.

Brugha strongly opposed the treaty, and during the treaty debates in the Dáil, he made a bitter personal attack on Michael Collins, accusing him of being a publicity seeker and questioning if he had ever fired a shot for Ireland. After the Dáil approved the treaty, Brugha was replaced as Minister by another Waterford man, Richard Mulcahy (see entry for May 10th). Cathal Brugha died on the 7th of July 1922 having been wounded in the opening week of the Civil War. His wife Caithlín Brugha was elected TD for Waterford in the 1923 general election (see entry for August 30th).

1919

21 AUGUST

Earliest Newspaper

There have been many newspapers published and printed in Waterford during the last few centuries (see entry for January 14th). The earliest reference is to a paper called the *Waterford Flying Post*. Although an original copy of this paper does not exist, there is a reference to it in another newspaper *The Waterford Mirror* in 1814 which states:

> *A friend had obliged us with a copy of the Waterford Flying Post published by Thomas Cotton, August 21st 1729. It is an object of curiosity more from its appearance than from its contents. It is printed on both sides of a half sheet of copybook paper with the royal arms at the left and the city arms at the right of the title.*

Ryland in his *History of Waterford* (1824) makes reference to it also. He states that its full title was:

> *The Waterford Flying Post, containing the most material News, both Foreign and Domestic*

Ryland goes on to conclude that the price was one halfpenny,

> *from the circumstance of a receipt having been seen for a shilling, as a quarter's subscription to a paper published twice a week.*

The earliest newspaper in the country is reputed to have been published in 1641 under the title of *Warranted tidings from Ireland*.

1729

22 AUGUST

The Exchange

On the 22nd of August 1932 the Ulster Bank opened new premises on the Quay. The location for the new premises was an historic one, as it was the site of the former City Exchange.

The Exchange (or Tholsel) itself was originally built around 1715 on the site of the old market on the Quay. The word Tholsel comes from the old English words "tol" and "sal" meaning the hall of taxes. It was home to Waterford Corporation until they moved to the present City Hall in 1816 (see entry for February 2nd). Smith in his *History of Waterford* (1746) states:

> *The exchange, together with the custom-house adjoining, are charmingly situated on the quay, …… The exchange is a neat light building, supported by pillars of hewn stone of the Tuscan order, the outside being adorned with the arms of the King, and those of the city with a handsome clock. It has an Italian hipt roof, with a beautiful octagon cupola, and a dome at the top, the cupola being surrounded by a balustrade, about which is a walk.*

Downey in his *History of Waterford* (1914) goes on to state:

> *The space below stairs where the merchants assembled was large and spacious. On one side was the office of the town clerk. Upstairs were the council chambers and a large assembly room and other apartments.*

Unfortunately the building was demolished in the middle of the 19th century. However, the Tholsel (or Town Hall) in Kilkenny is more or less an exact replica of the Waterford Exchange, having been built about the same time.

1932

23 AUGUST

Strongbow

In the late 1160s small parties of Normans gradually began to arrive in Ireland. In 1169 a larger party led by Robert FitzStephen arrived at Bannow Bay in Wexford. This was followed in May 1170 by Raymond le Gros who arrived in Baginbun with a small army. Baginbun is also in Wexford.

However it was the arrival of Richard de Clare, or Strongbow, that proved to be the turning point. He began his siege of Waterford on the 23rd of August 1170. While the city had built a stone wall around it some fifty years earlier, it was no match for Strongbow's army. Within two days the city fell. According to reports, a house which projected over the walls was supported by props outside the walls. The invaders cut away the props and the house collapsed, bringing down a portion of the wall. Strongbow's army entered the city through the breech, and began a slaughter of the inhabitants.

As part of his agreement with Mac Murchada, the King of Leinster, Strongbow married his daughter Aoife on the 25th of August in the ruins of Christ Church Cathedral. This wedding is the subject of an iconic painting by Daniel Maclise (1806-1870) now on display in the National Gallery.

The capture of Waterford by Strongbow in August 1170 marked the end of the Viking Age in Ireland, and the beginning of the Anglo-Norman age. It was to be 752 years later in 1922 before English forces finally left Waterford (see entry for March 9th).

1170

24 AUGUST

Tramore Train Accident

At 12.30pm on Saturday the 24th of August 1935, the engine of the Tramore train left the rails at Carricklong Bridge and plunged down the embankment into a field. Luckily the buffer planks on which the couplings were set snapped off and saved the coaches from following the engine. The engine did a complete somersault as it left the line and ended up lying on its side. Both the driver and fireman were injured but not seriously. None of the thirty-six passengers on the train were injured. Work at repairing the line began immediately, and normal service was restored later that night. The engine suffered a different fate. Due to its weight it could not be removed from the bog intact, so it was broken up and sold for scrap.

Although there were only three serious incidents in the 107 years that the Waterford-Tramore railway operated (see entry for August 14th), W.R. Le Fanu described another incident, in his book *Seventy Years of Irish Life* (1893).

> *Another time, when the line from Waterford to Tramore was just finished, I was riding on the engine, when we saw a boy placing a very large stone, which he could scarcely carry, on the rail. He then stood beside the line watching for the result. We pulled up as quickly as possible, and were going comparatively slow when we reached the stone, which the iron guard in front of the wheel threw off the line. We stopped the engine, jumped off, and gave chase to the boy, whom we soon captured. He was a small boy about ten years old. We led him back, weeping piteously, and took him up on the engine. He besought us not to kill him. We told him we would not kill him, but that we would bring him into Waterford, where he would be tried, and undoubtedly hanged next morning for trying to kill us. When we had gone about half a mile we stopped and let him off; and didn't the little chap run! He evidently feared lest we should change our minds again and deliver him to up to the hangman.*

1935

25 AUGUST

Public Lighting

Public lighting of streets was an issue of concern for the City Council in the early 1700s. In 1715 a committee was appointed to decide which was the best method of illuminating the streets on dark nights *for the convenience of the Inhabitants*. Soon after, a by-law was passed which obliged residents to place candles on their windows for certain hours of the evening, after which the town was in total darkness.

In October of 1729, the Corporation decided that it would seek an Act of Parliament in order to have the streets lit with lamps. They obviously had some success as in June 1733 a survey was done in order to decide what the best position for the lamps were and what tax should be levied on the citizens in order to fund the new venture.

Houses rented at less that £2 per annum were exempt from any tax, houses between £2 and £3 had to pay one shilling a year, between £3 and £5 one shilling and six pence, and above £5 two shillings. Eventually Peter St. Leger was entrusted with making the lamps and Thomas Alcock was selected to collect the *lamp tax* and *take care of said lamps*. Initially the lamps would only be lit from the 25th of August to the 1st of May.

The first time the lamps were lit was on the 25th of August 1733.

1733

26 AUGUST

Unfortunate Clash

On Sunday the 26th of August 1923, W.T. Cosgrave, First President of the Executive Council (equivalent of Taoiseach today), was due to attend a meeting in Waterford. However a delay in his arrival led to a riot and a number of injuries.

Captain William Redmond had arranged a political meeting to be held outside the Imperial Hotel at 8.30pm that night, which was to be preceded by a procession around the city in which a number of bands were to participate. However the previous day they were informed that W.T. Cosgrave was due to speak at a Cumann na nGaedheal meeting on the Mall at 8.15. Captain Redmond then decided to rearrange the route of his procession and agreed not to arrive at the Mall until 10pm (by which time the Cumann na nGaedheal meeting would be finished).

Unfortunately W.T. Cosgrave was delayed in Kilkenny and did not arrive on the Mall until just before 10pm. A few minutes later the Redmondite procession led by the Erin's Hope Fife & Drum Band arrived on the Mall just as the President was about to speak. As expected, mayhem ensued. Some of Cosgrave's minders drew their revolvers and shots were fired. A stampede followed. Some people were injured in the rush. Members of the band were attacked and their instruments thrown into the river. Captain Redmond later stated that President Cosgrave owed an apology to the people of Waterford for what had occurred. However, common sense prevailed over the following days and both sides agreed the whole affair was unforeseen and it was not expected that any bad feeling would result.

1923

27 AUGUST

Shipbuilding

Shipbuilding in Waterford was as its height in the 19th century as shown by Bill Irish in his excellent book *Shipbuilding in Waterford 1820-1882* (2001).

However, shipbuilding was carried on in the city throughout the ages.

According to the *Corporation of Waterford Council Books* for 1698 Patrick Moore was granted permission on the 27th of August 1698 to:

> *Build a ship at St John's Bridge in the waste ground over against the mill. And any other citizens that wanted to build ships were at liberty to do so on the other side of the river especially.*

Thomas Smith, who was Mayor in 1699 was also described as a shipbuilder and as such was *free of water bailiff's fees.*

Some years later in 1716, an order was made that:

> *each person who built either a ship or a boat on the waste ground at the west end of the Ring Tower should pay to the Corporation a shilling for each Ton according to each ship or boat built there measures, and a clear passage should be kept for horses and cars to pass.*

1698

28 AUGUST

Lord Roberts of Kandahar

Frederick Roberts was a great grandson of John Roberts, architect of some of Waterford's finest buildings. He was born in 1832 in Cawnpore in India where his father, General Sir Abraham Roberts, served. Educated in England, he joined the army and returned to India. During the Indian mutiny of 1857 he was awarded the Victoria Cross. He then spent the next months of his life in Waterford where he resided at Newtown Park. He married Norah Bews in St. Patrick's Church and returned to India at the end of 1859. In 1880 he was commander of the 10,000 troops that fought and won the battle of Kandahar in Afghanistan. His success led him to the title of Baron Roberts of Kandahar and Waterford. On his return to Ireland he was awarded the Freedom of Waterford City on the 28th of August 1893. To celebrate the occasion he was presented with a grandfather clock. This clock is now in the Granville Hotel in Waterford.

In 1895 he was made Field Marshal and Commander in Chief of the army in Ireland and lived in the Royal Hospital Kilmainham. The Boer War saw him transfer to South Africa in 1899. His only son Freddy also received the Victoria Cross in this war, but was killed on the battlefield. This was the first instance of a father and son receiving the Victoria Cross (there are two later instances of this happening). Following a number of victories in South Africa, Lord Roberts returned to a hero's welcome in Britain. He continued to serve in the army for a long number of years. He died on the 14th of November 1914 while visiting troops in France at the age of 82. An interesting aside is that the phrase *Bob's your uncle* was reputed to refer to Lord Roberts, as he was referred to as Uncle Bob by his troops.

1893

29 AUGUST

Sodality of Angelic Warfare

On the 29th of August 1927 a group of some four hundred Waterford boys went on an excursion to Dublin under the auspices of the Sodality of the Angelic Warfare. This sodality/confraternity was a Dominican grouping dedicated to the promotion of chastity. At the time only boys were permitted to join. A Dominican priest named Fr. Bernard Larkin had founded the sodality in Waterford earlier that year.

Fr. Larkin had a reputation as a very conservative priest. Two years later a sermon he gave while preaching in the Black Abbey in Kilkenny caused some controversy. In keeping with the aspirations of the Sodality of Angelic Warfare, he dwelt on the evils of bad literature, cinema, all-night dances and mixed bathing. The cinema was already stamped with a *doubtful character* especially now that the *talkies* had arrived. All-night dances *had borne deadly poisonous fruit as everybody knew*.

However he saved his best criticism for Tramore. The problem according to Fr. Larkin was that there was not enough bathing boxes, and neither was there a place set apart for men and another for women. *Mixed bathing meant mixed undressing and dressing in the open*. He blamed the council for doing nothing *to remedy this evil*.

1927

30 AUGUST

Caithlín Brugha

Caithlín Brugha (nee Kingston) was born in Birr, County Offaly in 1879, and married Cathal Brugha in 1912. Cathal Brugha had been TD for Waterford since December 1918 until his death in the Civil War in 1922 (see entry for August 20th).

When the Civil War ended in May 1923, a general election was held on Monday the 28th of August 1923. There were eight candidates in Waterford. Sinn Féin nominated Caithlín Brugha. The final results were declared on the morning of Wednesday the 30th of August. Brugha topped the poll and was elected on the first count. The other candidates elected were Captain Willie Redmond (Independent), John Butler (Labour) and Nicholas Wall (Farmer). See entry for December 8th for more on the involvement of farmers in this election.

However Caithlín Brugha did not take her seat in the Dáil, in accordance with Sinn Féin's abstentionist policy at the time. When de Valera left to found Fianna Fáil in 1926, she remained with Sinn Féin. She was re-elected in the June 1927 general election. The fifth Dáil only lasted three months and she did not go forward for nomination in the subsequent election in September. Thus while Caithlín Brugha was the first female TD elected for Waterford, she did not take her seat. It was in 1933 that Bridget Redmond, wife of Captain Willie Redmond, became the first female TD to sit in the Dáil representing Waterford.

1923

31 AUGUST

George I

In the 17th and 18th centuries, no opportunity was lost in displaying the city's loyalty to the monarch. The coronation of King George I occurred on the 1st of August 1714. On the 31st of that month the Corporation decided to send the new King an address stating:

> *that nothing was wanting to complete the happiness of the untouched city* but the *intercession of Divine Providence that for the Church's and our good he would delay for many years the duration of his majesty's life in order to make Waterford the Envy of the World.*

Whether it be the King's birthday or the date of his coronation, it was an excuse for a party. On the date of his coronation the Council held a celebration. They obviously had a good time as three weeks later on the 17th of August, John Hayes, vintner, was paid £6 19s 5d for the wine bill. The same year another party was held for the King's birthday on the 28th of May while the previous year his birthday party was held on the 21st of February, apparently a movable feast!

1714

1 SEPTEMBER

John Redmond

John Redmond was born in Wexford on the 1st of September 1856. The son of William Redmond, MP for Wexford, he was educated at Clongowes and Trinity College. Prior to becoming MP for Waterford in 1891 he had represented both New Ross (1881-85) and North Wexford (1885-91). He held the Waterford seat until his death in 1918.

Redmond never actually lived in Waterford. He divided his time between London and his home in Aughavanagh, Co. Wicklow, where he lived in Parnell's old hunting lodge. He visited Waterford at least once a year *to give account of his stewardship*. Torchlight processions, marching bands, and large demonstrations of loyalty generally accompanied these visits. While in London he made sure to fully represent his constituency in supporting a number of bills such as the *De La Salle Training College Bill* of 1890, the *Waterford Harbour Bill* of 1893, the *Waterford Corporation Bill* of 1896, in addition to bills relating to the Leper House, and railway amalgamation. His success in obtaining a £38,000 grant to help finance the abolition of the toll bridge (Timbertoes) and the construction of a new bridge was something of a coup. When Redmond arrived in Waterford to open the new bridge in 1913 (see entry for February 10th), he was welcomed by a crowd estimated at 25,000.

The outbreak of World War I proved his greatest challenge. The third Home Rule Bill was passed in 1914, but its implementation was to be delayed until after the war. Redmond backed the war effort in the belief that it would help deliver a united Home Rule Ireland when hostilities ceased. Like most people, he believed the war would be over by Christmas. It was a major miscalculation. When Redmond died four years later in 1918, Ireland was a very different country.

1856

2 SEPTEMBER

Start of Emergency

On Friday the 1st of September 1939 Germany invaded Poland and so began World War II. The next day, the 2nd of September, the emergency began in Waterford when a detachment of regular army soldiers arrived in the city and were quartered in the military barracks. Sentries were posted on the bridge and provided with gas masks and steel helmets. Dunmore Harbour was also placed under military supervision.

On that night a blackout of business and private residences in Waterford was initiated. Streetlights were switched off. Initially a number of residences ignored the blackout. Pedestrians were warned not to walk on the roadway after dusk due to restricted lighting. However within a week or so partial public lighting was restored, when one in five street lamps were lit.

While Hitler may have invaded Poland on the 1st of September, that did not stop the All-Ireland Hurling Final two days later on Sunday the 3rd (Kilkenny defeated Cork 2-7 to 3-3).

1939

3 SEPTEMBER

Light Opera Festival

The first Waterford International Festival of Light Opera was opened by the Minister for Education Dr. P.J. Hillary, on Thursday evening the 3rd of September 1959 with the hoisting of a festival flag over City Hall.

The shows presented at the first festival included *The White Horse Inn*, Gwaun-Cae-Gurwen Choral and Operatic Society; *The Quaker Girl*, London Operatic Society; *The Student Prince,* Dundalk Musical Society; *The Desert Song,* Imokilly Choral Society; *Oklahoma,* De La Salle Society; *Oklahoma,* Standard Telephones and Cables Operatic Society Newport; *The Gondoliers,* Fishguard County Secondary School Amateur Operatic Society; *Maritza,* Carmarthen Amateur Operatic Society, and *The Gipsy Baron,* Tredegar Amateur Operatic Society. The first winners of the International Waterford Glass Trophy were Standard Telephones and Cables Operatic Society from Newport in Wales with their performance of *Oklahoma.*

The only Waterford Society to enter was the De La Salle Light Operatic Society with *Oklahoma.* Commenting on the performance afterwards, the adjudicator Miss Lelia Mackinlay stated that:

> *the pace at which it was played was much too slow. American folk operas of this kind required pep, vitality and musical urgency of a kind which could only be achieved by months of hard, untiring rehearsal of a kind which amateurs could not be expected to do. The audience had not helped the players in this instance, and had not accorded them the enthusiastic welcome given to other competing societies. This had further militated against a good performance.*

However she did single out Des Manahan for particular praise as the pedlar man. Unfortunately they did not win any award.

1959

4 SEPTEMBER

Waterpark

The origins of Waterpark College can be traced back to Mount Sion in the 1880s when a "higher course" was taken on by Mount Sion School for "advanced boys". However as the numbers increased, it was decided to acquire separate premises. The residence of James P. Graves at Waterpark was purchased and following alterations, Waterpark School opened in August 1892. The early history of the school is sketchy. In a letter dated 1898 it was noted that there were 142 day pupils. The school also provided evening classes three nights a week and some forty pupils were attending.

A number of temporary structures were added over the next few years in anticipation of a more permanent structure, but it was to be another forty years before a new school was built. Building began in October 1938 by John Hearne & Son at a cost of £20,000. Bishop Kinane formally opened the college on Monday the 4th of September 1939.

An advertisement at the time stated:

> *Classes for pupils of all stages from the Kindergarten to the University, including classes for Banks, Junior and Senior Intermediate Professional Entrance, and Civil Service completive examinations, and County Council Scholarships. The College affords special facilities for the training of Students for Ecclesiastical Colleges. The curriculum includes Irish, Greek, Latin, French, English, Mathematics (all branches), Chemistry, Physics, Commercial Course, Drawing, Singing, Games, Physical Drill and Gymnastics.*

1939

5 SEPTEMBER

All-Ireland Final

In the annals of Déise hurling this day goes down in history as the day that Waterford won its first All-Ireland Senior Hurling Championship. Before a crowd of 61,743 in Croke Park, Waterford beat Dublin by 6-7 to 4-2. Making it even more special was the fact that the Minor team also won their final (their second, having already won in 1929).

When the teams returned home to Waterford on the Monday night, over thirty thousand people turned out to welcome them. Bonfires blazed from various heights including Bilberry and Mount Misery. At Newrath the teams were transferred to two lorries and they proceeded at a snail's pace across the bridge and down the Quay, led by six city bands. A civic reception was held at City Hall, after which each member of the team was presented to the cheering crowd from the second-floor window. The greatest applause was reserved for the Captain, Jim Ware, with the Liam McCarthy Cup. A reception and dinner was then held at De La Salle College.

However the celebrations were marred by tragedy on that Monday evening when a 15-year-old boy was crushed to death by the crowds on the bridge as the teams travelled past.

An interesting fact from that All-Ireland is that the late RTÉ broadcaster Seán Óg O'Ceallacháin played for Dublin that day.

1948

6 SEPTEMBER

All-Ireland Final

Waterford reached the hurling final again in 1957 but were beaten by Kilkenny 4-10 to 3-12. They were back in Croke Park two years later on the 6th of September 1959 again facing Kilkenny in front of a crowd of over seventy-three thousand.

Waterford took an early point in the first twenty-five seconds when a free taken by Phil Grimes dropped the ball into the goalmouth and Larry Guinan tapped it over the bar.

At half time, Waterford were leading 0-9 to 1-1, but soon after the start of the second half, Kilkenny scored two goals in quick succession, both by nineteen-year-old Tommy O'Connell. Waterford responded straight away with a point by Tom Cheasty. However ten minutes later, the young O'Connell got his third goal. With 90 seconds to go, Kilkenny had 5 goals and 5 points to Waterford's 17 points. A goal from Séamus Power equalised the match and Waterford survived for a replay three weeks later (see entry for October 4th).

It had been twenty-five years since an All-Ireland final resulted in a draw, when Limerick and Dublin drew in 1934.

Again, crowds turned out in the city on the Monday night when the team returned home and a civic reception was held in City Hall. Luckily there was no show scheduled in the Theatre Royal that night where the first Light Opera Festival was being held (see entry for September 3rd).

1959

7 SEPTEMBER

Catholic Emancipation

Catholic Emancipation dominated Irish politics following the Act of Union in 1800. A report from the *Waterford Chronicle* on the 7th of September 1811 stated:

> *At a meeting of the Catholics of the County and City of Waterford convened by Public notice and held at the New Rooms on Monday 2nd September 1811 Thomas Fitzgerald Esq in the Chair, the following resolutions were unanimously adopted:*
>
> *That we view with extreme regret and concern that attempts made to prevent and impede the undoubtedly right of his Majesty's Catholic Subjects of this Realm to petition Parliament for redress of those great grievances which affect them, a right established by the Bill of Rights itself and recognised specifically by the very act under colour of which exercise thereof is attempted to be defeated.*
>
> *That fully impressed with the importance of the measure and a sense of what we owe to our country and to ourselves, we will persevere in earnest and continued petition to Parliament for the attainment of that great national object, the Emancipation of the Roman Catholics of Ireland.*
>
> *That we are persuaded this right of petition which belongs alike and is equally dear to his Majesty's subjects of whatever denomination or the other advantages of the Constitution cannot long be secured to any without the cordial union and cooperation of all.*
>
> *That we name the following Gentlemen as possessing the confidence of the Catholics of this County and City to prepare the petition to present to Parliament early in the ensuing session with liberty to confer for that purpose with our general committee: - John Mansfield, Richard Power of Bonmahon, Thomas Wyse, Patrick Power of Tinhalla, Thomas Quan, Colonel O'Shea, William Barron of Carrickbarron, Alexander Sherlock, Thomas Fitzgerald and John Burke.*

1811

8 SEPTEMBER

Garter Lane

In the early 1980s the Corporation decided to donate two public buildings in order that an arts centre could be set up in the city. The first of these buildings was the former library premises in O'Connell Street, known as Barker House. Smith in his *History of Waterford* (1746) states:

> *This gentleman's house is on the outside of it nothing remarkable, more than the appearance of a large well built house; being which we are agreeably surprised, with a large hill, beautifully cut into slopes and terrace-walks at the bottom of which is an handsome canal, with other reservoirs higher up. In the lower canal are fountains which play to a considerable height, the sides of which, are beautiful with statues standing in niches. The end of this terrace is beautifully terminated by a fine ruined arch, being the remains of a gothic structure called St. Thomas's chapel, and which also gives name to the hill on which these improvements are made.*

Following extensive reconstruction and remodelling it was opened on Saturday the 8th of September 1984 by the actor Niall Tóibín.

The second phase of the Arts Centre was the former Society of Friends Meeting House (and former temporary courthouse), also in O'Connell Street, which was built in 1792. Being over 200 years old it also required extensive modernisation and was eventually opened in early 1988. In February 1992, a plaque was erected by President Mary Robinson *to re-dedicate the building to the causes of education and culture for the people of Waterford*. The name Garter Lane comes from the famous or infamous lane that once stood in the present day John Roberts Square, removed by the wide street commission in 1857 (see entry for June 2nd).

1984

9 SEPTEMBER

Corruption in Council

Corruption in politics is not a new phenomenon. An incident occurred in 1680 when Alderman Andrew Rickards was charged with misleading the Council in connection with property rents, tithes and cash belonging to the civic body. What made this so unusual was that Rickards was already a prosperous draper and indeed one of the auditors of the Corporation.

A total of ten separate and detailed charges were made, some of which included receiving £8 per annum rent abatement under false pretences, receiving rent on several cabins and gardens on Kilbarry Road without passing it on to the Corporation, withholding £4 of the £50 received from the Corporation to pay to a Mr. Watts in Dublin, and pretending that £6 of public money in his possession was stolen from him.

The Council met on the 9th of September 1680 to consider these charges and Rickards' response to them.

The decision reached was:

> *Upon serious consideration had of all the scandalous, dishonourable, mercenary, and deceitful practices, contempts, and miscarriages of the said Alderman Andrew Rickards, which are common honesty and justice of the trust reposed in him by this corporation or contrary to his oaths and duties of a freeman and member of common council of the city and one of the auditors of the corporation accounts, it is this day ordered and concluded by the mayor and council that the said Andrew Rickards be and is suspended from being an alderman of this city till he give satisfaction to the council.*

1680

10 SEPTEMBER

British Gun Boat

In early September 1965, a British naval gunboat, the *HMS Brave Border,* was on a courtesy visit to Waterford. While in the city, the British officers were accorded a Mayoral reception by Cllr. P. Browne. The reception also included representatives of the Irish Naval Service, the Harbour Board and the Chamber of Commerce. Later that evening a reception was held on board the ship. For the following two days the ship was open to members of the public.

However as she was leaving on Friday morning the 10th of September, shots were fired at the boat from the Kilkenny side of the river. A large force of Gardaí was quickly on the scene and three men were apprehended near the Barrow Bridge.

A number of people had also objected to the awarding of a civic reception by the Mayor, and a few weeks later the Mayor received Garda protection following an anonymous telephone call threatening his life and home.

It was to be twenty-nine years before another British Naval vessel docked in Waterford. The *HMS Guernsey*, a British fishery patrol vessel, arrived for a Maritime Festival during the June Bank Holiday weekend in 1999. On this occasion, she was accompanied by the Irish Navy vessel the L.É. Orla.

1965

11 SEPTEMBER

Cholera

A cholera outbreak resulting in 290 deaths occurred in Waterford in 1832 (see entry for July 2nd). A further outbreak occurred in 1849.

As the country was still ravaged by the fever and dysentery that followed the famine, it was not surprising that this outbreak was more disastrous than that of 1832. The famine had denuded the countryside of many small hamlets and villages, and the resultant gravitation of destitute people to the towns and cities led to extremely poor sanitary conditions. On the other hand, the workhouse system had been set up in 1838, and the Waterford workhouse opened in 1841 (see entry for March 30th).

The first case of cholera occurred in the workhouse on the 15th of April 1849 and it raged over the following six months. Some 249 people died from a total of 522 cases. The last recorded death was on the 11th of September 1849.

1849

12 SEPTEMBER

Sir Henry Barron

A plaque in the porch of Ferrybank Church reads:

> *This church was erected by Sir Henry Page Turner Barron, Bart. To the honour and glory of God and in memory of his relations, deceased, 1906.*

Sir Henry died on the 12th of September 1900. There is a story about this plaque and indeed of the Barron family relations with the Catholic Church. It begins with his father, Sir Henry Winston Barron of Belmont Park, who had been elected MP for Waterford on seven occasions between 1832 and 1869. In 1867 he funded the building of a bell tower on the front of an existing small Grecian chapel in Ferrybank. When he died in 1872, his son Sir Henry Barron intimated to the Bishop of Waterford that if he got permission to erect a monument to his father inside a church, he would make sure that the Catholic Church would be very generously looked after in the coming years. Eventually the bishop agreed and a monument was erected on the sidewall of St. John's Church. It reads:

> *Sacred to the memory of Sir Henry Winston Barron, Bar., born Oct 15, 1795 at Ballyneale in this county. Elected M.P. for Waterford 1832; 1835; 1837-1848; 1865; 1869. Died 19 Aug 1872, R.I.P.*

When Sir Henry died in 1900, he left the sum of £6,000 to build a new church in Ferrybank and a further £3,000 to build a mausoleum. But Sir Henry had included a number of very specific conditions in his will which caused some disquiet. Following numerous discussions and legal advice, a compromise seems to have been agreed by architects and the trustees. Ferrybank Church and adjoining mausoleum was built in 1906, six years after the death of Sir Henry.

1900

13 SEPTEMBER

Corporation

Sometimes in the 17th century Waterford Corporation did not have cash in hand to pay its bills. It seems to have been normal practice to set the amount against future rents. The council meeting held on the 13th of September 1671 gives a number of examples of this practice:

> *That Mr. Richard Watridge shall be allowed for entertaining the judges horses last assizes (criminal courts) out of his own rent due to the Corporation.*

> *That Mr. William Frith shall be allowed ten pounds sterling towards entertaining the judges this assizes, to be paid out of such branch of the city rents as Mr. Mayor thinks fit.*

> *Upon complaint of Mr. Thomas Prince about the repairing the gutter betwixt the Tholsell and his houses, the money whereof amounts to three pounds nineteen shillings, and six pence sterling, it is ordered the sheriff receiver do reimburse the said Mr Prince the said sum if he have so much of the cities moneys in his hands, otherwise it is to be paid by assignment out of next Michaelmas rent.*

1671

14 SEPTEMBER

Corporation

In the 17th and 18th centuries members of Waterford Corporation regularly took turns serving in various offices. The following excerpt from the Council Books for the 14th of September 1685 illustrates this very well:

> *Concluded, that Mr. Abraham Smith, lately elected sheriff for the year ensuing and having procured Mr. Francis Barker to serve in his stead, he being not at present in capacity to serve himself, shall be excused for serving that office till his turn comes about again.*

In practice, Francis Barker was the third sheriff elected in as many weeks. Fredrick Christian had first been elected sheriff on the 18th of August. Then a few weeks later on the 7th of September:

> *Mr. Fredrick Christian being excused at his request from serving sheriff of this City the ensuing year doth promise to serve the city in the year following. Then Mr. Abraham Smith was chosen.*

Francis Barker went on to become Mayor in 1693 and served again as Mayor in 1713.

1685

15 SEPTEMBER

The Bass Protest

In 1932 the new Fianna Fáil government under de Valera embarked on a protectionist policy with regard to Irish goods and introduced tariffs on imported goods from Britain. In addition de Valera decided to suspend payment of all land annuities. The resulting economic war lasted from 1932 to 1938. The desire to protect native industry and avoid foreign products sometimes took an unusual twist. In 1933 a campaign was initiated against Bass Ale which at that time was brewed only in England. In September of that year people began to take the law into their own hands.

In early September there were reports of men entering a number of licensed premises in Dublin and breaking bottles of Bass stored on shelves. The following week raids were carried out on four Bass Ale stores in Tralee and over two hundred dozen bottles of ale were broken. A raiding party of about ten men also stopped a goods train outside Dundalk. They removed a number of Bass kegs and bored a hole in each, draining the contents. In Monaghan thirty-five publicans were visited by various groups "requesting" that they sell no more Bass. They also "requested" that all Bass signs and publicity notices be removed. All the publicans complied.

The protest spread to Waterford where on the 15th of September 1933, it was reported that men bearing iron bars had entered public houses in Waterford and Tramore and broke Bass bottles on the shelves. Frank Edwards (see entry for January 6th) was also involved in this movement.

Note: In the 1960s Bass Ale was brewed in Ireland by Beamish and Crawford in Cork.

1933

16 SEPTEMBER

Corporation

The members of Waterford Corporation in the 17th century never lost an opportunity to curry favour in high places (see entry for January 28th). If the King or Queen did not visit the city, then the next best thing was his representative in Ireland, the Lord Lieutenant.

On the 16th of September 1679, the Duke of Ormond, Lord Lieutenant of Ireland visited the city. Some ten days earlier the corporation had decided:

> *That Mr. Mayor be desired to provide a dinner for his grace the Lord Lieutenant and the charge thereof to be allowed out of the revenue of the city, not exceeding twenty five pounds sterling.*

Obviously a good night was had, as a few weeks later they decided:

> *That eight pounds three shillings shall be added to the twenty-five pounds ordered by former vote for treating the Lord Lieutenant.*

It was not clear how large the Lord Lieutenant's party was but a few months later it was ordered that the ferryman Henry Keating be paid two pounds fifteen shillings *for ferriage of the Lord Lieutenant.*

1679

17 SEPTEMBER

Captain Patrick Clooney

When you wander through the graveyard in Ballybricken Church you may come across a fairly substantial memorial to Captain Patrick Clooney who died on the 17th of September 1862 during the American Civil War.

Clooney was born in Ballybricken in May 1840. In June 1860 he went to Italy to join the Irish Brigade of the Papal Army. This army was raised by the Pope to protect the Papal States against nationalist forces in Italy. However, by September he was captured and interned in Genoa. Following his release in October 1860, he returned to Waterford.

The American Civil War began the following spring. Many veterans of the Papal Brigade crossed the Atlantic to join up with Thomas Francis Meagher's Irish Brigade. Clooney enlisted as a Private, was promoted to Sergeant and saw action at the battle of First Bull Run in July 1861. He was commissioned Captain of the new 88th Regiment in October. Over the following months the 88th were involved in a number of engagements at Fair Oaks and Seven Days.

Captain Patrick Clooney died on the 17th of September 1862 at the Battle of Antietam and was buried in the field. He was 22 years old. Sometime later his remains were exhumed and reburied in Queens in New York. The monument in Ballybricken graveyard was unveiled in 1863.

1862

18 SEPTEMBER

Portlairge

Many Waterford people will remember the *SS Portlairge* or the Mud Boat, as she was affectionately known. She completed seventy five years of service dredging the channel.

Although launched in Dublin in early September 1907, she was announced to the world by an article in the *Syren and Shipping* magazine published on the 18th of September 1907. Replacing the previous dredger named *Urbs Intacta* (see entry for June 3rd), she was 140 feet long and capable of carrying five hundred tons of spoil. In her day she was one of the most modern vessels afloat and could operate both as a dredger and a tugboat. She was the last working steamboat of her type, powered by coal and steam throughout her entire life.

There is a record of an incident during the Civil War when in October 1922 she was commandeered by officers of the Provisional Government to take them to Youghal. It returned the same day.

She broke down in December 1982, and was sold to the Scottish Steam Preservation Co. for a scrap value of £3,000. However, local outcry caused the cancellation of the sale and for the following five years she lay dormant on Scotch Quay. She was eventually sold (again for scrap) in 1987 and on the 26th of August 1987 she steamed down the Suir for the last time. She got as far as Saltmills in Co. Wexford where she now lies on the shoreline, a complete wreck.

1907

19 SEPTEMBER

SS City of Waterford

The ship the *City of Waterford* was originally built in Belfast in 1879 as the *Fair Head* for the Ulster Steam Company. At 1175 tons she was 232 feet long. She was purchased by the shipping company Palgrave Murphy Ltd. in 1934 and renamed *City of Waterford*. This company named all their ships after the ports they served.

In September 1941 she joined a convoy at Milford Haven with a cargo of coal for Gibraltar. On the 19th of September she collided with a Dutch tug in the convoy and sank. The five crew were rescued and transferred to the ship *Walmer Castle*. The following morning aircraft attacked the convoy and the *Walmer Castle* was sunk with heavy loss of life, including the five crew from the *City of Waterford*.

An unusual postscript to this event was that when the families of the dead men made life assurance claims they were refused, as at the time of death the men were not crew of the *City of Waterford* but passengers of the *Walmer Castle*.

After the war Palgrave Murphy Ltd. named another ship *City of Waterford*. This was the twenty-five year old steamer *Skerries II*, which they had purchased from the Clyde Shipping Company. This ship had been used on the Liverpool-Waterford route for years. Three years later in April 1949 while en route from Antwerp to Cork, she ran into fog off the south coast of England and collided with a very large Greek ship called the *Marpessa*. The *City of Waterford* sank, however all the crew were saved.

1941

20 SEPTEMBER

Corporation

The *Council Books of the Corporation of Waterford 1662-1870* records all the decisions made by the Council during that time, however mundane or trivial. For example on the 20th of September 1693 the Corporation agreed to pay a wine bill to the total of nineteen shillings and three pence for a Mr. Mathew White. It is not recorded what the wine bill was for. The only other record for this Mathew White is that he was admitted a Freeman of the City seven years earlier in 1886.

Another example of a trivial decision comes from December 1673 when the following decision was reached:

> *Ordered that the surveyors report at the next meeting how far Mr. Joseph Osbernes tenant near the great Quay is to clean the street before his house.*

1693

21 SEPTEMBER

Jacob's Biscuits

In the late 1600s the Jacob family fled Britain to Ireland because of their Quaker religious beliefs. Eventually Isaac Jacob ended up in Waterford in 1722. His son Joseph Jacob married into the Strangman family and set up home in King Street (the city end of O'Connell Street). The firm of Jacob, Watson and Strangman, shipping agents, was set up but it collapsed following a war between Holland and England in 1780. One of his children, Thomas Strangman Jacob, overcame this setback and established a flourishing corn business.

It was his son Isaac that set up a bakery in Bridge Street. Although a general baker he soon saw the potential of making "sea biscuits", as at that time Waterford had a thriving maritime trade. On his death, his sons William Jacob and Robert Jacob decided to concentrate on the biscuit business. On the 21st of September 1850 William and Robert Jacob opened their biscuit factory in Bridge Street.

An advertisement later that year stated: *Waterford General Bakery. We beg respectively to inform our numerous customers and the public of Waterford that we intend opening next week the premises No 69 Quay for the sale of the various articles of the General and Fancy Baking Trade on connection with our establishment in Bridge Street.*

The business flourished with customers in many parts of Ireland and England. In order to fulfil this thriving demand the Jacob brothers decided to move their business to Dublin, and the Waterford factory was closed down. Tragedy struck in 1861. Robert drowned while on holiday in Tramore. He is buried in the Quaker burial grounds in Newtown. William continued with the business and Jacob's went on to become one of the best-known biscuit brands in Ireland.

1850

22 SEPTEMBER

WRTC

The original Regional Technical College building was built in 1969/70 by MacMahon & McPhillips Ltd. of Kilkenny and handed over to the Minister for Education at the end of July 1970. On the 22nd of September the college formally opened its doors to new students, although some students had been in temporary accommodation during the previous year.

Five months later in a report to the College Council, the principal Mr. R. Langford stated that the building was designed to hold seven hundred comfortably, and was accommodating about three hundred at any one time. Almost one thousand students used the building during the first term. There were twenty-four full-time teaching staff and another twenty-three part-time staff. It was expected that progress would be made in the next year by getting support staff for the workshops and perhaps some administrative staff. Mr. Langford reported that that there were six classes of full time students for 74 students, nine block release courses for 117 students, twelve day release courses for 256 students and ten part-time courses for 313 students. With other short courses the total enrolment was 969.

The first conferring in 1972 was a small affair with 32 parchments presented and a total attendance of 112 people including graduates, staff and visitors.

In January 1997 the RTC was upgraded to Waterford Institute of Technology.

1970

23 SEPTEMBER

Chamber of Commerce

Waterford as a merchant city, had always engaged in trade since being granted its original charter in 1215. Its merchants would have cooperated with each other in some form down through the years. While a Chamber of Commerce or Body of Merchants may have existed in some formal way, the earliest recorded existence is in 1787 (a minute book from that year survives to this day). This is generally known as the founding date of the Chamber of Commerce.

However, the Chamber of Commerce was incorporated on the 23rd of September 1815. This date was confirmed in 1994 by chance, when an official at the Bank of Ireland on the Quay opened two tin boxes, which had been placed in the bank vault in 1927. Inside the boxes were the original charter for the Chamber dated the 23rd of September 1815 and a supplementary charter dated the 19th of May 1908. A written record kept with the boxes showed that they had been placed by the chamber for safekeeping in the old National Irish Bank at 50 The Quay in September 1927. In the late 1960s the National was taken over by the Bank of Ireland and all the items in safekeeping were transferred to its vault at 60 The Quay. These charters were handed over to Waterford Museum of Treasures in April 2013 where they are now on display.

It appears that towards the end of the nineteenth century, it was felt that the original charter from 1815 was too rigid, and rather than amend it, a new one was sought. Edward VII granted this new one on the 19th of May 1908.

1815

24 SEPTEMBER

Charles Bianconi

Charles Bianconi was born in Italy on the 24th of September 1786. Having moved to Ireland in his teens, he worked initially in Dublin selling pictures on the street. In 1806 he moved to Waterford where he set up a shop in Georges Street. In 1809 he moved to Clonmel. In July 1815 Charles Bianconi began his first transport route from Clonmel to Cahir. The Clonmel-Waterford route opened the following year in 1816. Over the next thirty years he established a coach network throughout Munster and Leinster.

In 1832 Bianconi purchased a house belonging to Thomas Meagher Snr. on the Quay. This house, where Thomas Francis Meagher was born, became Cummins Hotel (now the Granville Hotel) and served as the terminus for the Bianconi transport business in Waterford. A biography of Charles Bianconi, published in 1878 by his daughter, includes the following:

> *Mr. Edward Cummins, the proprietor of Cummins's Commercial and Family Hotel, was Mr. Bianconi's agent at Waterford. This connection dates back to the year 1821 or 1822, and was continued through the Cummins family up to the period of the selling of the establishment, when the Dungarvan, Passage, and New Ross lines passed by purchase to Messrs. W. K. and P. Cummins. In the heyday of the establishment, Waterford was one of the most important depots in the country. On Sundays, when all the horses working into that city were resting, the stables usually contained forty animals. The hotel being the centre of this traffic, was naturally a place of great business and bustle.*

1786

25 SEPTEMBER

Leper House

On the 25th of September 1661 an inquisition was taken before the Sheriff and Mayor of Waterford regarding the Leper Hospital in Stephen Street. A transcript of its findings was published in the *Journal of Waterford & South East of Ireland Archaeological Society* in 1894. The introduction is as follows:

> *We find that the Lazar or Leper house in the suburbs of Waterford, in St. Stephen's Parish, was erected and founded by King John and hath given the same house immunities and a charter to a Master, Brethren and Sisters of the said House for the maintenance of Lepers for ever and of which immunities they had a liberty that if any assault, battery, or bloodshed was committed within the precincts of said Lazar House, the Baron or Master of said house were sole judges of any such fact. We do also find that it is further part of the immunities of said House, that if any with the Leprosy, and not taking their licence and freedom of members of the house to live abroad and so dying, their estate is forfeited to the said Leper house.*

The document continues to deal with the vast array of land and properties which they found belonged to the Leper Hospital including:

> *We find that Leperstown in the Barony of Gaultier and Parish of Kilmacom esteemed were plough lands with the tithes thereof great and small to belong to the said House.*

In 1662 the Corporation were informed that:

> *there are in the house two men and three women all lepers, and one servant, viz, Philipp Walsh, Phill McGrath, Ellan Grant, Joan Garvey, Joanny Hea and Margaret Walsh, all maintained within the leperhouse and by its revenue.*

1661

26 SEPTEMBER

Civil Survey

On the 26th of September 1653 an act was adopted in the British Parliament which allowed the Civil Survey of 1654 - 1656 to take place. This survey was set up by Cromwell's Government in Ireland to gather information about the location and quality of the confiscated land. The survey is based on the old division of land into baronies and the smaller subdivisions of parishes and townlands.

Twenty-seven counties were surveyed but unfortunately the original records were lost in the fire at the Four Courts in 1922. However copies for twelve counties including Waterford had been made, and survived. In the 1930s and '40s the Irish Manuscripts Commission published the surviving records including *The Civil Survey A.D. 1654-1656 County of Waterford* which was published in 1942.

In Waterford City the survey identified fifty-nine streets or lanes in the city and over three hundred and fifty *tenants or posssessors*.

The amount of information given in this survey is quite detailed as illustrated by the following entry for a house in Broad Street:

Present Tenant:	*John Hill*	
Denominations:	*A dwelling house to ye street, stone walls and part cadge work slated*	
	A yard backwards (length 29, breadth 11)	
Length	*47*	
Breadth	*31*	
Proprietors in 1641:	*Peter Dobbin.*	
Worth to be set for a lease of 21 years:		*£16*
Value of ye house as it is worth to be sold at eight years purchase:		*£128*

1653

27 SEPTEMBER

Bar Extensions

At the Annual Licensing Court held on Monday the 27th of September 1982 the *pathetic* level of drunkenness amongst young people late at night was a cause of concern. The Garda Superintendent stated that every Saturday night there was a steady stream of young people from public houses towards places of entertainment. Too often these people were unfit for entry and lay on the roadway or fell around on the streets. In addition the number of arrests for drunken driving was much higher than on any other night of the week. The Garda Superintendent told the court that *it is pathetic to see the number of young people involved* and suggested that if the attraction of dances with 2am closing times did not exist on a Saturday night, the problem of drunkenness would not be so bad.

The District Justice decided to take the Superintendent's advice and banned all dances after midnight on a Saturday night. This ban not only took place in the city, but also in Tramore, Dunmore East and South Kilkenny. Only a few exceptions were allowed, for example at private functions where there was a full four-course dinner supplied.

However three city hotels (the Bridge, the Ardree and the Tower) appealed the ban to the Circuit Court. In a sitting at Carlow Circuit Court some four weeks later the ban was overturned. The Circuit Court Judge decided that dancing would be allowed up to 1am in winter and 1.30am in summer.

1982

28 SEPTEMBER

The Great Parchment Book

The Liber Antiquissimus Civitatis Waterfordiae or *The Great Parchment Book* is one of the most remarkable historical compilations of any municipality in Ireland. The book, which is on display in the Medieval Museum, covers three centuries from the middle of the 14th century to the middle of the 17th. The contents include statutes passed by Waterford Corporation, annual entries giving names of Mayors, Bailiffs, Sheriffs, and admission of Freemen, rental of Corporation property, lists of leases granted by the Corporation, judgments against specific people, and various miscellaneous records.

In an entry for 1604, it gives the details of the number of people killed by the plague in the twelve months prior to the 28th of September:

> *Also about the 23rd day of October there began a plague in this city, whereof there died in all this year ending the 28th of September 1604, 2256 of which infection the city is now almost freed (God be thanked) so as there died within the city the week but fewer, where the same was so hot that there died a month ago weekly a hundred and sixteen.*

1604

29 SEPTEMBER

Housing Conditions

In late 1910 the Local Government Board instigated an enquiry into the sanitary circumstances and administration of Waterford. Public sittings were held in the courthouse, and various witnesses were examined. Their report was published on the 30th of September 1911. It included the following:

> *The central portion of the city contains the main business streets, which are lined with shops and offices. Between these streets, many of them narrow, there is a ramification of old and narrow lanes and courts, where the houses are huddled together without due regard to proper hygienic considerations. Many of the lanes and courts have in front of the houses high walls which are within five or six feet of the doors and windows. The courts are for the most part cul-de-sacs and the covered passages leading to them have a damp and unpleasant odom. Some of the houses in these courts have neither back windows nor doors, and consequently there is no through ventilation. In many the windows cannot be opened and the houses are dark and damp on account of the want of air and sunshine. No person having any knowledge of sanitary requirements would contend that such houses are fit for human habitation. Yet when one of these so called houses becomes vacant, there are as much as twenty applicants seeking to become the tenant such is the famine for the cheapest habitations.*

The report went on to state:

> *There are eighty-seven tenement houses, two, three and four storeys situated principally in Little Michael Street, Alexander Street, New Street, Patrick Street, Kneefe's Lane and Little Patrick Street. Many of them are old and in an unsanitary condition and owing to want of space, structural and other defects are incapable of being put into a proper sanitation state or made fit for human habitation and consequently should be closed up.*

1911

30 SEPTEMBER

Lifeboat

When the Clyde steamer arrived in Waterford on Sunday night the 30th of September 1911, on board was a new lifeboat for Dunmore East Life Boat station. The new lifeboat, named *Fanny Harriet,* was built at the Thames Iron Works. At 37 feet, she was the same size as the previous boat (*Henry Dodd*) but had the added advantage that she could be worked efficiently with ten oars instead of the twelve which the previous boat required. She also came fitted with complete sail equipment. The lifeboat was rowed to Dunmore East the following morning.

The *Fanny Harriet* was launched only once while in Dunmore and that was for the infamous *Mexico* incident on the Keeragh Rocks on the 20th of February the following year. Although the Fethard lifeboat, *The Helen Blake,* was lost with the death of nine local lifeboat men, the Dunmore East boat, along with the Rosslare boat, rescued the crew of the *Mexico* and the other five Fethard lifeboat men.

The *Fanny Harriet* was replaced at the Dunmore Station in 1914 by a motor driven lifeboat, the *Michael Henry.*

For a full account of the various lifeboats in Dunmore East see the entry for March 19th.

1911

1 OCTOBER

Central Technical Institute

On the 1st of October 1906 the Central Technical Institute (CTI) officially opened its doors on Parnell Street.

The impetus for the foundation of the CTI lay in the *Agricultural and Technical Education Act of 1899*. In 1900 the Waterford Technical Instruction Committee met for the first time in July of that year under the chairmanship of Dr. Richard Sheehan, Bishop of Waterford and Lismore. This committee immediately started work on securing suitable premises.

A site was identified in Parnell Street and tenders were sought. In October 1905 the contract was awarded to a local builder, Patrick Costen, for a price of £3,283. This was the same builder who had built the Carnegie Library which had opened that same year. The building was handed over in mid-August 1906, and the opening ceremony was held on the 17th of September.

There were six teaching staff in that first year, most of whom came from similar technical colleges in England and Wales. The first principal, Bernard O'Shaughnessy, was a chemist and a member of the Institute of Chemistry and came from London. During the first year some 544 individual students attended the CTI. The staff had doubled to twelve by 1912. Gradually more Irish staff were employed due to a high turnover in the first few years of operation.

In 2006 the CTI celebrated its centenary.

1906

2 OCTOBER

Richard II

According to a number of sources this is the date that King Richard II arrived in Waterford for the first time. This was the first expedition to Ireland by an English King in 184 years, since King John in 1210. It was also one of the largest expeditions, as Richard arrived with over 4,000 soldiers and 30,000 archers in 500 sailing ships. By the time Richard departed in May 1395, virtually all of Ireland had submitted to his rule.

Richard's life was documented by a Frenchman called Jean Froissard. In his *Chronicles* is found one of the greatest contemporary accounts of 14th century life. Interestingly, Froissard wrote about Richard's visit to Waterford. He tells for example that Richard and his army had to *wade up to their waist in ooze* getting from the ships to dry land. There is also an illustration of the landing in Waterford which shows artillery being unloaded. This was the first time artillery was used in Ireland.

Froissard gives a general description of the country as follows:

> *Ireland is one of the worst countries to make war in or to conquer, for there are such impenetrable and extensive forests, lakes, and bogs that there is no knowing how to pass them and carry on the war advantageously; it is so thinly inhabited that wherever the Irish people please they desert the towns and take refuge in the forests, living in huts made of boughs like wild beasts.*
>
> *They are a very hardy race of great subtlety, and of various tempers, paying no attention to cleanliness, nor to any gentleman, although the country is governed by kings of whom there are several; but seem desirous to remain in the savage state in which they have been brought up.*

1394

3 OCTOBER

Captain Walter Farrell

As mentioned numerous times throughout this book, Waterford has an extensive maritime history. There are many records of shipbuilding, shipwrecks and shipping trade. However, there are very few accounts of the Waterford men who sailed these ships.

One exception is the account given by Captain Walter Farrell in the autumn 1988 edition of *Decies*. He states that on the 3rd of October 1888 he arrived back in London after a 14-month voyage on board the *SS Lodestar* where he was second mate. She had left Hull in August 1887 and sailed for Bombay. Having discharged her cargo, she took on a new cargo of salt and headed for Calcutta. She then took on a cargo of wheat and arrived back in London in October 1888. The article in *Decies* outlines fascinating details of the eleven separate voyages of Walter Farrell. Born in July 1862 at 10 Sion Row, he first went to sea as a cabin boy on board the barque *Queen of the North* at the age of sixteen. His first voyage lasted twelve months, from London to Madras in India and back. The ship never docked on dry land, as her cargo was discharged from two miles off shore.

Over the next twenty-five years Walter sailed all over the world, working his way up through the ranks. In 1891 he left sailing ships for steam powered ships and thus ended up with the Waterford Steamship Company in 1892. In 1895 he became Captain of the *SS Ardnamult* with the Limerick Steam Ship Company. His last ship was the *SS Comeragh* on the Waterford-Liverpool route. In October 1903 Captain Farrell retired from the sea and became harbour master of the Port of Waterford.

1888

4 OCTOBER

All-Ireland Hurling Final

On the 6th of September 1959, the All-Ireland Hurling Final between Waterford and Kilkenny had resulted in a draw, thus both teams were back in Croke Park on Sunday the 4th of October. The attendance of 77,285 was a record for an All-Ireland Final replay in either hurling or football. In fact it was the third highest attendance ever at a hurling final, the previous best being 84,856 in the 1954 final and 83,096 in the 1956 final. It was to be another sixty-four years in 2003 before a redeveloped Croke Park was able to accommodate a larger attendance. Although the match did not live up to the heights of the first drawn game, the final score of 3-12 to 1-10 saw Waterford the decisive winners.

An estimated twenty thousand people turned out in the city on the Monday night when the team returned home. As the crowds waited for the returning heroes, they were entertained by a tape recording of the commentary of the drawn match played a month earlier by Mícheál O'Hehir. Eventually traffic had to be diverted from the Quay onto O'Connell Street, but even then the crowds became so great that all traffic was diverted up through Ballybricken. The team was escorted in a colourful cavalcade down the Quay, led by torch bearers and all the city bands, to the Mall and City Hall where they were received by the Mayor and members of the Corporation.

Bonfires blazed from Mount Misery and in many streets. However a number of bonfires got out of control and the fire brigade was called out on eight occasions that night. This included a gorse blaze at Mount Misery.

1959

5 OCTOBER

Knockaderry Water Works

The earliest water supplies for the city were from springs or wells both inside and outside the city walls. Each of the wells was named after the local churches. St. Patrick's Well was located at the junction of Patrick Street and Stephen Street and is reputed to have been thirty feet deep. St. Michael's Well was in Manor Street, St. Stephen's Well was in the southern end of Stephen Street and St. Catherine's Well on Catherine Street.

Gradually during the 17th and 18th centuries conduits or channels were used to distribute water. However these conduits were open and very easily polluted. In 1670 it was reported that water in the conduits was *much abused by infectious matter washed into the fountains and springheads* seemingly as a result of the *abundance of filth in Stephen St. caused by the slaughtering of cattle there and the keeping of pigs*. In 1731 there is a reference to wooden pipes being used while in 1758 there is a reference to lead pipes being used. In 1786 forty stopcocks were purchased. In 1789 Water Commissioners were appointed by an act of parliament. Cast iron pumps first made their appearance in 1838.

By the mid-19th century a proper water supply for the city was clearly needed. Two possibilities arose, Ballyscanlon Lake and Knockaderry Brook. Knockaderry was chosen and an Act of Parliament was obtained allowing the corporation to take over the existing water works from the Water Commissioners and to proceed with work at Knockaderry. *The Waterford Water Act of 1871* enabled contracts to be signed and on the 5th of October 1875 the first sod was turned for the Knockaderry Water Works.

1875

6 OCTOBER

Donncha Rua Mac Conmara

Donncha Rua Mac Conmara is best remembered as the author of the song *Bán Chnoic Éireann Ó*. Born in Co. Clare in 1715, he travelled to Rome with the intention of becoming a priest. However he was expelled from the college. On his return back to Ireland he ended up in the Sliabh gCua area of Co. Waterford, where he taught in a hedge school. In 1745 he was reputed to have gone to Newfoundland for a short time, but no one is sure if he ever got there. He did travel to Europe and it was in Hamburg that he is said to have composed *Bán Chnoic Éireann Ó*. A few years later Donncha did travel to Newfoundland. It was here that he composed his bilingual ballad. He was in a public house in St. John's, Newfoundland, when some English sailors asked him for a song. On the spot, he sang a new song with alternate English and Irish lines to the delight of the sailors who understood the English patriotic part, and to the double delight of the Irish present, as the Irish words were scurrilous of the English nation in general. This ballad is known today as *MacNamara's Bilingual Ballad*.

In Waterford a few years later, and poverty stricken, he pretended to convert to Protestantism which enabled him to get a job as a parish clerk in Newtown near Kilmacthomas. Very soon he was found out and sacked from this position. He spent the last years of his life as a Latin tutor to a Power family. He died on the 6th of October 1810 at the age of 95. He was buried in Newtown. His grave was unmarked for over a hundred years until a head stone was erected in the early 1900s. This is still visible today.

1810

7 OCTOBER

Arundel Ballroom

A gala opening of the Arundel Ballroom in Arundel Square was held on Friday the 7th of October 1955. Dancing was from 9pm to 3am and over nine hundred people attended. The resident band, under the leadership of Jack Barrett, provided the music. The new ballroom sported a new polished maple sprung oval shaped floor, which was modelled on the floor of the Aberdeen Hall in the Gresham Hotel, Dublin. In addition the decorated alcoves were furnished with blue Rexine armchairs and Dunlopillo foam seating. A fully equipped kitchen adjoined the supper room. Hundreds were turned away on that first night, but patrons were glad to hear that dancing would be held six nights a week (excluding Mondays) with the resident Jack Barrett Orchestra.

In October 1961 the ballroom closed down and the premises was purchased by Irish Rubber Products in The Glen with the intention of converting it into a factory to recondition rubber printing and industrial rollers. This factory opened in May 1962. The old factory at The Glen had been destroyed by fire in July of the previous year. In 1981 it was sold to John O'Sullivan, Amusement Caterers, with the intention of converting it into a shopping arcade.

Note: The site of the ballroom was where Cherry's opened their first Waterford brewery in 1806 (see entry for June 4th).

1955

8 OCTOBER

Jenny Lind

In 1908 the great Irish tenor Count John McCormack appeared in the Theatre Royal (see entry for March 23rd). Another famous international artist to do so was the Swedish Nightingale, Jenny Lind, who appeared on the 8th of October 1859.

Jenny Lind was born in Stockholm in 1820. By 1838 she had enraptured audiences with her soprano voice in her own native Sweden. Very soon her fame spread across Europe. Her description as the Swedish Nightingale came from her association with the author Hans Christian Anderson whose unrequited love for her led to Anderson writing the story *The Nightingale* as a tribute to her. Lind herself experienced unrequited love with the composer Frederic Chopin.

The American showman P.T. Barnum organised a tour of America in 1850 and his advance publicity turned her into a celebrity before she arrived. Forty thousand people turned up when her ship docked at New York. An article in the New York Herald in September 1850 stated that she was the most popular woman in the world.

She married in 1852 and moved to England in 1858 where she was appointed the first professor of singing at the Royal College of Music. It was the following year that the Swedish Nightingale appeared on the stage of the Theatre Royal.

Jenny Lind died in 1887. While buried in Worcester, there is a plaque dedicated to her on the walls of Westminster Abbey.

1859

9 OCTOBER

Fever Hospital

The Fever Hospital was originally established in 1799 by a Dr. Barker in a house called The Turrets on John's Hill. This was reputed to have been the first fever hospital in Ireland and as Ryland says in his *History of Waterford* (1824), *the second in the empire.* In 1815 land was leased from the Waterford Leper Hospital and the building of a new Fever Hospital began. Designed by John Roberts, the hospital opened on the 9th of October 1816.

Its opening proved fortuitous as a typhoid epidemic broke out in 1817 and lasted two years. At its height in July 1818 some 313 cases were admitted to the Fever Hospital. Over four hundred people died in Waterford during this epidemic. Ryland stated in 1824:

> *The Waterford Fever Hospital is an admirably conducted establishment, posing every requisite which the ingenuity of man can deliver, as likely to contribute to the comfort and recovery of its unhappy inmates.*

In 1894 the sisters of St. John of God took charge of the hospital and they remained there until its closure in 1960.

For a long time the Infirmary had attempted to subsume the Fever Hospital into its operation but various legal impediments prevented it. Finally in September 1962 the lease was handed back to the Infirmary. The building then lay idle as the Minister for Health refused to sanction any money for its refurbishment. Gradually it fell into disrepair. Lead was stolen from the roof and the building became derelict. It was eventually demolished in January 1977.

1816

10 OCTOBER

Corporation

Greasing the corridors of power was a fairly common occurrence in the 17th and 18th centuries. On the 10th of October 1669 the Council decided to present an address to the Lord Lieutenant and in addition, to give his secretary *a piece of plate of sixteen pounds value*. It was left to the Mayor to decide whether this *present* should be made in plate or gold. It obviously had the desired effect as the Mayor was told to come to Dublin on the first week of November to make his address to the Lord Lieutenant.

This approach was not universally approved. In particular, an Alderman William Bolton complained the Mayor and the Corporation to the Lord Lieutenant. It seems that such *presents* were the convention of the time. The Mayor was aghast with the suggestion that the present might be seen as corrupt. The result was that Alderman Bolton was dismissed and struck off the list of Freemen.

William Bolton had only arrived in Waterford some twenty years beforehand with the Cromwellian Army. He was granted several town lands including Faithlegg (see entry for March 1). When the monarchy was restored in 1660 Bolton had no difficulty in changing with the times. In 1662 he was made a Freeman, and soon after became a Councillor and Alderman. He was also elected Mayor that year. However, he caused deep division within the Council, and his enemies finally succeeded in moving against him following the incident referred to above.

1669

11 OCTOBER

Harry Power, Bushranger

Most people have heard of Ned Kelly the Australian bushranger (1855-1880). Another famous bushranger named Harry Power was born in Waterford in 1820. Having found work in Manchester, he was arrested in 1841 for stealing a pair of shoes. His punishment was to be transported to Van Diemen's Land for seven years. He was released after five years and made his way to New South Wales.

In March 1855 Harry was stopped by the police on suspicion of being a horse thief. In the resulting scuffle one of the police was wounded. This time his sentence was thirteen years hard labour on the roads. He escaped in 1862 and remained at large for another two years. After his capture he was sentenced to another seven years.

Five years later in 1867 he escaped again, and took to the life of a bushranger, robbing coaches and homesteads. He was reputed to have introduced Ned Kelly to the life of crime when he was only fifteen years of age, and taught him how to survive and elude the police. Although he never murdered any of his victims and seldom took money from the poor, a reward of £500 was put on his head, dead or alive. In 1870 he was arrested and sentenced to a further fifteen years.

Due to declining health he was released in 1877. On the 11th of October 1891 Harry Power died by accidental drowning in the Murray River in South Australia, a very long way from his birthplace in Waterford.

1891

12 OCTOBER

Brendan Bowyer

Brendan Bowyer was born on Wednesday the 12th of October 1938 in Baileys New Street. His father was Stanley Bowyer, organist at the Cathedral and first musical director of the Waterford Light Opera Festival.

The Royal Showband was formed in 1957 with Brendan playing trombone. The other members were Michael Coppinger, sax; Tom Dunphy, bass; Jim Conlon, guitar; Eddie Sullivan, trumpet; Gerry Cullen, keyboard and Charlie Matthews, drums. All were aged between eighteen and twenty. Initially there was no front man, and different members of the band alternated with different songs. Eventually Brendan Bower ditched the trombone and became the lead singer.

The Royal's first appearance was in September 1957 in the Olympia Ballroom on Parnell Street. Six months later they were billed as *Waterford's up-and-coming orchestra*. They turned professional in March 1958 with their first professional performance in the Olympia Ballroom in Dublin on the 11th of March. Their first professional performance in Waterford occurred some days later on St. Patrick's night in the Olympia in Waterford.

The rest is history. Brendan Bower and the Royal Showband became Ireland's biggest pop stars of the 1960s. In 1971 Brendan left the Royal and moved to Las Vegas with his new band The Big Eight.

In February 2001 Brendan Bowyer, along with Val Doonican, was awarded the Freedom of Waterford (see entry for February 3rd).

1938

13 OCTOBER

Rosamond Jacob

Rosamond Jacob was a novelist, feminist, nationalist, historian and political activist. She was born in Waterford on the 13th of October 1886 to a middle-class Quaker family. Educated at Newtown and the Protestant School, she also spent much of her time being home schooled due to ill health. From an early age she displayed an interest in the Gaelic League and joined Sinn Féin and Cumann na mBan. She also became a member of the Irish Women's Suffrage League

In 1919 she moved to Dublin. Following the War of Independence she opposed the treaty and was imprisoned for a time. After the Civil War she remained an avid campaigner on a variety of issues. As a writer of fiction, she is not well known today. Her first novel was called *Callaghan* and was published in 1915. Her other publications include *The Troubled House*, based on the experiences of the Civil War, *The Rebel's Wife*, loosely based on the wife of Henry Joy McCracken, and a children's book *The Raven's Glen*.

Rosamond Jacob kept a diary almost all of her life. Beginning when she was a schoolgirl in Waterford in 1897 to just before her death in 1960, these diaries are more than just a chronicle of events, they provide a fascinating commentary of the political events which occurred during her life, and the causes she was involved in. Her diaries are now housed in the National Library.

She died in October 1960 and was buried in Dublin on the 13th of October on what would have been her 72nd birthday. Her biography *Rosamond Jacob, Third Person Singular* by Leeann Lane was published in 2010.

1886

14 OCTOBER

Talkies

Talkies or talking movies arrived at the Theatre Royal on the 14th of October 1929. Over £3,000 had been spent by the lessee of the Theatre Royal, a Mr. Breen, on installing the latest talkie apparatus. The equipment included a *dynamo of 350 volts being laid down in a closed off area in the kitchen at the back of the stage and connected with a projection apparatus in the operation box at the back of the pit by wires led through pipes under the ground floor.*

The first film to be shown was *The Singing Fool* with Al Jolson in the title role. A comment made at the time was that the accents were decidedly "yankee". There were two performances, one at 6.45pm and the other at 9pm.

The success of these talking movies in the Theatre Royal did not please everyone. Twelve months later in October 1930 concern was expressed at a meeting of the Finance and Law Committee of Waterford Corporation that there seemed to be a reduction in the proportion of theatrical performances to cinema projections. The management noted in a response that *there was now a difficulty in attracting first-class travelling shows owing to the scarcity and quality of the shows available in consequence of the large numbers of legitimate theatres which have installed "talkie" equipment thus preventing first-class shows from arranging tours.* They assured the council that their efforts would always be directed towards giving the Waterford public the best and cleanest entertainment possible and stated that *already they had booked a pantomime for the 5th of January following a two-week engagement in Cork.*

1929

15 OCTOBER

Coliseum

For generations of Waterford people the Coliseum at Adelphi Quay was an institution. Known affectionately as *The Col* it originally opened as a skating rink in May 1910 but it closed two years later. The Animated Picture Company took it over and it opened as a movie theatre on the 15th of October 1915. However instead of a picture on the first night, there was a cabaret concert.

During the days of the silent movies there was a full time orchestra employed to provide the background music. This Coliseum Orchestra provided much needed employment for many musicians in the city. It supplied music for many functions and balls in the city for a long number of years. With the arrival of the talking movies, the need for the orchestra disappeared and the musicians had to find alternative employment.

Although it operated as a cinema, for the next 52 years until it closed in January 1966, the Coliseum also held concerts and even boxing tournaments. During that time it closed for short periods, such as Lent and Holy Week. It was also refurbished a few times and re-roofed in 1949.

The Harbour Commissioners bought the building in 1966 and used it as a storage shed for many years. In August 1984 Southern Electrical Services set up in the premises. Gradually the building fell to rack and ruin and was finally demolished in 1992 to make way for the new Adelphi Quay development.

Another cinema, the Broad Street Cinema, also opened in Waterford in 1915. It later became the Savoy and is now the Book Centre.

1915

16 OCTOBER

Luke Wadding

Luke Wadding was born in Waterford on the 16th of October 1588 into a prominent affluent family. Members of both his father's family and his mother's family (Lombards) served as Mayor of Waterford on a number of occasions. He was also related to a number of Irish bishops. Luke was the eleventh of fourteen children. His mother died from the plague in 1602 (she was buried outside the city walls along with all plague victims). His father died around the same time but presumably not from the plague, as he was buried inside the walls in the family burial plot in Greyfriars.

At the age of 16 in 1604 Luke moved to Portugal with his older brother Matthew, and he was never to set foot in Waterford again. Educated in Portugal, he entered the Franciscan Order in 1607 and was ordained in 1613. What followed was a meteoric rise through the ranks of the Catholic Church. He became President of the Irish College at Salamanca, and founder and rector of St. Isidore's Irish College in Rome. He was a prolific writer and produced a vast array of scholarly works. He was the official agent of the Irish Bishops in Rome and continually used his influence in Irish matters. It was thought that St. Patrick's Day became a feast day by his efforts.

He died in November 1657 and is buried in St. Isidore's Church in Rome.

In the 1950s a statue of Luke Wadding was erected on The Mall in Waterford. This was later moved to Greyfriars. This statue is a replica of the one outside St. Isidore's in Rome.

1588

17 OCTOBER

Arthur Young

Arthur Young was an English author who toured Ireland in 1776-77. In 1780 he published an account of his travels in a book entitled *A Tour in Ireland*. As part of this tour he arrived in Waterford on the 17th of October 1776. The following are excerpts from his visit:

> *The staple trade of the place is the Newfoundland trade. This is very much increased; there is more of it here than anywhere. The number of people who go as passengers in the Newfoundland ships is amazing; from sixty to eighty ships, and from three thousand to five thousand annually. They come from most parts of Ireland, from Cork, Kerry etc. Experienced men will get eighteen to twenty-five pounds for the season, from March to November.*

With reference to the pig trade, he mentions: *they kill here three to four thousand a week, the price being 50s to £4 each; goes chiefly to Newfoundland.* He continues: *There is a foundry at Waterford for pots, kettles, weights and all common utensils; and a manufactory by Messers. King and Tegent of anvils to anchors, twenty hundredweight, etc. which employs forty hands. Smiths earn from 6s to 24s a week. Nailers from 10s to 12s.*

With regard to shipping he states: *Eighty sail of ships now belong to the port, twenty years ago not thirty. They pay to the captains of ship of two hundred tons £5 a month; the mate £3 10s. Ten men at 40s, five years ago only 27s. Building ships £10 a ton. Wear and tear of such a ship, £20 a month. Ships provisions, 20s a month.* He reserves his highest praise for the Quay. *But the finest object in this city is the Quay, which is unrivalled by any I have seen. It is an English mile long; the buildings on it are only common houses, but the river is near a mile over, flows up to the town in one noble reach, and the opposite shore a bold hill, which rises immediately from the water to a height that renders the whole magnificent.*

1776

18 OCTOBER

Henry II

The Anglo-Norman age arrived in Ireland in 1170 with the capture of Waterford by Strongbow (see entry for August 23rd). The success of Strongbow alarmed the English King Henry II, who feared that Strongbow might contemplate setting up a rival kingdom in Ireland. Henry therefore decided to sail for Ireland to ensure that he would remain in control of all Anglo-Normans. Henry II arrived in Waterford on the 18th of October 1171 having landed in Passage the day before. Henry came with over four hundred knights and four thousand soldiers. This was the first visit by an English monarch to Ireland.

One of the first things Henry did on his arrival was to imprison an Anglo-Norman by the name of Robert FitzStephen (who had led an attack on Wexford in 1669) in Reginald's Tower. This action was a reminder to the rest of the Anglo-Normans that irrespective of how well they had succeeded in securing Irish cities up to then, he was now in charge. It also secured the good will of the Irish lords.

Strongbow formally surrendered Waterford to Henry. Delegates from Cork and Wexford also acknowledged him as sovereign. Henry stayed six months in Ireland travelling to Lismore, Cashel and Dublin. While in Ireland he confirmed Strongbow as the heir to the McMurrough lands in Leinster with two exceptions. Both Waterford and Dublin were retained as royal cities under his direct control.

He left Ireland from Wexford on the 17th of April 1172, while his army had sailed from Passage the previous day.

1171

19 OCTOBER

Carnegie Library

In 1896 Waterford Corporation adopted the *Public Libraries Act of 1855* and the first public library was opened that year at Adelphi Terrace, with John Morrin as the librarian. In 1901 the Corporation applied for grant aid from the Carnegie Foundation. Following the award of a grant of £5000, a site (donated by Mayor Alexander Nelson) was identified in Lady Lane and plans were drawn up. The architect was Albert Edward Murray of Dublin and the building contractor was Patrick Costen of Waterford.

On the 19th of October 1903 Andrew Carnegie himself laid the foundation stone for Lady Lane Library. Earlier that day Carnegie had received the Freedom of the City from Mayor James Power at a ceremony at City Hall (this was the same James Power who was knighted by King Edward VII a few months later in May 1904). The building, which opened in 1905, was described as a five-bay two-storey classical style building with a smooth sawn Kilkenny limestone facade. It included living accommodation for the librarian. Initially the librarian John Morrin lived there. His daughter Miss P. Morrin, who became librarian after him, also lived there.

The library remained in Lady Lane until 1953 when it was moved to Barker House in O'Connell Street. The Lady Lane premises was then used as a health centre and motor tax office. In 1982 the library moved back to Lady Lane. In 2003, an extension to the library was built, taking in the undertaker's yard next door. While this building was going on, the library moved temporarily to the former Bank of Ireland building in Ballybricken. During excavations a portion of the city wall was discovered. This was preserved and can be seen in the entrance foyer of the new library.

1903

20 OCTOBER

Bull Post

The Bull Post is to Waterford what the Treaty Stone is to Limerick, and the Blarney Stone is to Cork.

So stated Alderman John Redmond at a meeting of the Corporation in 1884. To put this statement in context we need to go back 170 years, when at a meeting of the Corporation held on the 20th of October 1714, the following decision was recorded: *Ordered, that a bull-rope be provided at the charge of the city revenue.*

This decision refers of course to the 18th century pastime of bull-baiting. The book *Ireland Sixty years Ago* by John Edward Walsh, published in 1847, gives the best description of this pastime:

> *The south of Ireland, connected by several ties with Spain, adopted many Spanish usages and sports; among the rest, bull-fighting, which degenerated into bull-baiting. In Waterford on the election of every Mayor, he was surrounded by a mob who shouted out, "a rope, a rope, a rope!" And the new Mayor never failed to grant their demands. A rope two inches in diameter, with a competent leather collar and buckle, had been previously prepared, and was then delivered to the claimants, who bore it away in triumph, and deposited it in the city gaol-yard, to remain there till wanted.*

> *We have an extract before us from the old corporation books of Waterford, dated 1714 October, in which month the slaughtering season commenced: "Ordered, that a bull-rope be provided at the charge of the city revenue". Under this sanction, the populace assumed the authority of seizing all the bulls, and driving them to the bull-ring to be baited before they were killed. The place for baiting them was an open space outside the city gate, called Ballybricken. It was surrounded with houses, from which spectators looked on, as at a Spanish bull-fight. In the centre was a ring through which the rope was passed.*

1714

21 OCTOBER

Francis Hearn

In May 1798 seventeen students were expelled from Maynooth as a result of *being associated with the United Irishmen*. One of these was Francis Hearn from Waterford. Born in Dungarvan, he had studied in Louvain before attending Maynooth. However as he had three uncles who were priests in Waterford, he succeeded in gaining entry into Carlow College.

A year after the rising in October 1799 Francis Hearn was arrested in Carlow College and brought to Waterford. This arrest shocked the people of Waterford, as one of his uncles was a very popular and respected priest, Fr. Thomas Hearn. It was Fr. Thomas who had sought permission from Waterford Corporation in 1792 to build the cathedral in Barronstrand Street and who had also raised the necessary finance to build it. Another uncle, Francis, was parish priest of St. Patrick's and a third, Timothy, was parish priest of Crooke.

Francis Hearn, on the advice of his uncles, pleaded guilty on the understanding that he would be sentenced to transportation. However, he was sentenced to death. Three days later he was hanged from Waterford Bridge at 2pm on the afternoon of Monday the 21st of October 1799.

Another Dungarvan man, Edmund Power, was arrested at the same time as Hearn. He was also found guilty and sentenced to death. Brought to Dungarvan, Edmund Power was hanged on the following day, the 22nd of October.

1799

22 OCTOBER

Presbyterian Church

Early on Sunday morning the 22nd of October 1961 the sexton of the Presbyterian Church in Lady Lane, Mr. Alex Bell, struck a match to light the gas boiler which operated the central heating in the church. An explosion followed and the sexton was hurtled across the room. The entire roof of the church was blown off and smashed against the wall of the Franciscan Church. Windows were blown out, and many of the walls were cracked. Eight o'clock mass was being said in the Franciscan Church at the time. The priest asked for calm and continued as if nothing had happened.

In 1964 the Church of Ireland offered the use of St. Patrick's Church in Patrick Street. The Presbyterian congregation then joined with the Methodist congregation to form St Patrick's United Church.

The church in Lady Lane was sold at auction in 1965. It was described as a valuable cut limestone building with the extensive assembly hall adjoining. *The church is a comparatively new structure splendidly built of limestone measuring inside 55 x 28 ft or thereabouts with arched roof and supported by ornamental timber.*

Waterford Badminton Club bought the damaged property for the sum of £3,150. Following renovation work it opened for play with two courts in 1966. In 1982 a major repair programme commenced with the assistance of an ANCO community scheme.

The church was originally built between 1910 and 1912 at a cost of £2,500. However due to lack of funds a steeple was never built.

1961

23 OCTOBER

Garda Barracks

Previously we mentioned that the Garda Barracks had moved from the Infantry Barracks in Barrack Street to the Country Club in Adelphi Quay in 1940 (see entry for June 23rd). Here it remained for the next twenty eight years until 1968.

The Country Club premises was owned by the Holy Ghost Hospital Board who rented it to the Garda Síochána. However in early 1968 the entire block at Adelphi Quay was leased to the Adelphi Hotel. The owners of the Adelphi intended to develop the site and erect a new luxury eighteen-storey hotel (see entry for May 25th).

The Garda authorities then leased a large premises at 15 South Parade and the barracks moved there on the 23rd of October 1968. In February 1970 the ceiling of the public office in this premises fell in, but luckily no one was injured. Following an architect's report which stated that the building was not suitable for the purpose, plans were made for a new station in Ballybricken.

This new garda divisional headquarters station at Ballybricken was opened in September 1973, by Minister for Justice Mr. Patrick Cooney TD. The opening was not without controversy. The list of invited guests was drawn up by the Department of Justice. While the Mayor was invited, other members of the Corporation were not. This caused some disquiet and one Corporation member went so far as to say that the opening was "unofficial" due to the absence of Waterford Corporation as a body.

1968

24 OCTOBER

Press Gangs

Impressment was a mechanism of taking men by force and putting them on board Royal Navy ships as crew. This occurred especially during wartime when there was a lack of qualified seamen. These press gangs roamed the streets and pubs of port towns and also ventured out to the surrounding countryside in search of able-bodied men. These innocent young men simply disappeared from their homes and families and found themselves serving in the Royal Navy for a number of years. Waterford was no exception to this practice and a number of incidents are recorded down though the years.

Press gangs favoured pressing experienced crewmen from merchant ships. An incident occurred in October 1779 when an attempt was made by a Lieutenant Rudsdale from the *HMS Licorne* to impress all the merchant crew without exception from the ships and vessels lying at Cheekpoint. In his deposition to the Admiralty dated the 24th of October 1779, he reported that all did not go according to plan.

The night started well when the Lieutenant came across a small boat rowing out to one of the ships. He immediately pressed all the occupants and set the boat adrift. Having deposited the pressed men back on board his ship, he then approached the merchant ship the *Triton*. Finding the crew asleep, he took as many as he could fit, and deposited them back on board the *Licorne*. By the time he returned to the merchant ship, the remaining crew were ready for him. His attempts to board resulted in a fusillade of bottles and billets of wood. Armed with hatchets and crowbars, the crew managed to repel Rudsdale and his press gang. At that stage the element of surprise was gone as every other ship at Cheekpoint became aware of the fracas. Lieutenant Rudsdale wisely decided to call it a night.

1779

25 OCTOBER

Fanning Institute

In 1806 James Fanning, a native of Waterford, died in France. In his will he left the sum of £31,000 to the poor of Waterford. This was no small sum. In today's terms it would be over one million euro. At that time a war was raging in Europe so the money could not be returned from France. In 1820 a commission was set up to deal with the bequest but it took another twenty years before the money was finally released. The Fanning Institute was opened on the 25th of October 1842 on the site of the old House of Industry on The Glen.

Egan writing in his *History of Waterford* published two years later in 1894 states:

> *The charities of the Fanning Institute are confined to natives of Waterford, and who though indigent and helpless by old age or infirmity, should be considered of a class who from their respectability would decline to enter the union workhouse.*

By 1863 there were 140 living in the Institute with another 55 seeking admission. Vacancies only occurred due to deaths, however expulsion could occur due to "drink".

In 1969, following a submission to the High Court, the Fanning trust was amalgamated with the Holy Ghost Hospital (see entry for October 28th). At that stage there were only four people resident in it and these were transferred to the Holy Ghost. With the agreement of the Commissioners of Charitable Donations and Bequests the vacant building and grounds were handed back to Waterford Corporation. In the mid-1970s the building was demolished to make way for new government buildings.

1842

26 OCTOBER

Merchants' Guilds

While control of trade within the city of Waterford was the prerogative of the Corporation, the merchants' guilds controlled what might be called quality assurance within each craft. In the same way a merchant could not trade within the city without becoming a Freeman of the City, a craftsman could not operate his trade without belonging to a guild. The operation of merchants' guilds in Waterford has a long history. We learn from the Great Parchment Book of Waterford that their history goes back to 1205 where in a entry for October 1626 it states:

> *Whereas King John of famous memory, by his letters, patents dated at Marlebridge, the 3rd June on the seventh year of his reign, among other privileges granted to the citizens of Waterford that they should have and enjoy other reasonable guilds.*

Initially the guilds were completely autonomous, however in 1552 the Corporation decided that following allegations of corruption they needed to be controlled. Thereafter the guilds operated on the basis of a charter granted by the city.

The question as to whether the charter issued to the Tailor's Guild should be withdrawn was considered by the Corporation on the 26th of October 1670. An internal dispute had occurred between tailors, but after discussion it was decided not to withdraw the charter. However eleven years later in 1681 the Tailor's Guild was split up and the following crafts were separated into a new guild:

> *clothiers, stuff workers, weavers, worsted combers, shearmen, dyers, cotners and tuckers.*

1670

27 OCTOBER

St John's College

The original St. John's College can be traced back to College Street (the site of the present Good Shepherd / WIT building) where it was founded around 1810. It was both a lay school and a seminary, although by 1854 the lay school had closed. As the number of students began to increase, the college also used a number of adjacent buildings although it was noted that students who used these *were exempt from regular discipline*. In 1868 the lease on the building in College Street expired and a new building was planned.

A site was obtained on John's Hill. An architect, George Goldie, was appointed and the contract to build was awarded to McMullan from Cork (who had previously built Thurles Cathedral and St. Peter and Paul's in Cork). On Tuesday the 27th of October 1868 the Bishop of Waterford & Lismore, Rev. Dr. O Brien, laid the foundation stone at John's Hill. In less than three years the structure was completed at a cost of £23,000. It opened in September 1871.

At its peak in the 1940s St. John's had over one hundred students. In total over one thousand of its students became priests. Due to declining vocations St. John's College closed in 1999. At that time there were just thirteen students.

1868

28 OCTOBER

Holy Ghost

In the 17th century Waterford Corporation was not slow in exerting its authority, as Andrew Lynn, Master of the Holy Ghost Hospital found to his cost in 1672. He had refused to furnish an account of the revenues of the hospital and so on the 28th of October 1672, the Council declared he was dismissed from his office and Alderman Henry Seager appointed in his place.

The origins of the Holy Ghost can be traced back to the Franciscan Friary or Greyfriars. In 1539 their property was confiscated and the friars ordered to leave the city (see entry for April 2nd). In 1543 the property was divided and two merchant brothers, Henry and Patrick Walsh, purchased the Friary. Two years later in 1545 they successfully sought a Royal Charter from Henry VIII to set up a hospital in the Friary for the sick and poor and called it the Holy Ghost Hospital. Elizabeth I issued an improved Charter in 1600. For a number of years, the Walsh family looked after the affairs of the hospital but eventually they handed over control to the Mayor and Corporation.

In 1878 the Commissioners of Charitable Donations and Bequests issued a new scheme of governance with the introduction of a hospital board with nominating rights from various bodies. The hospital itself was maintained solely from ground rents from a considerable portion of city property. At the time this land was granted to the friars it consisted of gardens and open land. However the development of the city meant that quite a large proportion of the city was built on land owned by the Holy Ghost. In 1960 the High Court sanctioned the amalgamation of the Fanning Institute with the Holy Ghost (see entry for October 25th).

1672

29 OCTOBER

Corporation

Waterford Corporation had a robust system of standing orders for the orderly conduct of its meetings in the 17th century. The *Council Books of the Corporation of Waterford 1602-1700* gives numerous examples of these. An order adopted on the 29th of October 1681 illustrates this:

> *The former order for fining absentees renewed and also that of speaking in the council whilst others is speaking to pay to the box, every alderman 1s., each assistant 6d.*

Other examples include:

> *That if any member of council depart out of the council chamber after his appearance without leave of Mr. Mayor for his so doing, he shall forfeit the sum of one shilling sterling each default.*

An example of this put into practice occurred in June 1681 when:

> *Mr. Benjamen Powell for departing this council without Mr. Mayor's leave is fined ten shillings sterling.*

They also deal with the need for a quorum by the following order adopted in November 1662:

> *It is ordered by the mayor and council that in case a council shall be summoned and but twelve of them appear, it is and shall be lawful for the said mayor and those twelve that do appear to act and do such thing and things as the whole council might or could do only excepting disposal of the city revenue and the disposing or expelling of any member of court or council.*

1681

30 OCTOBER

Victoria Cross

Patrick Mahoney was born in Waterford in 1827. He joined the British Army and was stationed as a Sergeant in the 1st Madras European Fusiliers (later the Royal Dublin Fusiliers) in India. On the 21st of September 1857 during the Indian Mutiny he distinguished himself in capturing the Regimental Colours of the 1st Regiment Native Infantry, and was awarded the Victoria Cross as a result.

Sergeant Mahoney was killed in action the following month at Lucknow on the 30th of October 1857. His burial site is unknown. His Victoria Cross medal is on display in the British Library in London.

Other famous Waterford recipients of the Victoria Cross were Lord Roberts of Kandahar and his son Freddy (see entry for August 28th).

1857

31 OCTOBER

St. Thomas Church

What was described as an act of absolute barbarism took place in 1967 when the ruins of the ancient church at Thomas Hill were demolished. A letter to the editors of the local papers dated the 31st of October 1967 stated:

> *Dear Sir,*
> *A bulldozer last week demolished the old gable wall of the Church of St. Thomas which stood until last week at Thomas Hill. The surrounding cemetery and tombstones were also completely obliterated. Alas no traces now remain of the ancient church founded in 1210 A.D. and dedicated to the memory of Thomas A Becket. What would our tourists prefer to see, a square court or a gable of a church 750 years old. Surely Ballintubber Abbey provides the answer. Where were the Waterford Corporation, An Taisce, Junior Chamber of Commerce, Old Waterford Society. It's too late now – it's gone.*
> *Yours faithfully*
> *"PARVA ROMA"*

The Church of St. Thomas was reputed to be the oldest in Waterford. Canon Power in his *Parochial History of Waterford and Lismore* (1912) states:

> *It is difficult to estimate the particular character of St. Thomas church, the ruin of which stands within an ancient, badly kept graveyard on Thomas Hill. It is evidently by far the most ancient ecclesiastical structure in Waterford and appears to date from the later Danish period. Originally it may have been a Hiberno-Danish church, converted later by the Normans into a votive chapel and dedicated to St. Thomas and finally made a chapel-of-case to Trinity Within. The ruin itself which consists of little more than a Romanesque chancel arch, is situated in that portion of the parish which lay beyond or outside the city walls.*

1967

1 NOVEMBER

Crystal Manufacturing

Crystal manufacturing originally began in Waterford on the 1st of November 1783 when George and William Penrose opened the Waterford Flint Glass Company. This factory was in Anne's Street and employed between fifty and seventy people. The company was sold to Gatchell, Ramsey and Barcroft in 1799. In 1811, Gatchell took complete control.

Ryland in his *History of Waterford* (1824) states:

> *A glass manufactory, of a superior description, was established in Waterford on 1783 by the Messers. Penrose. It is now conducted by Messers. Gatchell and Co. who have a large export trade, particularly to America: the number of persons employed average seventy weekly.*

Forty years later in 1851 Gatchell decided to close the business. In early October of that year the following notice appeared in Waterford newspapers:

> *The well known Waterford Glass manufacturing being about to close, the proprietor, George Gatchell, order to be sold on Wednesday October 20th 1851 the entire stock of glass, including dinner and table lamps, gas chandeliers, one crystal chandelier for six lights, together with beautiful specimens of Bohemian and Venetian glass.*

Crystal manufacturing did not take place in Waterford again until 1947 when Karel Bacik founded the modern Waterford Glass (see entry for June 25th).

1783

2 NOVEMBER

Shipwrecks

Previously we mentioned how the 17th of January seemed to be an unlucky date for shipping. Four ships were wrecked on that day in the 61-year period from 1748 to 1809. Another unlucky date was the 2nd of November. Over a 101-year period from 1806 to 1907 four ships were lost on this date off the Waterford coast.

On the 2nd of November 1806, the brig *Cheshire* was lost. En route from Newport in Wales to Cork with a cargo of coal, she was driven onshore in Tramore Bay. All of the crew were saved.

On the 2nd of November 1876, the schooner *Janet* was lost off Mine Head. She developed a leak on a voyage from Bangor to Limerick with a heavy cargo of slate. The onslaught of a force 6 storm made the leak worse and she had to be abandoned.

On the same date in 1899, the barque *Hansa* was arriving in Waterford having sailed from St. John in New Brunswick when she struck Creaden Head in force 10 wind conditions. Another boat towed her off but she was stranded again on the bar. Again she was towed off but sank on Drumroe Bank below Passage.

Finally on the 2nd of November 1907, the schooner *Peri,* on a voyage from Newport to Cork, was driven ashore between Helvic and Mine Head by force 8 winds. Two of the crew were drowned but the captain and another crew member were found clinging to a bush at the bottom of a sheer cliff face.

1806 - 1907

3 NOVEMBER

Irish Chancery Letters

The level of sophistication of the legal system in 14th century Waterford is illustrated by the following entry, dated the 3rd of November 1375, from the Rolls of the Irish Chancery:

3 Nov. 1375

Kilkenny

To the Kings's beloved and faithful John Keppok, chief justice at pleas following the governor and keeper of Ireland.

William Tany, prior of the hospital of St John of Jerusalem in Ireland, Chancellor of Ireland, is engaged on the King's service in various parts of Leinster and cannot be in person at the city of Waterford, where the King's next session is to be held, with the great seal used in Ireland to seal writs. Not wishing that the King's business or that of anyone else should be delayed by reason of the lack of that seal and having full confidence in his loyalty and industry, GRANT to John Keppok, chief justice at pleas [etc.], full power to make and prosecute all writs of novel disseisin, mort dancestor, attainder, trespass, accounts, debts and all other writs concerning the King or county Waterford to be delivered into the hands of the sheriff of the said county by John's own hand in the absence of the said seal. The sheriff of the county is to receive the said writs from John [Keppok], although they are not sealed, and he is to execute them.

William [Windsor], governor [and keeper] of Ireland. By the council.

1375

4 NOVEMBER

Valentine Shortis

On the 4th of November 1895 one of the longest trials in the history of the Canadian justice system came to an end. The accused, Valentine Shortis, was sentenced to death for murder. Shortis was born on The Mall in Waterford in February 1875. The only son of a wealthy cattle merchant, he moved to Canada in 1893 at the age of eighteen. On the night of the 1st of March 1895 he shot and killed two men. Valentine was arrested and charged with murder.

A long trial then followed. The defence pleaded insanity. To support their case they succeeded in moving proceedings to Waterford in July 1895 where testimony was gathered from over sixty witnesses all of whom recounted "strange" incidences involving the defendant which had occurred over the previous years. In addition, a number of doctors gave evidence of mental illness in several family members. Back in Canada, some of the leading psychiatrists in Canada supported the view that Shortis was insane. However the evidence did not sway the jury and on the 4th of November 1895, Shortis was found guilty of murder and sentenced to death. This sentence was later commuted to life imprisonment. Shortis spent the next forty-two years of his life in prison in Canada until he was released in 1937. He died in 1941 and was buried in an unmarked grave in Toronto.

Although the case of Valentine Shortis is not remembered in Waterford today, it is well known in Canada as it dealt with various legal, psychiatric, political and constitutional issues. A book called *The Case of Valentine Shortis, A True Story of Crime and Politics in Canada* was written about the case by Martin Friedland, Professor of Law at the University of Toronto.

1895

5 NOVEMBER

Adam Torrie

The L&N supermarket was an institution in Waterford for many years. Originally founded by A.L. Game as the London and Newcastle Tea Company in the 19th century, it grew into a chain of over fifty shops throughout England, Scotland and Ireland. In 1886, the L&N Company sold off each of its stores to its managers.

Adam Torrie, originally from Scotland, came to Waterford as manager of the L&N store. This store was situated at 3 & 4 Broad Street. In 1886 he availed of the opportunity to purchase the Waterford and Kilkenny stores. A few years later he purchased the Cork and Carlow stores. In 1927 the company Adam F. Torrie Ltd. was incorporated. Adam Torrie died the following year on the 5th of November 1928.

His sons Robert and William then took over the business. They succeeded in purchasing over twenty more L&N stores in Munster and Leinster. There were five shops in Waterford City: Broad Street, Roanmore, Morrisson's Avenue, Lower Grange and Ferrybank.

Eventually the growth of big supermarket chains changed the way the grocery business operated. In 1973 the company broadened out with the opening of the Hypermarket in Waterford and other larger stores throughout the country.

The last of the original L&N stores in Broad Street closed in 1986. The company was finally sold to Musgraves in 1995 and any remaining stores came under the Supervalu banner.

1928

6 NOVEMBER

Council Books of Munster

The continuity of the King's authority was a matter of concern to the Lord President of Munster in 1620. In an order dated the 6th of November 1620 in Waterford he delegated his authority to Henry Bryan and Sir Thomas Browne as he would have to travel to Dublin and his *return from there being uncertain*.

The order is quite specific and legalistic as follows:

And for that in my absence there may be intelligences and other daily business may happen and arise which may not be protracted until such time as they may be sent to me and receive my direction, I have therefore thought good hereby to authorise you to receive all letters or other such intelligences as shall be sent to me thither which shall or may concern the state and therein to do whatever you in discretion and for the general good shall hold fit and convenient. And also to give direction upon all Civil Bills by way of referment, issuing of process or otherwise as if I were personally present. During my time out of the province giving unto you authority to do whatsoever that does concern the public or civil government as you in discretion shall hold most requiset provided that all such occurrences that are needful, and shall in my absence happen, you advise the Lord Deputy from time to time with the conveniences of speed you may: whereof not failing this shall be your warrant given under his Majesties privy. Signed of this Province at Waterford 6th November 1620.

1620

7 NOVEMBER

RNLI

Although it was not until 1884 that a RNLI lifeboat station was established in Dunmore East, the RNLI itself was founded in 1824. Its original name was the National Institution for the Preservation of Life from Shipwrecks, but became the Royal National Lifeboat Institution in 1854. From the beginning it awarded gold and silver medals for acts of outstanding gallantry. In the years prior to the setting up of the Dunmore East station, many rescues were carried out in the waters close by. These were recognised by the Institute and silver medals were awarded in 1834, 1835, 1838 and 1841.

The first such silver medal resulted from a rescue on the 7th of November 1834. The sloop *James* had run aground off Dunmore East. Lieutenant Thomas Stuart from the Royal Navy, along with other coastguards and local fishermen, dragged a boat along the beach and rowed it out to the stranded vessel. The crew of six men, who at that stage had climbed the rigging, were rescued. As the rescue boat made its way back to safety it capsized. Fortunately everyone was helped back to dry land by those waiting on the beach. Lt. Stuart was awarded the silver medal for his gallantry.

1834

8 NOVEMBER

Graves

William Graves founded Graves Timber Merchants in New Ross in the year 1811. Within a few years, William had also established a shipping business, advertising for passengers from New Ross to Canada and importing timber on the return journey. One of his ships was the original *Dunbrody,* built in Quebec in 1845. Designed as a cargo vessel, she was converted to carry passengers once the famine broke out and emigration was at its highest. In 1851 one of William's sons, John P. Graves, opened up the business at the Park Road in Waterford.

In 1894 Graves became a limited company with J.P. Graves as chairman. In 1896 new offices were built at their premises on the Park Road which at that stage extended over four acres and included an extensive steam-powered saw mill and a private wharf. The last of the Graves to be involved in the family business was Anthony Graves who died in 1917.

In 1934 the company was taken over by Robert S. Elmes who had originally started working for Graves in 1898 and Edward B. McBride, who joined Graves in 1906. By the mid sixties the company employed over 180 people in Waterford and New Ross. In 1971 Graves was sold to the Fitzwilton Group which also owned Dockrells Builders Providers (Dublin & Cork). By 1982 a recession in the building industry forced a reduction in staff and some seventy employees were made redundant. In 1983 short time was introduced, more redundancies were sought in 1984 and finally on the 8th of November 1985 Graves closed its doors for the last time. An attempt to revive it was made in October 1986 when "Graves of Waterford" was set up. This in turn was taken over by Brooks in 1990.

1985

9 NOVEMBER

Seduction

An unusual case came before the circuit court on the 9th of November 1928. A Mrs. K. McElligott from Arundel Square sued Guard W. Lyons, from Lismore Civic Guard Station, for damages amounting to £300 for the seduction of her daughter.

Council for the guard stated that the defendant admitted the charge, but questioned whether the mother had shown proper parental control, and the issue was more a breach of promise case. He stated that: *he might have old ideas, but the sooner the old ideas are reverted to the sooner will the young girls of the country have their reputation and character restored.* The council continued *that the girl could have brought a breach of promise case, but she could do this later and then another case for the maintenance of the child.*

The council for Mrs. McElligott stated that the man had disowned the girl in public. *She had been seduced under the promise of marriage. There was nothing in modern times against the mother leaving her daughter alone with the man to whom she was engaged.*

The judge agreed with the council for the guard and agreed that if the old times were reverted to, it would be for the better. He suggested that *if young girls attended court and heard a case such as this, it would show them the consequences of being seduced under a vague promise of marriage. The people of this country had great respect for Civic Guards, and this girl's mother thought perhaps that he would make a good catch for her daughter.* However he continued that the man would be dismissed from the force and this was a greater punishment than any he could inflict. He considered £300 was too much and he awarded the mother the sum of £50.

1928

10 NOVEMBER

Ballinamona Fire

Ballinamona Park on the old Tramore Road was the seat of the Carew family for over 300 years. The original house was recorded as being built on the site of a house or castle dating back to 1488. The Carew family was identified with Waterford for many generations. A Robert Carew was High Sheriff of the county in 1614, and again in 1621 and 1622. There is a legend that a Tomas Carew who lived there from 1775 to 1853 haunts the grounds with a ghostly pack of hounds on the night of a full moon. Another famous ancestor was Sir George Carew, the officer commanding the *Mary Rose* at the time when that ship went down with all hands in 1545.

Charles Smith in his *History of Waterford* (1746) states:

> *Ballinamona, the seat of Thomas Carew, Esq. is a well built house. The improvements, which are carrying on, are designed in a good taste. On the east side of the house is a handsome canal, and about it are considerable plantations, gardens etc. On a commanding hill in the deer-park is a handsome turret that affords a prospect of part of Tramore Bay, with a view of the City of Waterford, and the counties of Wexford and Kilkenny.*

On the morning of the 10th of November 1894 a disastrous fire broke out, which more or less completely destroyed the entire mansion, with only the wings being saved. The house was subsequently rebuilt. The last of the family was Major R.J.H. Carew who died in 1982 (his wife died in 1934 following a road accident). A three-day auction of the contents of Ballinamona was held in April 1983 (the auctioneers were Mealy & Sons, who were also the same auctioneers for the Mount Congreve auction in 2012). The proceeds of the sale was £300,000, which exceeds €1,000,000 in today's terms.

1894

11 NOVEMBER

World War I

Although WWI ended on the 11th of November 1918, it was a day too late for one Waterford soldier. Private James Kenneally from the Royal Army Service Corps died on that date. He is buried in a communal cemetery in Belgium.

Of approximately 4,800 men from Waterford who served in the war, over 700 men died in, or as a result of, the conflict.

One particular family that paid a very heavy price was the Collins family from Philip Street. Of the eight children of Thomas and Agnes Collins, seven enlisted in the army. Four of these died: Stephen on the 19th of October 1914, Michael on the 8th of May 1915, John on the 9th of September 1916 and Patrick on the 29th of March 1918.

Another family who suffered great losses was the Shine family from Tramore. Three sons of Colonel J.M.F. Shine and his wife Kathleen died: John (Captain) on the 25th of August 1914, Hugh (Lieutenant) on the 25th of May 1915 and James (Captain) on the 16th of August 1917.

While 14-year old John Condon from Waterford is well known as the youngest soldier to die in the war in May 1915, the oldest person from Waterford to die was Patrick Casey, aged 73, from Stradbally. He was an able seaman on board the *SS Dotterel* which sank in November 1915 having struck a mine.

1918

12 NOVEMBER

Ardree Hotel

In January 1969 the demolition of Fleming's Castle began. This was on a prominent position on the slopes of Mount Misery overlooking the city. The commanding residence had previously been known as Larry Forristal's Castle, as he had been its first resident when it was built in the 19th century. The building was then purchased by the Congreves of Mount Congreve, who subsequently sold it to John Fleming in 1908.

In 1968 the Breen family, who already owned the Bridge Hotel and the Majestic Hotel in Tramore, purchased the property. They planned a £750,000 luxury hotel on the site. Building continued through 1969 and 1970, the main contractor being P.J. Hegarty & Sons Ltd.

The Ardree Hotel finally opened on the 12th of November 1970. It had one hundred bedrooms and six private suites. The bedrooms all had *bathrooms with shower, bidet, and toilet attached; radio, telephone and baby alarm are laid on; television can be installed on request.*

The Ardree was sold to Jurys Hotel Group for £2 million in January 1990. They in turn sold it to the McEniff Hotel Group in July 2002. The McEniff group purchased the Ardree and the Jury's Skylon hotel in Dublin for a combined price of €14 million.

The Ardree finally closed on the 23rd of December 2005.

1970

13 NOVEMBER

Irish Chancery Letters

The following appeared in the Irish Chancery Letters on the 13th of November 1378:

> APPOINTMENT of Thomas Founte and John Webbe as controllers of John Symcok in the port of Waterford.

This begs the question as to who was John Symcok. The answer can be found in the previous entry in the Chancery Letters dated the 12th of November 1378:

> APPOINTMENT, during pleasure, of John Symcok as collector of customs great and small in the port of Waterford, rendering his account at the exchequer.

John Symcok went on to become Mayor of Waterford in 1380 and held the position for two years.

John Symcok is mentioned again in the Chancery Letters in January 1384:

> John Symcok, formerly mayor of the city of Waterford, has shown that John and Donatus, sons of William Odwyr, and Molaghlyn son of Mkraigh Omolryan, formerly hostages for the King's peace were delivered to Edmund Mortimer, late earl of March and Ulster Lieutenant; and the Lieutenant sent the hostages to John, then mayor of the King's city, for safe keeping at the King's expense. John received them by letters of the Lieutenant under his privy seal asking that he might keep the hostages at reasonable expenses of the King; and John kept the hostages for 36 weeks at his own expense by virtue of the said letters. He seeks his expenses in sustaining the said hostages. Wishing to do what is just towards John, we (the King) grant John Symcok 10m of our gift for the above reasons. ORDER to pay him the said 10m.

1378

14 NOVEMBER

Great Charter Roll

The Great Charter Roll on display in the Medieval Museum in Waterford is one of the great treasures of this period. Compiled circa 1373 during the reign of Edward III, it is a compilation of royal charters and other documents dated back to 1215. Four metres in length, its illustration of Waterford is the earliest illustration of any Irish city. In addition it has sixteen other illustrations including stunning depictions of five medieval kings of England.

The manuscript was produced to help Waterford's case in an enquiry held in London in the 1370s regarding the monopoly that Waterford claimed over the port of New Ross. All the documents included in the roll are in some way linked to the claim. The problem for Waterford was that there was no actual charter conferring the monopoly on the city except for the charter of Edward III, which stated that all ships entering the harbour must unload at Waterford. The purpose of the Charter Roll was to back up Edward's charter with legal precedence over the previous 157 years. By lavishly illustrating the document, they were giving it credibility and authenticity.

As mentioned, the one specific charter that Waterford could point to was that of Edward III. This charter was issued on the 14th of November 1356. Indeed the last document in the Charter Roll is a writ sent to the King's Lieutenant in Ireland in 1371, which quotes from this charter of November 1356.

1356

15 NOVEMBER

Joseph Hansard

As mentioned in the entry for the 1ˢᵗ of January, there are six standard works published on the history of Waterford. Joseph Hansard's *History of Waterford* is one of these works. Originally published in 1870, a modern edition edited by Donald Brady was published by Waterford County Council in 1997.

Joseph Hansard's place of birth is unknown. Research suggests he was born in either Limerick or Tipperary circa 1835. Having served his apprenticeship as a printer in Clonmel he moved to Dungarvan in 1861. In 1870 he published his book. The full title is:

> *The History, Topography and Antiquities (natural and ecclesiastical), with biographical sketches of the nobility, gentry and ancient families and notices of eminent men, of the County and City of Waterford. Including the towns, parishes, villages, manors and seats.*

This book was published and printed in Dungarvan.

The following year he established *The Dungarvan Gazette & County Advertiser*, a weekly paper of four pages priced at 2d. However the arrival of the railway to Dungarvan with regular deliveries of other newspapers caused the *Gazette* to fold. Hansard moved to Killarney in 1880 and set up a bookshop and stationery business. Here he developed a reputation as having the largest stock of any bookseller in the south of Ireland. Joseph Hansard died on the 15ᵗʰ of November 1909.

1909

16 NOVEMBER

Ernest Walton

Ernest Walton was born in Dungarvan in October 1903, the son of a Methodist minister from County Tipperary. In 1915 he was sent as a boarder to the Methodist College, Belfast, and in 1922 he entered Trinity College Dublin, on a scholarship. He graduated in 1926 with a first class honours degree in Physics and Mathematics, followed by a M.Sc. in 1927.

The same year he was awarded a Research scholarship to work in the Cavendish Laboratory in Cambridge, and received his Ph.D. in 1931. In April 1932, while working with J.D. Cockcroft, they succeeded in splitting the atom for the first time. The results were published in the scientific journal Nature two weeks later. The scientific community immediately seized upon the significance of this work, as it was the first experimental verification of Einstein's mass energy relationship. In 1934 Walton returned to Trinity. On the 16th of November 1951, the Swedish Royal Academy of Sciences announced that the 1951 Nobel Prize for Physics was to be jointly awarded to Walton and Cockcroft. It is the only time an Irishman has won a Nobel Prize in a scientific subject. The actual award took place at a ceremony in Stockholm in December that year.

The citation for the award recognised *their pioneer work on the transmutation of atomic nuclei by artificially accelerated atomic particles*. It went on to say *their discoveries initiated a period of rapid discovery in atomic physics*, and continued *indeed this work may be said to have introduced a totally new epoch in nuclear physics*.

Walton retired from Trinity in 1974 and died in June 1995.

1951

17 NOVEMBER

Plane Crash in Barrack Street

During the War of Independence, the interception of mail was a tactic used by the IRA for intelligence gathering. Eventually the only way the British Army could ensure dispatches were delivered to various barracks was to use RAF planes. In the south of the country a plane would take off from Fermoy barracks and drop mail at Dungarvan, Waterford, Kilkenny and Clonmel before returning to Fermoy.

However the flight on the 17th of November 1920 did not go according to plan. As the plane flew over the city it appeared to have engine trouble. Arriving over the barrack square, it hit the wireless aerial, went out of control, and crash-landed on the roof of two houses in Barrack Street, just opposite the gate of the barracks. One house was Aspel's licensed premises and the other belonged to a Mrs. McSweeney.

Luckily no one in either house was injured. Soldiers for the Devon Regiment ran from the barracks with ladders. In their enthusiasm one of them fell through the roof, but was not injured. The two pilots were unconscious and were taken down by stretcher and removed to hospital in Fermoy.

A military guard kept the excited crowd back while the plane was being dismantled.

1920

18 NOVEMBER

Dock Strike

The start of the ten year long dock strike at Waterford port can be traced back to this day, the 18th of November 1980. A Japanese ship, the *Wakafui,* docked at the North Wharf with a consignment of fertiliser. The off-loading gang made up a three-man shortfall by using men from another gang. Casual dockers then mounted a picket, bringing the deep-sea section to a halt.

The dispute had its origins in a 1974 rationalisation agreement which cut the labour force in the deep-sea section of the port to thirty (three gangs of ten each). They were to be supplemented by casual labourers as required. Over the passage of time, the strength of the full-time gangs had reduced to twenty-two, due to deaths and long-term illnesses. However, these full-time vacancies were not filled by the casual dockers, and therein lay the problem. When an AGTWU (Amalgamated Transport and General Workers Union) directive was ignored, the full time dockers broke away and joined the MPGWU (Marine Port and General Workers Union). Pickets were placed, court injunctions were sought, and closed shop agreements were questioned. Accusations that the wages of the thirty men were being shared out by the remaining twenty-two were made.

The strike lasted ten years having defied the intervention of independent mediation, rights commissioners and the labour court. Over the ten years there were sit-ins, scuffles and arrests, alleged assaults on union officials, alleged sabotage and a hunger strike. A resolution was arrived at in 1988 only to break down immediately. The strike finally ended in January 1990.

1980

19 NOVEMBER

Suir Bridge

It is generally accepted that the first bridge across the Suir was *Timbertoes* which was built in 1794. However Downey in his *Story of Waterford (*1914) makes reference to a document dated the 19th of November 1697 in which a John Newport makes a financial claim on the basis he had *supplied the timber to make up the broken bridge over the river Suir.*

The difficulty with this assertion by Downey is that the records of Waterford Corporation for 1662 - 1700 have been preserved and were published by the Irish Manuscript Commission in 1964 (see bibliography). Nowhere in this publication is there any reference to a John Newport or any bridge over the Suir. Where Downey got his information from is a mystery.

The full quote from Downey's book is as follows:

> *In a petition dated November 19th 1697, John Newport claimed some forfeited estate on the score that he had "supplied the timber to make up the broken bridge over the river Suir". This was a temporary bridge or pontoon which was thrown across the river by Cromwell in 1649 and was in 1690 made staunch and strong "to carry the army and carriages to reduce Waterford". Some time before Newports petition was forwarded to the Lords of the Treasury, James Roche, "the Swimmer" had got a grant of the ferry of Waterford (in 1693).*

1697

20 NOVEMBER

Keily's Brewery

Keily's on New Street was know for years as wholesale bottlers and mineral water distributors. However, a brewery operated on that site for a long number of years. The original Keily family were bakers in Barronstrand Street in the early 1800s. On the 20th of November 1859 they opened a brewery in New Street. This seems to have been the amalgamation of three other breweries which existed in New Street, Stephen Street and Newgate Street. Here they traded under the name Patrick Keily and Sons.

The name St. Stephens's Brewery was used from the early 1900s. It was known for the strength of its products such as *Draught XX Porter, Draught XXX Pale Ale* and *Keily's XXX Pale Ale.*

In 1947 brewing ceased and Keily's concentrated on the wholesale bottling and producing of mineral waters.

In 1957 the company was taken over by Donohoe Beverages Group. It continued as a wholly owned subsidiary and traded as Patrick Keily and Sons (1957) Ltd. The company still trades today and operates from the Lacken Road Business Park in Kilbarry.

1859

21 NOVEMBER

Annie Brophy

There are very few Waterford families that do not have an Annie Brophy photograph in their albums. Getting your photograph taken by her was a rite of passage for most young people in the Waterford of the forties, fifties or sixties.

Annie Brophy was born in 12 Johnstown in 1899. Her father was an RIC constable. The family moved to Kilmacthomas for a time. Having attended the Mercy convent, she began her training as a young photographer in 1916 with Hughes Photographers in Manor Street.

In 1922 she set up her own photographic studio in Barker Street and remained there for the rest of her life. She did not retire until the age of 79. During that time she photographed all walks of Waterford life. A meticulous person, she organised and catalogued all the names and addresses of her customers and built up a collection of over 60,000 negatives during her lifetime. The collection covers subjects such as weddings, christenings, communions, May processions, hurling victories, light opera casts, showbands and city mayors.

Annie Brophy died on Friday the 21st of November 1986 at the age of 87.

In 2005, Waterford City Council purchased Annie Brophy's collection of over 60,000 negatives. These are held in the city archives. Each year a selection of her photographs are exhibited.

1986

22 NOVEMBER

Newfoundland

Many authors have told the story of emigration from Waterford to Newfoundland during the 18th and 19th centuries. When vast quantities of cod were first found off the coast of Newfoundland, the emigration there was seasonal. Gradually as time passed the fishermen brought out their wives and families and settled there.

At this time, the Penal Laws were still in force in Ireland. The British Government was not about to allow a *popish colony* to be established in one of its overseas possessions. Therefore no priest was allowed in Newfoundland, although the Irish Catholics could build as many churches as they liked. This caused all sorts of problems for celebrating marriages and baptisms. Special dispensations were allowed for civil marriages, as long as a church ceremony was held as soon as possible. This resulted in many Waterford emigrants returning home to Waterford and getting married in a church, years after their original marriage in Newfoundland. Often the same happened with baptisms.

On the 22nd of November 1759, for example, the parish records of the cathedral show that the four children of Henry Miller and Catherine Scurry were all baptised on the same day. They were named Mary, John, James and William, all of whom were born in Newfoundland. Another record exists for the same month when *Robin Holly and Jane Broders married about three years ago in Newfoundland according to the custom of the place renewed and ratified their consent.*

1759

23 NOVEMBER

Sir William Goff

Waterford people will recall the Goff bicycle track that once existed in the People's Park. This track was presented to the Waterford Bicycle Club by Sir William Davis Goff, who was born in September 1838 in Cathedral Square. The son of Mr. Strangman Davis, he changed his name in accordance with his father's will.

Educated at Trinity College, he joined the army and became a Captain in the 2nd Dragoon Guards. In 1866 he married Anne Hassard, daughter of Michael Dobbyn Hassard, MP of Glenville. Inheriting much of his wealth, he took a very active part in the business and public affairs of the city. He was a member of the corporation for over forty years, and was sheriff of the city on two occasions. A keen athlete, he was one of the first in Ireland to ride a high wheel bicycle and, as mentioned, presented the Goff Track to the old Waterford Bicycle Club. He went on to become chairman of the Dunlop Cycle Company. A keen yachtsman also, he kept a motor yacht on the Suir. He presented the Goff Challenge Shield to the Waterford Rowing Club. Sir William was the owner of the first car registered in Waterford City, a Napier with the registration number W1-1. A director of W. F. Peare & Co, the first garage opened in Ireland (forerunner of Kelly's Garage in Catherine Street), he was also the founding chairman of the Irish Automobile Club. His business connections extended to being a director of Strangman's Brewery, Waterford Steamship Company and the Tramore Railway Company.

Sir William died on the 23rd of November 1917 and is buried at Ballinakill Church (now the Dunmore Badminton Club at the Brasscock).

1917

24 NOVEMBER

Battle of Fenor

In the month of November so late in the year
When the workers of Fenor one day did appear
To uphold their union the best way they should
And to pull down the farmers the best way they could.

On a fine Monday morning 'twas a beautiful scene
With rifles and hurleys and some dressed in green
To shout Up Labour no threshing today
And to hell with the farmers we'll burn the hay.

The above is the first two verses of a ballad called the *Fenor Melee*. It commemorates the Battle of Fenor which took place on the 24th of November 1919.

In the years following WWI the trade union movement began to grow amongst agricultural workers. In Co. Waterford, the farm labourers were very well organised by the ITGWU. Small strikes amongst agricultural workers began to break out. These reached a climax on Saturday the 22nd of November 1919 when the labourers were locked out of their farms. On the following Monday the 24th, the farmers in Fenor decided to arrange their own threshing using outside help. As the threshing machine made its way to the farms, protected by about 120 partially armed RIC, they met almost about 300 labourers. A pitched battle ensued in which revolvers, batons and bayonets were used freely. Many injuries were reported on both sides.

1919

25 NOVEMBER

People's Park

Although the People's Park was officially opened in August 1857 (see entry for August 19th), a stone tablet on the Park Ranger's house at the entrance to the park states that on the 25th of November 1857 the park was handed over to the citizens of Waterford. This plaque was erected forty-three years later in 1900 during the mayoralty of A. Nelson.

The wording of the plaque is as follows:

> *The formation of these grounds into a Public Park was initiated by the late Mr. J.A. Blake M.P. Mayor 1855-6-7, Chairman of a committee of citizens and Lieut. Col. Roberts Hon. Secretary completed and handed over to the corporation for the use of the citizens on 25th Nov. 1857.*
>
> *1st Park Ranger Ald. W. Johnson J.P. 1857 – 1881. 2nd Ald. W.E. Keily 1881 – 1892.*
> *3rd Ald. R. Hearne J.P. 1892 – 1920, 1925-1929.*
>
> *This Lodge was erected A.D. 1900. A. Nelson D.L.J.P. Mayor.*

1857

26 NOVEMBER

Edmund Ignatius Hogan

The name of Edmund Ignatius Hogan will not be familiar to many in Waterford, especially as he was born in Cork and died in Dublin on the 26th of November 1917. His link to Waterford is through a book he published in 1878 based on unpublished manuscripts from the archives in Rome. The title of the book is *The Description of Ireland and the State thereof as it is at this present in anno 1598*.

The description of Waterford and its citizens in 1598 is worth quoting:

> *Waterford is properly built, and very well compact, somewhat close by reason of their thick buildings and narrow streets. The citizens through the intercourse of foreign traffic in short space attain to abundance of wealth. The soil about it is not all of the best, by reason of which the air is not very subtle; yet never the less the sharpness of their wit seemed to be nothing dulled by reason of the grossness of the air. They are, as students, pregnant in conceiving, quick in taking, and sure in keeping; very heady and wary, loving to look before they leap, cheerful in their entertainment of strangers, hearty one to another, nothing given to factions. They love no idle bench whistlers nor luskish faitors. The men are addicted to trafick, the women to spinning and carding. As they distil the best Aqua vita, so they spin the choicest rug in Ireland. The city was never dusked with the least freckle of treason, and therefore the city's arms are decked with the words 'Urbs Intacta'.*

1917

27 NOVEMBER

Militia

There seems to have been a lot of resentment by the inhabitants of Waterford at the end of the 17th century regarding the presence and cost of maintaining soldiers within the city, not to mention the frequent disputes which broke out. On the 27th of November 1678, in an attempt to foster a citizen army the City Council declared;

> *that every man hereafter admitted into the City Freedom shall be sworn in his bodily harness and arms and shall swear the arms to be his own goods.*

The following May a meeting was called to consider how to provide arms and ammunition for the militia. The meeting was informed:

> *that arms and ammunition had arrived and ready to be given out at certain rates ... yet the said troop and militia companies still remain unarmed and out of a posture of defence (if any foreign invasion or internal disturbance should happen) occasioned partly by the citizens and inhabitants neglect and partly for want of money to purchase arms.*

It was agreed that:

> *A sum of money shall be forthwith apportioned assessed, collected, and raised by equal levy on the city and liberties to purchase and provide arms and ammunition to the said militia troop and company not exceeding two hundred and sixty pounds ten shillings sterling.*

A detailed breakdown of the arms to be purchased included one hundred firelocks, eight hundred pikes, ten barrels of powder, ten barrels of ball, twenty cases of pistols and holsters, two hundredweight of pistol bullets, twenty carbines, and one hundred and fifty collars of bandoliers.

1678

28 NOVEMBER

SS Iowa

Some forty iron steam ships were built by the Neptune Shipyard in Waterford between 1843 and 1882. The largest of these was the *SS Iowa*, which was launched on the 28th of November 1863. Taking just twelve months to build, the *Iowa* was 316 feet in length and weighed 1781 tons, and was the largest ship built in Ireland at that time.

Having been fitted with her engines on the Clyde, she made her maiden voyage on the London - Le Havre - New York route in July 1864. A few months later she ran aground near Cherbourg. It was a testament to the quality of the ship that although she was not refloated for six months, only very minor damage had occurred.

In 1866 she was sold to the Anchor Line of Glasgow, and served on the Glasgow - New York route. In 1873 she was sold again, this time to the Henderson Brothers of Glasgow, who renamed her the *Macedonia*. Initially she sailed between Glasgow and Bombay before she went back to the Atlantic.

The *Macedonia* was wrecked in May 1881 when she ran aground on the Mull of Kintyre during fog. No lives were lost.

1863

29 NOVEMBER

Corporation

Downey in his *Story of Waterford* (1914) refers to a rather unusual matter which came before a meeting of the Council on the 29th of November 1684. A debate arose:

> *upon the question whether any member of this board did hear any such words spoken by any alderman of this council as that he had rather the Devil should come sit here than a Blackcoat, resolved in the negative by all the members save one namely Alderman William Fuller.*

William Fuller had been Mayor the previous year and was obviously in dispute with the new Mayor as a later meeting recorded:

> *That this council shall petition the Lord Lieutenant and council setting forth that whereas certain articles have been exhibited to the government by Alderman William Fuller late mayor against the mayor, recorder, Alderman Seay and Malbanke and others of the council praying that they may be heard in vindication of themselves.*

Two months later it becomes clearer that the issue was concerning his position as master of the Leperhouse of St. Stephen's, as the council took action against Fuller when they decided:

> *That Alderman William Fuller having abused by accusing to the government several members of this board and reflected on the whole council in general and contesting with the council for the mastership of the leperhouse of St Stephens in the suburbs of Waterford be and is suspended from the board till the said members and council have finished their vindication and the cities right to the choice of master of the lepers be determined.*

1684

30 NOVEMBER

Clover Meats

The origin of Clover Meats can be traced back to the Irish Co-operative organisation which was set up in order to provide better markets and prices for farmers. In the early 1920s a new factory was set up in Christendom in Ferrybank. Initially only bacon was produced, but by 1935 the carving of beef began. The production of Erinox cubes began in 1937. These beef extract cubes, similar to the Oxo cube, became very popular during the emergency when they were also used as a tea substitute.

In 1948 Clover began to expand, taking over the Limerick plant of W.J. Shaw, and the Wexford Co-op bacon factory in 1949. During the next thirty years Clover Meats prospered. In May 1979 the Clover Sports and Social Centre opened.

A downturn occurred in the early 80s. In 1982, Clover closed for ten weeks due to a rationalisation dispute. This was complicated by a Department of Social Welfare decision not to pay any unemployment benefit. They took the view that the workers were really part of a trade dispute and were not unemployed as such.

Clover Meats finally closed on the 30th of November 1984. The closure did not go smoothly and workers were left many months waiting for their redundancy payments.

1984

1 DECEMBER

Sir Thomas Wyse

The Wyse family in Waterford is reputed to have its origins from Sir Andrew Wyse who landed here with Strongbow. Members of the family filled the office of Mayor of Waterford fifteen times between the years of 1478 to 1639. Recall it was a William Wyse that received the Cap of Maintenance and a sword from Henry VII in 1536 (see entry for April 30th).

Sir Thomas Wyse was born in Newtown on the 1st of December 1791. Following his education at Stonyhurst and Trinity College, he went to London to study law. Having travelled in Europe, he married a young Letizia Bonaparte (niece of Napoleon Bonaparte) in 1821. By coincidence her birthday was also the 1st of December, but she was thirteen years younger than Wyse. This marriage broke down in 1828 (see entry for July 4th).

In 1830 he was elected MP for Tipperary and became the second Catholic MP after Daniel O'Connell. In 1835 he was elected MP for Waterford, a position he held until 1847. He played a leading role in parliament driving the Catholic struggle. He also had a great interest in educational reform. He was instrumental in the founding of state-funded elementary schools in Ireland some forty years before this occurred in England and was also the prime mover in the establishment of the Queens Colleges, later UCC, UCD and UCG.

After he lost his seat in the general election of 1847 he became British ambassador to Greece. He died in Athens in 1862.

1791

2 DECEMBER

Lord Waterford

On the 27th of April we heard the story of the tragic deaths of various holders of the Lord Waterford title in the 18th and 19th centuries. This misfortune continued into the 20th century when the sixth Marquess of Waterford, Henry de la Poer Beresford, also died accidentally, this time from drowning. This occurred on Saturday the 2nd of December 1911 when Lord Waterford fell into the Clodagh River having gone out to check his kennels. His body was found the following morning. He was thirty-six years old when he died.

Twenty-one years later in September 1934, the seventh Marquess was found dead in the gunroom at Curraghmore with a bullet wound in his right temple. A freshly discharged .22 rifle was found beside him. At the subsequent inquest, it was found that Lord Waterford was in the habit of shooting at hares from his bedroom window. On that particular morning he saw a hare on the lawn and went to the gunroom to get his rifle. It appears he slipped on the stone floor and in doing so discharged the rifle. He was thirty-three years old when he died.

This same Lord had a previous brush with death in the last months of the Civil War. In April 1923 he was returning home from a hunt in Kilkenny when his car came across a firefight between irregulars and the national army close to Carrick on Suir. It appears the irregulars mistook his car for a military vehicle and starting firing at it. The Marquess escaped injury but his chauffeur was wounded.

1911

3 DECEMBER

New Protestant Corporation

In 1650 Waterford surrendered to Cromwell's General Ireton, who immediately dissolved the Corporation. In 1656, the Corporation was restored but membership became exclusively Protestant. However, Catholics continued to exert some influence. Cromwell died in 1658 and the monarchy was restored in 1660 with Charles II being proclaimed King. The new Protestant Corporation adapted to this new state of affairs and quickly assured the King of their support, but the continued influence of Catholic merchants became a cause of concern. Finally on the 3rd of December 1662 they decided to act with the following decision:

Whereas sundry freemen of this city have heretofore taken apprentices of the Irish nation and popish religion, by which their inconsiderate and imprudent practice, the city will in a short time become a popish plantation again, the Mayor and council taking the same into their serious consideration do think fit to order and declare by common consent that if any merchants, shopkeepers, artificers or tradesman shall presume to take any apprentice from and after the 28th day of this instant December that is not educated in the Protestant religion and confirmed therein by ecclesiastical authority shall forfeit for every his or their offence ten pounds sterling to be levied upon his or their goods and chattels by distress or otherwise by the sheriffs of this city.

1662

4 DECEMBER

Suir Froze

There are a number of recorded instances of the Suir freezing over. The most recent was on Christmas Day in 2010 at Fiddown Bridge. The river froze over in Carrick on Suir in 1947 and in Cahir in 1903. However the biggest freeze occurred on the 4th of December in 1878, when ice formed on the surface at Waterford. On the following day the river between Carrick and Waterford was covered with ice. The ebb and flow of the tide, combined with a strong west wind, piled the ice in miniature icebergs which then floated down river and became jammed across the wooden bridge in Waterford. This blocked the river to any shipping traffic.

The blockage caused problems for the Suir Steam Navigation Company, who plied their trade between Waterford and Carrick on Suir. The owner of the company, Ernest Grubb, was piloting their steam tug, towing a boat behind it, when he came across the ice. Eventually after about an hour the tug broke through the ice to the cheers of the many spectators. The ice melted on Christmas Day following a rise in temperature.

Two years later in January 1881 a similar freeze occurred, and the Waterford Bridge Commissioners contracted Grubb to keep the channels open. At that stage the ice at Grannagh was thick enough to support a loaded horse and cart. Ernest Grubb himself stated that he stood on ice in the middle of the river.

Of interest is the fact that Ernest Grubb was a great supporter of the temperance movement and named his tug the Father Matthew. Hence, the Suir Steam Navigation Company never got involved in the transport of any intoxicating liquors.

1878

5 DECEMBER

Bishop of Waterford Hanged

In 1636 John Atherton (a native of Somerset in England) was appointed Bishop of Waterford. On his arrival he immediately set about recovering lands which had been lost to the Anglican Church. One of his main opponents was Richard Boyle, Earl of Cork. Gradually Atherton began to make progress. The Bishop's Palace was recovered and a number of suits were filed against Boyle, and also against Piers Butler, the Recorder of Waterford.

However his success at recovering lands made him many enemies. His lifestyle eventually led to his downfall. In June 1640, his steward, John Child, accused him of sodomy, acts of fornication, adultery and homosexual relations. Bishop Atherton admitted the charges of fornication but denied the other charges. After a trial he was found guilty of all charges.

On the 5th of December 1640 Bishop John Atherton was hanged in Dublin. His body was buried in a rubbish dump.

After his death, various theories were put forward suggesting he was framed by his opponents. These were responded to with new allegations including the circulation of an anonymous pamphlet titled *The Case of John Atherton, Bishop of Waterford in Ireland who was convicted of bestiality with a cow & other creatures.*

1640

6 DECEMBER

James Rice

Of all the tombs and memorials in Christ Church Cathedral, probably the most striking is the cadaver tomb of James Rice. It was consecrated by the Bishop of Ossory on the 6th of December 1482.

James Rice was born sometime in the early 1400s. He claims a remarkable place in Waterford history as he held the office of Mayor a record eleven times between the years 1467 and 1485 (see entries for July 6th and September 28th). His father Peter Rice was also Mayor, but only three times between 1426 and 1436.

A deeply religious man, he prepared a tomb for himself prior to his pilgrimage to Santiago de Compostela in Spain in 1483, in case he did not survive the hazardous journey. The tomb was housed in a side chapel in the medieval Christ Church Cathedral and was consecrated on the 6th of December 1482.

James Rice is believed to have died in 1488 and was buried in the tomb which had been consecrated six years earlier. The tomb was later removed from the side chapel into the body of the old cathedral. It was then erected in the burying ground opposite the west door. Finally in 1880 it was moved into its present position in the new cathedral which was built in 1779.

The inscription, which is in Latin, is translated as follows:

Here lies James Rice, late citizen of this city, and by his direction is interred Kathleen Brown, his wife. Whose thou art that passeth by, stop, read, mourn I am what thou wilt be, and I was what thou art.

1482

7 DECEMBER

Dunmore Rescue

We already mentioned that a number of rescues were carried out on the Waterford coast prior to a lifeboat station being established in Dunmore East in 1884 (see entry for November 7th). Another such rescue was carried out on the 7th of December 1840.

The *Glencoe* was on a voyage from Glasgow to Calcutta when she was forced into Waterford Harbour by strong winds. She was an unusual type of ship called a snow, which was a two-masted sloop but with square sails on both masts. The ship was driven ashore close to Creaden Head.

The chief officer of the coastguard, Charles French, along with six other men succeeded in getting lines on board from nearby rocks. All thirteen members of the crew were saved before the ship broke up. The RNLI awarded a silver medal to French for his gallantry.

1840

8 DECEMBER

Farm Labourers Strike

During World War I the growing demands for food supplies coupled with the shortage of manpower, led to better pay and conditions for farm labourers. At the end of the war, farmers began to claw back the concessions made. In County Waterford the farm labourers became particularly militant. Recall the Battle of Fenor in 1919 (see entry for November 24th).

A final bitter conflict between the Irish Farmers Union and the ITGWU occurred in Waterford in May 1923 when the farm labourers went on strike. This dispute lasted seven months. Various commentators describe it as probably the most bitter dispute to have ever occurred in Ireland. In the beginning the labourers managed to stop all movement of farmers' goods with the support of workers in creameries, railways, docks and factories. In June 250 troops, members of the Special Infantry Corps, arrived in Waterford to help maintain order. The struggle then evolved from an industrial dispute into open class conflict. In July the army, under the command of Major-General Prout, imposed a curfew on all of east Waterford (except the city) and martial law was declared. The tide gradually began to swing to the farmers' side.

In the midst of it all, a general election was held on the 27th of August. Both sides put forward candidates. While the traditional Redmond and Sinn Féin camps held two of the seats, the other two seats went to a farmers' candidate and a Labour candidate, emphasising the polarisation which had occurred. Eventually, the ITGWU took the view that the strike was unwinnable, and it ended on the 8th of December 1923. It was estimated that only about 30% of farm labourers got their jobs back.

1923

9 DECEMBER

Robert Manning

Very few Waterford people have heard of the scientist and engineer Robert Manning except those engineers who may have used *The Manning Formula*. This formula dealing with open channel flow is now a fundamental formula used in fluid mechanics worldwide. However the Waterford connection is not well-known.

Manning was born in Normandy in 1816. His father, a Lieutenant in the Wicklow Militia, married his mother, Ruth Stephen, when he was stationed in Geneva Barracks. On the death of his father in 1826, the family returned to Waterford where his mother's family still lived in Dromina. Robert Manning worked as an accountant in Waterford for a number of years. In 1846 he took up a position with the Office of Public Works. Before long he was working in engineering, in the field of arterial drainage. Although he had no engineering education, he taught himself the principles of hydraulics from a French book on the subject. Over the next few decades he became involved in a number of major projects, such as the construction of Dundrum Bay Harbour, a water supply for Belfast, and the mapping of the Marquis of Downshire estates in Down, Wicklow and Offaly. In 1877 he was president of the Institute of Civil Engineers of Ireland.

Manning's formula was first mentioned in a paper *On the flow of water in open channels and pipes* published in 1891. Robert Manning died on the 9th of December 1897.

1897

10 DECEMBER

William McCleverty

A visitor to Christ Church Cathedral will see many plaques and monuments. Those with an interest in the sea will be intrigued by one plaque which has a tall ship engraved on it. This plaque is dedicated to the memory of Captain William McCleverty from County Antrim who died in Waterford on the 10th of December 1779. As a young man, William McCleverty was one of those who accompanied Commodore Anson on his memorable expedition around the world in the middle of the 18th century. This expedition started out in 1740 with seven ships and some 1900 men, however only one ship and 188 men returned four years later.

Following that expedition McCleverty rose quickly through the ranks of the British Navy. In 1777 he was Captain of the *Hind*, stationed in Waterford. One of his main duties was to impress men for the Navy. An incident occurred in December 1779 when families of the pressed men attempted to recover their loved ones from the *Hind* docked on the Quay. The Mayor of Waterford Mr. Alcock, in supporting Captain McCleverty, is reputed to have said to him in a loud voice *have you no powder of shot* to which McClerverty replied he had, *then use it and I will support you,* said the Mayor. The crowd quickly dispersed.

Captain William McCleverty died in Waterford on the 10th of December 1779.

1779

11 DECEMBER

Temperance Movement

In 1833 there was a total of 190 licensed premises in Waterford. In 1838 some 60% of the people tried before the Mayor's Court were charged with drunkenness. In the last three months of 1838, 964 people were arrested in the city and locked up in Reginald's Tower for being drunk. In January 1839, fifteen extra policemen were recruited to enforce the Drunkenness Act.

As seen from these figures alcohol was a problem in Waterford, as it was in the rest of the country. It was estimated that Irish people drank over twice the amount of spirits that the English did (some 13 pints per person in 1838).

It was against this background that the temperance movement of Fr. Matthew grew. On the 11th and 12th of December 1839 Fr. Matthew visited Waterford and administered the pledge. The crowds were so great in Ballybricken that Fr. Matthew had to take refuge in the courthouse. Approximately two hundred people at a time entered and took the pledge to abstain from alcoholic drink. Over the two days it is estimated that over eighty thousand people took this pledge.

The effect was instantaneous. The following Saturday not one person was arrested and committed to Reginald's Tower, something which had not happened in the previous twenty years.

1839

12 DECEMBER

Death Rate

In the mid 19th century the condition of some of the housing and tenements in Waterford was as bad, if not worse, than in many other cities. In addition, the water supply was completely inadequate Knockaderry water works was not opened until 1875 (see entry for October 5th).

As a result it was reported by the Register-General's Office on the 12th of December 1874 that Waterford had the highest annual death rate of any city, with forty-seven deaths per year per thousand of population. Cork had thirty-eight while Limerick had only fifteen.

A later report into the conditions of the housing of the working classes in 1885 found:

- *All the tenement houses were situated in the old part of the city*
- *Some of these tenements were described as wretched*
- *Sixty-six people were living in three small houses in Usher's Arch.*
- *In some single rooms there were as many as eight or nine people of both sexes*
- *There were about 180 tenement houses in the city, each containing on an average five families. These were built as private dwelling houses, and where one family dwelt in the first instance, there were now five, and sometimes more families representing up to twenty human beings.*

Over the next thirty years some major new housing schemes were completed including Ballytruckle, Doyle Street, Philip Street, Morley Terrace, Summerhill, Alphonsus Road and others. Despite all this building, the local government enquiry in 1911 still identified major problems with much of the city centre (see entry for September 29th).

1874

13 DECEMBER

Tramore Sand Dunes

The back strand in Tramore was first reclaimed in 1863. Financed by the Malcomsons, an embankment was built to hold back the sea. Over a thousand acres were reclaimed. Initially the reclaimed land was ploughed and farmed, and in 1880 a racecourse was built on it. In 1894 a nine hole golf course was laid out between the racecourse and the embankment.

However the back strand was always exposed to the elements. In 1896 severe damage was done to the golf course following a storm. Another storm in 1898 also caused damage.

In the early months of 1911 the embankment was breached in a storm, but was quickly completely repaired. The golf club and racecourse were back in action soon after. The August races went ahead as planned (see entry for August 16th).

On the 13th of December 1911 a severe gale struck the south east coast. Again the embankment was breached. Engineers who had been working on the bridge in Waterford went to Tramore and erected a timber barrier and piled sand bags against it. Some £2,000 was spent in trying to repair the breech. However all attempts were unsuccessful. The back strand remained flooded and both the golf club and the racecourse had to move to different locations.

1911

14 DECEMBER

Pernicious Literature

On the 14th of December 1911 a public meeting was held in the City Hall complaining about *Pernicious Literature*. The meeting was organised by the "Vigilance Committee", whose chairman was Monsignor Flynn PP. The Bishop of Waterford and Lismore Dr. Sheehan presided. The Church of Ireland Bishop of Cashel and Waterford, Dr. O'Hara, also attended the meeting. A number of resolutions were adopted at the meeting, including:

> *That this public meting of the citizens of Waterford conscious of the grievous injury to Christian faith and morals effected by the tide of debased foreign literature which now inundates our country, views with feelings of gratification the country's uprising against it and pledges itself by all moral influence and legal means within its power of each individual present to put an end to the evil.*

The previous Sunday a number of sermons by priests exhorted:

> *The Catholic people not to read or allow into their homes a Sunday newspaper from England, which makes a special feature of serving up all the immoral English news of the week. An Irish Catholic paper or periodical should find a place in every Catholic household in the country.*

Some priests were glad to report:

> *That local newsagents when approached by the clergy on the matter consented at once to give up selling the objectionable Sunday English papers.*

Other priests referred to:

> *Indecent postcards which are hidden under the counter in shops and were passed around from person to person.*

1911

15 DECEMBER

SS Formby

The *SS Formby* was the flagship of the Clyde Shipping Company. Built in April 1914, she was 270 feet in length with a gross tonnage of 1283 tons. Although built primarily for the cattle trade, she also had accommodation for thirty-nine first class passengers and forty-five in steerage.

The *Formby* left Waterford for the last time on the afternoon of Tuesday the 11th of December 1917. She reached Liverpool the following morning and began discharging her cargo. A new cargo was loaded and at 11am on the morning of Saturday the 15th of December she left the quayside at Liverpool and sailed down the Mersey to open sea. At approximately 6pm she rounded off Holyhead and headed south. At the same time she was spotted by the German submarine U-62. At 7.35 pm the sub fired one torpedo. It hit amidships and after a few minutes the *Formby* sank with all hands. There was no time to radio a mayday or to launch a lifeboat. The thirty-seven crew and two passengers were lost. All but five of them were from Waterford.

The *Formby* was expected back in Waterford the following Sunday morning. A very bad storm hit the Irish Sea overnight so when she did not arrive, all assumed that she was sheltering from the storm. By Monday morning she was twenty-seven hours overdue, and officials at the Waterford Clyde office began to worry. While it was always possible that she had sunk in the storm they were also worried about U-Boat activity. They tried to contact Liverpool to warn her sister ship the *Coninbeg* but because of the storm damage the telephone lines were down (see entry for December 17th).

1917

16 DECEMBER

Clyde Shipping Company

We tend to forget today that prior to air travel, regular passenger ships were the lifeblood of any travel outside the country. For example on Saturday the 16th of December 1911, one of the Clyde steamers left Waterford for Southampton at 4pm. This was a regular weekly service. To illustrate the regularity of these services, here is a weekly schedule for the Clyde Shipping Company in 1911 for services out of Waterford.

To Glasgow: Every Monday (direct) and every Wednesday (via Plymouth).
To London: Every Saturday, via Southampton and rail.
To London: Every Monday (via Glasgow) Cargo only.
To Southampton: Every Saturday (direct).
To Newhaven: Every Saturday (via Southampton).
To Dover: Every Saturday (via Southampton and Newhaven).
To Plymouth: Every Wednesday (direct).
To Belfast: Every Saturday (direct).
To Dublin: Every Saturday (via Belfast).
To Cork: Every Thursday (direct).

Their advertisements claimed: *New and Powerful Steamers, Excellent Passenger accommodation, Electric Light and Stewards and Stewardesses carried.*

1911

17 DECEMBER

SS Coninbeg

The *SS Coninbeg* was a sister ship of the *Formby* (see entry for December 15th). Although built in 1903 for the Waterford Steamship Company, she was transferred to the Clyde Shipping Company in 1912 and was completely refitted in 1913. At 270 feet also, she was 1278 tons. Her cargo was mainly cattle although she was fitted out for eighty-five first class passengers and seventy-four in steerage.

The *Coninbeg* left Waterford on the afternoon of Wednesday the 13th of December 1917 and arrived in Liverpool on Thursday the 14th. She stayed in port until Monday the 17th when she sailed at 1pm. Late that night she was off the Wicklow coast, south east of Arklow, when she was spotted by the same U-Boat that had sunk the *Formby*. At 11.45 pm one torpedo was fired by the submarine. A direct hit caused a massive explosion which broke the vessel in two. A few minutes later she sank with all hands. Again there was no time to radio a mayday or to launch a lifeboat. The forty crew and four passengers were lost. All but eight of them were from Waterford.

Back in Waterford, the wives and families of the crew and passengers waited in vain for the *Formby* and the *Coninbeg*. It was two days after Christmas before the Clyde Shipping Company accepted that both ships were lost (see entry for December 27th).

1917

18 DECEMBER

Piracy

There are very few accounts of piracy involving Waterford ships in any of the histories of the city with the exception of one involving the O'Driscolls of Baltimore (see entry for February 20th and December 25th). The most famous account of piracy in Ireland also involves Baltimore, when Algerian pirates attacked the town in 1631 and took the inhabitants back to the Barbary Coast of North Africa.

An article in the *Journal of the Waterford and South-East of Ireland Archaeological Society* in 1897 states that Baltimore was not the only place in the south of Ireland to suffer at the hands of Algerian pirates. It refers to a report published on the 18th of December 1772 regarding the piracy of a Waterford ship that October by Algerian pirates which reads:

> *A merchant in Waterford has received the melancholy account that the Rose in June, vessel belonging to that port, with wine and fruit for Alicant (Spain) was taken the 20th October last near the entrance of the Straits of Gibraltar by a Moorish cruiser and carried into Larache in Barbary, where the unhappy crew and passengers are made slaves.*

The article goes on to say that the *Rose in June* was doubtless a trader between the south of Ireland and Spain and was at the time of her capture bringing home the red wine of Spain. It was not known who her passengers were, but their *fate must have occasioned many a sad heart in the City of Waterford*. This Algerian piracy continued until 1816 when Lord Exmouth's expedition finally put an end to Christian slavery in Algiers.

1772

19 DECEMBER

The Mall

Old maps of Waterford show that the present day Mall was actually covered in water and known as Miller's Marsh. The name Miller came from the fact that there was a mill here in ancient times. First mentioned in the 13th century, a map of 1673 shows Colbeck's Mill and a Mill Pond. In 1728 the Corporation purchased the Mill Pond.

In 1735 a bowling green was laid out on the site of the present Tower Hotel. Two years later in 1737 the Mall itself was laid out as a tree-lined promenade. Smith in his *History of Waterford* (1746) states:

> *The Mall is a beautiful walk, about 20 yards long and proportionally broad situated on the east end of the city. The draining and the levelling of the ground which was formerly a marsh, was done at a very considerable expense, is planted with rows of elms, and the sides of the walk are fenced with a stone wall.... Here the ladies and gentlemen assemble on fine evenings, where they have the opportunity of each other's conversation. Nothing can be more agreeable than to see this shady walk crowded with the fair sex of the city, taking the air, enjoying the charms of a pleasant evening, and improving their health; nor need I inform the reader, that this city has been long since peculiarly celebrated for the beauties of its female inhabitants.*

In 1783, the building of the Assembly Rooms and Playhouse (the present City Hall) began. However, the tree-lined promenade had become an eyesore and was dilapidated. On the 19th of December 1792 the corporation decided to cut down the trees and replace the promenade with paving stones. Thus the modern Mall took shape.

1792

20 DECEMBER

Jute Factory Closes

The origins of the Jute factory in Tycor can be traced back to the Waterford Sack Factory owned by the Denny family. The Denny's concern was in major need of an upgrade. Approaches were made to Goodbody Ltd., who at that stage had a plant in Co. Offaly. With the backing of the Corporation, who handed over a 4.5 acre green field site in Tycor, the sod was turned for the new factory on the 17th of December 1936. There was some delay initially as the site was originally earmarked for housing. The building was completed in 1937 and production started in 1938. By the end of 1938 over 180 people were employed and 2.5 tons of jute was being produced weekly.

During the war, the factory had to close down due to inadequate supplies of raw jute. Production restarted in 1944. By 1951 over six hundred were employed, with some 80% female (average wages for females were about 55% of male wages). In 1956 the plant went on short time to allow fitting of new equipment, which allowed it to diversify into high-class yarn for carpets. By the '60s competition came from synthetic fibres, which gradually led to a reduction in demand for its products.

On the 20th of December 1974 the Jute factory closed for the last time.

1974

21 DECEMBER

John Horn

While it was the Malcomsons who had the money to develop shipbuilding in Waterford in the 19th century, it was John Horn and his shipbuilding expertise which brought it to a fine art. John Horn was born on the 21st of December 1814 in Scotland. At an early age he was apprenticed to Robert Napier's marine engineering business. Napier has been described as the father of Clyde Shipbuilding. Horn became foreman at the early age of 18. As his reputation grew in shipbuilding circles he was head-hunted by Joseph Malcomson to lead the new iron shipyard in Waterford.

Horn arrived in Waterford in September 1849 to take up the position of Managing Superintendent of the Neptune Ironworks. Initially his work involved ship maintenance, but in 1852 he began a project to lengthen the *SS Neptune,* followed by construction of the *SS Sylph* and *SS Leda*. Under his stewardship the Neptune yard prospered and in its heyday built some of the largest ships in Ireland. In 1855 he adopted watertight compartments and in 1856 he used cement on the inside bottom of the hull to prevent rusting and deterioration. The *SS Avoca,* launched in 1861, was the first steamship to force the ice at Odessa while under contract to the Russian Government.

John Horn retired from Neptune in 1870 and was replaced by his son Andrew as designer and shipbuilder. He died in 1895.

1814

22 DECEMBER

Corporation

The 17th century Corporation was not slow to assert its authority when it was felt the office of Mayor was slighted, or the property of the city was not treated with respect. The following excerpt from the *Council Books* dated the 22nd of December 1662 shows an example:

> *The Mayor and council take note that James Shinckler of this city, ferryman, had build a boat upon the quay of Waterford and had broken up the pavement thereof, and thereby had done much damage to the said quay, and for as much as Mr. Mayor did reproach the said Shinckler for so doing, and instead of mending the same, he gave uncivil language to Mr. Mayor, therefore the mayor and council have and do hereby think fit to fine the said Shinckler six shillings eight pence sterling for his said offence, without favour or abatement, and 20s sterling in case he does not put right the Quay into as good repair as it was before he built his boat upon the same (by the 6th January next) then the sheriff is to levy the said summons of 20s upon his goods and chattels without grace.*

At the same meeting they also dealt with a William Keyes:

> *Whereas William Bamlett and Mr John Wright hath informed this council that William Keyes of this city, butcher hath scandalised and abused the whole council in general and scandalised and abused Alderman John Haughton, Heaven, Rickards and Tomlinson in particular by calling them traitors and rebels and in saying the council had turned out honest men and taken in knaves and fools into the council instead, the mayor and council taking the same onto consideration do think fit to fine the said William Keyes for his abuse of this council in six shillings eight pence, without grace, and that he stand committed till he ask the mayor and council forgiveness for his said offence.*

1662

23 DECEMBER

Modern Bakeries

At about 8pm on the night of Sunday the 23rd of December 1962, a large fire occurred at the premises of the Modern Bakeries Ltd. at Canada Street and Newton Road. The fire, which was believed to have started in the canteen, rapidly spread to the rest of the building and the entire premises was gutted. However the adjoining flour and yeast storage buildings were saved. The damage was estimated to be in the region of £250,000.

As the bakery supplied about 16,000 loaves of *Gold Crust Bread* throughout the south of the country, there were fears of a shortage of bread for Christmas. Panic buying started in the other bakeries, resulting in a rationing system. Many of these smaller bakeries employed some of the bakers from the burnt-out bakery to help increase their output and quell the panic. In addition, a bakery in Arklow supplied bread to many customers of Modern Bakeries.

Further problems occurred the following week when the worst snow blizzard in over twenty years hit the southeast, and vans from Modern Bakeries were unable to collect supplies in Arklow.

On a side note, the snow blizzard which hit on Sunday the 30th of December 1962 caused major disruption in the south east. An ESB high tension cable crossing the river from Mount Misery was brought down, a trawler sank in the harbour in Dunmore East and a hearse on its way to a burial in Ballygunner could not travel up Ballygunner Hill and had to divert around Callaghan. It was also reported that it was the first time in history that the weather caused the cancellation of a dance in the Olympia Ballroom.

1962

24 DECEMBER

Great Western

To a generation of Waterfordians the ship the *Great Western* was as familiar a presence on the Suir as the *Portlairge*. Her high superstructure distinguished her from other ships and both her steam siren and foghorn were easily recognised by their distinctive sounds. Built in 1933 at Birkenhead, she was 283 feet long. She came into service in 1934 and for the next thirty years sailed between Waterford and Fishguard. Named after the railway company, her usual cargo was live cattle. She could take six hundred head of cattle and five hundred tons of cargo.

The *Great Western* also had accommodation for first class and steerage passengers. Departing from Adelphi Quay at 6.30pm, she landed in Fishguard at 2am, from where passengers could get the 4am train to London and arrive in Paddington by early morning. On the return journey passengers took the 3.45pm train from Paddington in time for the midnight sailing from Fishguard. They could eat their breakfast as they sailed up the Suir before docking at Adelphi Quay.

During the war service was interrupted a number of times. She was placed on the Rosslare service for nine months in 1941. At one stage she was attacked by German bombers but only suffered slight damage. She was requisitioned by the Admiralty for three months in 1944. Passenger numbers declined in the 1950s, and in 1959 the small cabins were removed to make way for containers, which were becoming the modern method of shipping goods. As the livestock trade dwindled and container traffic grew, it became apparent that she could not be fully adapted and a specific container ship was required. The *Great Western* left Adelphi Quay for the last time on the 24th of December 1966.

1966

25 DECEMBER

O'Driscolls of Baltimore

The long conflict between Waterford and the O'Driscolls of Baltimore has already been mentioned (see entry for February 20th). It was on Christmas Day in 1413 that the Waterford fleet arrived in Baltimore. We first hear of the O'Driscolls in September 1368, when having joined with the Powers of Dunhill, they sailed towards the city with plunder in mind. The Mayor of Waterford, John Malpas, sailed out to meet them with the Sheriff and a volunteer force. It did not end well for Waterford however, as their forces were routed and the Mayor, Sheriff, and sixty of their forces were killed. The city itself escaped capture but the bad blood was to last for years.

To avenge this defeat, a later Mayor, Simon Wicken, set sail for Baltimore on Christmas Eve 1413 with a strong band of men in armour. They arrived in Baltimore on Christmas night. The guards of Baltimore accepted the Mayor's assurance that he had come with a ship full of wine, whereupon the gate was opened. The Waterford force quickly captured the O'Driscoll castle, and carried the owner and his family as hostages back to Waterford. A suitable ransom was paid, but the conflict continued for over a hundred years.

In 1461 the O'Driscolls were "invited" by the Powers to Tramore. The Mayor put an army together and went out to do battle. Victory ensued for Waterford again, and this time several of the O'Driscolls and ten of the Powers were slain. In addition, the prisoners included The O'Driscoll Óg with six of his sons, and three of their galleys. Perhaps there is a connection between these three galleys and the galleys emblazoned on the Waterford coat of arms. The long conflict finally ended in 1538.

1413

26 DECEMBER

De La Salle

The De La Salle Brothers first came to Waterford in October 1887 when the primary school in Stephen Street was opened. The following year the order purchased a large house in Newtown. In November 1890 they made a formal application for the approval of a training college in Waterford for both members of the De La Salle order and other secular students.

On the 26th of December 1890, the Provincial of the order sent a letter to his superior in Paris stating that they had received approval for the new training college.

The following year plans were drawn up for a new building at Newtown. Meanwhile some forty lay students were enrolled in the training college in addition to a number of student brothers. The lay students slept in the Adelphi Hotel while waiting for the new building to be opened.

The new building was opened in July 1894. Over two thousand primary teachers were trained here during the next forty-five years (including this author's father) until a government decision was made in 1939 to close the training college. During the next ten years the college was used for the training of brothers only. In September 1949 the college was opened as a boarding and lay secondary school.

1890

27 DECEMBER

Formby and Coninbeg

The two Waterford steamers, the *SS Formby* and the *SS Coninbeg*, belonging to the Clyde Shipping Company, were lost on the 15th and 17th December 1917 respectively. Neither ship managed to get out a distress call before sinking. Back in Waterford, relatives waited anxiously for news of their loved ones. Finally on the 27th December, management at the Clyde Shipping Company accepted that the two steamers were lost and the following letter was sent to the relatives of each of the eighty-three casualties:

Date 27th December 1917

Dear Madam,

SS Formby and SS Coninbeg

It is with feeling of the deepest grief that we have to inform you that the company now consider that they must give up hope concerning these steamers, and I have been instructed to convey to you the very deepest sympathy of the Directors in your great sorrow.

I would like to add an expression of my own heartfelt sympathy with you and of my desire to be of any assistance I can to you in connection with this terrible calamity.

It would be necessary for certain papers to be filled up in connection with the procuring of compensation, pensions, etc. and all possible help in that connection will be gladly at your disposal. As soon as the forms are ready you will be advised.

I would like to have called personally on relatives of all the members of crews and cattlemen but have found this to be quite impossible.

Yours faithfully,

G.A.Watt.

1917

28 DECEMBER

First Bishop of Waterford

It was only at the end of the 11th century that the Catholic Church in Ireland began to be organised into dioceses. Prior to that time, it was the monasteries that led the way in terms of church organisation. Dublin was the first dioceses to be set up and was then followed by Waterford. This organisation came about as a request from the people of Waterford themselves. A letter with a request for a bishop was sent from the clergy and people of the city, and supported by King Murchertach Ua Briain, to Anselm, the Archbishop of Canterbury. Murchertach Ua Briain was a great-grandson of Brian Boru. This letter had also identified who they wanted as their bishop, an Irish monk by the name of Malchus who was at the Cathedral Priory of St. Swithun in Winchester.

Before Anselm would agree, he insisted that Malchus swear on oath of obedience to him as Archbishop of Canterbury, which made Waterford in effect a suffragan diocese of Canterbury. Bishop Malchus, the first Bishop of Waterford, was consecrated on the 28th of December 1096. He remained in Waterford until 1110 when he moved to Lismore and from there to Cashel. He is believed to have been involved in the building of Cormac's Chapel in the Rock of Cashel.

While in Waterford, Malchus is credited with the building of the original Christ Church Cathedral. The historic St. Peter's Church (now visible in City Square shopping centre) was reputed to have been built by Malchus. However, the archaeological excavation which took place prior to the City Square development provides evidence that places the building of St. Peter's Church in a period thirty years after Malchus' time in Waterford.

1096

29 DECEMBER

John J. Hearne

When passing through William Street you will see a Blue Plaque erected by Waterford Civic Trust dedicated to John J. Hearne who was born in the street in 1893. The plaque also mentions that he was the architect of the Irish Constitution which came into force on the 29th of December 1937.

John J. Hearne was born in 8 William Street in November 1893. His father, Richard Hearne, was proprietor of Hearne and Cahill Boot Manufacturers and held the office of Mayor of Waterford in 1902 and in 1903. Educated at Waterpark and University College Dublin, John Hearne entered public service and became Assistant Parliamentary Draftsman from 1923 to 1929. He joined the Department of External Affairs in 1929 as a legal advisor. Following Fianna Fáil's return to power in 1932, he was given the task by Éamon de Valera of drafting the heads of a new constitution. The text of the draft constitution with minor amendments was approved by the Dáil in June 1937, and adopted by a referendum in July. It came into force on the 29th of December. On that day the Taoiseach Éamon De Valera dedicated a copy of the constitution to John Hearne. It reads:

> *To Mr. John Hearne, Barrister at Law, Legal advisor to the Department of External Affairs, Architect in Chief and Draftsman of this Constitution, as a Souvenir of the successful issue of his work and in testimony of the fundamental part he took in framing this the first Free Constitution of the Irish People.*

John Hearne was appointed High Commissioner to Canada and later Ambassador to the United States, where he remained for the next ten years. Hearne then served as a legislative consultant to the governments of Nigeria and Ghana. He died in Dublin in 1969.

1937

30 DECEMBER

Robert Boyle

Robert Boyle of Boyle's Law fame, was born in Lismore in January 1627. He was the fourteenth child and seventh (and youngest) son of Richard Boyle, the Earl of Cork. At the age of eight he was sent to Eton. At eleven he was sent with his tutor on a grand tour of Europe which lasted six years. On his return he lived initially in Dorset in England where he set up a scientific laboratory. In 1655 he moved to Oxford, where he joined a group of natural philosophers that foreshadowed the Royal Society which was founded in 1660.

He continued his scientific experiments and employed Robert Hooke as his assistant (Hooke went on to develop Hooke's Law, which deals with the force needed to extend springs). Together they built an air pump used to create vacuums, with which Boyle carried out many experiments on the nature and importance of air. He was able to demonstrate the necessity of air for combustion, for animal breathing, and for the transmission of sound. His most recognised research involves the inverse relationship between the volume and pressure of a gas, now known as Boyle's Law.

Boyle was also a devout Christian and was a prolific writer on theology. He also wrote widely on philosophy.

Boyle died in London on the 30th of December 1691.

1691

31 DECEMBER

Sabbath Day

We mentioned earlier (see entry for June 18th) the concern of Waterford Corporation in observance of the Lord's Day in 1692.

The issue of the opening of a public house on a Sunday was still a cause of concern for the Mayor in 1831. An article published in the *Waterford Chronicle* on Saturday the 31st of December 1831 reports on the Mayor of Waterford taking action against publicans who were opening illegally on a Sunday. He had purposely made sure the constables were on duty the previous Sunday morning to check if any public houses were open. The fact that the previous Sunday was the 25th of December, Christmas Day, did not merit any attention. The issue was purely about public houses opening on a Sunday.

> *Violation of the Sabbath*
>
> *The Mayor finding that several of the publicans (not withstanding the repeated cautions given them) still continue the unlawful practice of selling spirituous liquor on Sundays, ordered the constables to be on duty on the 25th instant, in order to detect such as might be concerned in selling on that morning in consequence of which seven publicans were fined on Monday last the penalty of seven pounds each before him and Doctor Poole, which sums the magistrates have divided equally between the Sick Poor and Mendicant Asylum Institutions.*
>
> *Sick Poor: The Treasurer (Mr Ryland) acknowledges the receipt of £17 10s from the Mayor and Doctor Poole being part of fines levied on publicans for selling spirit on Sunday last December 25.*
>
> *Mendicity Asylum: John Blake Collector to the Mendicity Asylum acknowledges the receipt of £17 10s from the Mayor and Doctor Poole being part of fines levied on publicans for selling spirit on Sunday last December 25.*

1831

BIBLIOGRAPHY

Anderson, E. B. *Sailing Ships of Ireland* (Dublin 1951)

Battersby, W. J. *Brother Potamian, Educator and Scientist* (London 1953)

Barnard, N. *The Political Balance, for 1754. The Mock–Patriot for 1754. To which is added the case of John Atherton, Bishop of Waterford in Ireland, who was Convicted of Beastiality with a Cow and Other Creatures* (Dublin 1754)

Bonaparte-Wyse, O. *The Issue of Bonaparte-Wyse: Waterford's Imperial Relations* (Waterford 2004)

Bonaparte-Wyse, O. *The Spurious Brood* (London 1969)

Brady, D. *Waterford Scientists, Preliminary Studies* (Waterford 2010)

Brennan, D. *Tramore Golf Club 1894-1994* (Waterford 1994)

Burke, J. *History of Snowcream Dairies 1952-2009* (Waterford, 2011)

Burnell, T. *The Waterford War Dead* (Dublin 2010)

Byrne, N. J. (ed) *The Great Parchment Book of Waterford* (Dublin 2007)

Byrne, N. *The Waterford Leper Hospital of St. Stephen and the Waterford County and City Infirmary* (Dublin 2011)

Colclough, B. & O'Neill, W. *Waterford & Thereabouts* (Waterford 1993)

Cowman, D. *Perceptions and Promotions, The Role of Waterford Chamber of Commerce 1787-1987* (Waterford 1988)

Cummins, P. J. *"Emergency" Air Incidents South-East Ireland* (Waterford 2003)

Curtis Clayton, M. (ed) *The Council Book for the Province of Munster c. 1599-1649* (Dublin 2008)

Cowman, D. & Brady, D. *The Famine in Waterford 1845-1850* (Dublin 1995)

de Courcy Ireland, J. *Ireland and the Irish in Maritime History* (Dublin 1986)

Dooley, T. P. *Irishmen or English Soldiers? The Times and World of a Southern Catholic Irish Man (1876-1916) Enlisting in the British Army During the First World War* (Liverpool 1995)

Doonican, V. *The Complete Autobiography, My Story My Life* (London 2009)

Dowling, D. *Waterford Streets Past and Present* (Waterford 1998)

Downey, A. *The Glamour of Waterford* (Dublin 1921)

Downey, E. *The Story of Waterford, From the Foundation of the City to the Middle of the Eighteenth Century* (Waterford 1914)

Egan, P. M. *Historic Guide & Directory of County and City of Waterford* (Kilkenny 1894)

Fayle, H. & Newham, A. T. *The Waterford & Tramore Railway* (Devon 1964)

Ferguson, P. *Troubled Waters, Shipwreck and Heartache on the Irish Sea* (Dublin 2008)

Fewer, T. N. *Waterford People, A Biographical Dictionary* (Waterford 1998)

Finnegan, F. *Do Penance or Perish, A Study of Magdalen Asylums in Ireland* (Kilkenny 2001)

Fitzpatrick, T. *Waterford during the Civil War 1641-1653* (Waterford 1912)

Flenning, H. *The Waterford Dominicans 1226-1990* (Waterford 1990)

Fraher, W. & Ui Uallachain, P. *The Newfoundland Emigrant Trail* (Waterford 2010)

Friedland, M. L. *The Case of Valentine Shortis, A True Story of Crime and Politics in Canada* (Toronto 1986)

Griffin, E. *Waterford Boat Club 1878 – 2012, A Piece of History* (Waterford 2012)

Hansard, J. *The History, Topography and Antiquities of the County and City of Waterford* (Dungarvan 1870)

Hartery, J. *The Waterford-Fishguard Service* (Waterford)

Havel, B. F. *Maestro of Crystal, The Role of Miroslav Havel and his Role in Waterford Crystal* (Dublin 2005)

Healy J. N. *Ballads from the Pubs of Ireland* (Cork 1965)

Hearne, J. M. *Waterford Central Technical Institute 1906-2006, A History* (Waterford 2006)

Hogan, E. *The Description of Ireland and The State Thereof as it is at this present in Anno 1598* (Dublin 1878)

Hurley, M. J. *Links and Landmarks being a Calendar for the year 1900, recording curious and remarkable events in the History of Waterford City from the earliest times to the present day* (Waterford 1900)

Hutchinson, J. R. *The Press Gang Afloat and Ashore* (London 1913)

Inglis, H. D. *Ireland in 1834: A Journey Throughout Ireland During the Spring Summer and Autumn of 1834* (London 1835)

Irish, B. *Shipbuilding in Waterford 1820-1882: A Historical, Technical and Pictorial Study* (Wicklow 2001)

Irish, B. & Kelly, A. *A Century of Trade & Enterprise in Waterford, A Photographic Essay 1880s-1980s* (Waterford 2009)

Irish, B. & Kelly, A. *Two Centuries of Tall Ships in Waterford, A Photographic Voyage* (Waterford 2011)

Kennedy, T. *Waterford Through the 20th Century* (Waterford)

Keohan, E. D. (ed) *Waterford City & Region: An Historical & Pictorial Almanac of Waterford City and County* (Waterford 1987)

Kiely, B. *The Connerys, The Making of a Waterford Legend* (Dublin 1994)

Lane, L. *Rosamond Jacob Third Person Singular* (Dublin 2010)

Larn, B. T. & R. *Shipwreck Index of Ireland* (London 2002)

Le Fanu, W. R. *Seventy Years of Irish Life* (London 1893)

Mackey, P. (ed.) *Housing in Waterford* (Waterford 1988)

Mackey, P. *Life in Waterford 1800-1900* (Waterford 1990)

Mackey, P. *Selected Walks Through Old Waterford* (Waterford 1984)

Mackey, P. *Talk of the Town* (Waterford 1985)

Mackey, P. *Reginald's Tower and the Story of Waterford* (Waterford 1980)

Mackey, P. *Waterford Fireside Stories* (Waterford 1989)

McEneaney, E. *Discover Waterford* (Dublin 2001)

McEneaney, E. (ed.) *Waterford Treasures* (Waterford 2004)

McEneaney, E. (ed.) *A History of Waterford and its Mayors, from the 12th to the 20th Century* (Waterford 1995)

McElwee, R. *The Last Voyages of the Waterford Steamers* (Waterford 1995)

McRonald, M. *The Irish Boats Volume 2, Liverpool to Cork and Waterford* (Gloucestershire 2006)

Mooney, T. *Cry of the Curlew* (Waterford 2012)

Morris, J. *The Story of the Dunmore East Lifeboats* (Waterford 2003)

Murphy, S. & S. *Waterford Heroes, Poets & Villains* (Waterford 1999)

Murphy, S. & S. *The Comeraghs "Gunfire & Civil War"* (Waterford 2003)

Nolan, W. & Power, T. P. (ed.), Cowman, D (associate ed), *Waterford History & Society. Interdisciplinary Essays on the History of an Irish County* (Dublin 1992)

Olden, M. G. *The Life & Times of Patrick Comerford O.S.A. 1586-1652* (Waterford 2012)

O'Connell, M. J. *Charles Bianconi, A Biography 1786-1875* (London 1878)

O'Connor, E. *A Labour History of Waterford* (Waterford 1989)

O'Daly, J. *The Poets and Poetry of Munster: A Selection of Irish Songs* (Dublin 1860)

O'Donoghue, F. *The 5-Minute Bell, History of the Tramore Train 1853-1960* (Waterford 2012)

O'Maitiu S. *W&R Jacob Celebrating 150 years of Irish Biscuit Making* (Dublin 2001)

O'Neill, J. *A Concise History of Waterford* (Waterford 2011)

O'Neill, J. *Waterford and the Way We Were* (Waterford 2010)

O'Neill, J. *Waterford through the Lens of Time* (Waterford 2009)

O'Neill, J. *Waterford Its History and People* (Waterford 2008)

O'Neill, J. *A Waterford Miscellany* (Waterford 2004)

O'Neill, J. *Waterford A History* (Waterford 1992)

O'Neill, M. (ed.) *Reminiscences of Waterford* (Waterford 1997)

O' Reilly, T. *Rebel Heart, George Lennon Flying Column Commander* (Cork 2009)

Patton, B. *Irish Sea Shipping* (Kettering 2007)

Pender, S. (ed.) *Council Books of the Corporation of Waterford 1662-1700* (Dublin 1964)

Phelan, R. *William Vincent Wallace, A Vagabond Composer* (Waterford 1994)

Power, D. *Historic Photographs & Anniversaries of Waterford City* (Waterford 1994)

Power, D. *The Street Where You Live* (Waterford 1993)

Power, D. *The Ballads & Songs of Waterford, Volume 1 & 2* (Waterford 1992 & 1996)

Power, D. *Waterford A Hidden History, A Collection of True Stories* (Waterford 2009)

Power, J. *A Maritime History of County Wexford, Volume 1 1859-1910* (Wexford 2011)

Power, J. A. *A Mayor's Holiday* (Dublin 1906)

Power, P. *A Short History of Waterford* (Waterford 1937)

Power, P. *Parochial History of Waterford and Lismore during the 18th and 19th Centuries* (Waterford 1912)

Power, P. C. *History of Waterford City and County* (Cork 1990)

Power Kelly, M. *A Tale of Two Hospitals* (Waterford 2002)

Quinn, M. *The King of Spring, The Life and Times of Peter O'Connor* (Dublin 2004)

Rich, E.E. (ed.) *The Staple Court Books of Bristol* (Bristol 1934)

Ryland, R. H. *The History Topography and Antiquities of the County and City of Waterford, with an account of the present sate of the peasantry of that part of the south of Ireland* (Dublin 1824)

Sheehan, W. *British Voices from the Irish War of Independence 1918-1921* (Cork 2005)

Sheridan, M. *Murder in Monte Carlo* (Dublin 2011)

Simington, R. C. *The Civil Survey A.D. 1654-1656 County of Waterford* (Dublin 1942)

Smith, C. *The Ancient and Present State of the County and City of Waterford* (Dublin 1746)

Taylor, A. *Tramore of Long Ago* (Waterford 1996)

Thackeray, W. M. *The Irish Sketch Book* (London 1887)

Tiernan, D. *Souls of the Sea, The Tragic Story of Seven Lives Lost* (Dublin 2007)

Walsh, J. E. *The great charter of the liberties of the City of Waterford, with explanatory notes. To which is added a list of the mayors, bailiffs & sheriffs of the City of Waterford, from the year 1377 to the year 1806 inclusive* (Kilkenny 1806)

Walsh, J. E. *Ireland One Hundred and Twenty Years Ago* (Waterford 1911)

Walsh, K. (ed.) *Waterford Memories, 150 years with the Munster Express* (Dubin 2010)

Walsh, J. J. *Waterford's Yesterdays & Tomorrows* (Waterford 1968)

Walton, J. C. *The Royal Charters of Waterford* (Waterford 1992)

Wigham, M. J. *Newtown School Waterford, A History 1798-1998* (Waterford 1998)

Williams, G. *The Prize of all the Oceans* (London 1999)

Young, A. *A Tour in Ireland 1776 – 1779* (London 1897)

Other

Decies – the Journal of Waterford Archaeological & Historical Society Vol. 1-68

Journal of the Waterford and South East of Ireland Archaeological Society Vol. 1 – 18 1895 - 1915

Old Waterford Society Journal Vol. 3 1972

A Brief Account of the Cathedral Church of the Blessed Trinity (Christ Church) Waterford (Waterford 1950)

Ballybricken & Thereabouts C.A.R.A. (Waterford 1991)

The De La Salle Brothers Waterford 1887- 1987 A Century of Service (Waterford 1987)

The Duncannon Wreck, a Seventeenth Century Ship in Waterford Harbour (Dublin 2004)

Saorstát Eireann Irish Free State Official Handbook (Dublin 1932)

St. Paul's Silver Jubilee 1972-1997 (Waterford 1997)

Waterford Where I Live School Workbook (Waterford 2012)

A Parcel from the Past Waterford Civic Trust and Griffin, D. (Waterford 1994)

Shadows of the Past Waterford Civic Trust & Waterford Museum of Treasures (Waterford 2005)

Waterford & Suir Valley Railway Guide (Waterford)

Mealy's, Mount Congreve the House Sale (Waterford 2012)

INDEX

Adelphi Hotel	May 25
Advertisements	Jan. 19, May 29, July 27, Aug. 9
Aircraft Crash	Feb. 17, July 31, Nov. 17
Airmount	Mar. 22, July 25
Air Show	May 16
All-Ireland	Sept. 5, Sept. 6, Oct. 4
Ardree Hotel	Nov. 12
Arundel Ballroom	Oct. 7
Atherton, Bishop John	Dec. 5
Bacik, Karel	Jan. 12, June 25
Ballinamona	Nov. 10
Ballinaneeshagh	Mar. 15, July 13
Ballybricken	July 20, July 28, Oct. 20
Baltimore	Feb. 20, Dec. 25
Bands	April 23, Aug. 26
Banks	Mar. 6, Mar. 28, June 6, July 20, Aug. 22
Bar Extension	Sept. 27
Barracks	Mar. 9, July 16
Barron, Sir Henry Page	Sept. 12
Barronstrand Street	June 2
Bass Protest	Sept. 15
Battle of Fenor	Nov. 24
Bianconi, Charles	Sept. 24

Bicycle Club	Jan. 16
Boat Club	Aug. 18
Bonaparte Wyse, Letizia	July 4
Boot Factory	Aug. 13
Bowling Green	May 9
Bowyer, Brendan	Oct. 12
Boyle, Robert	Dec. 30
Brennan on the Moor	April 8
Brewery	Jan. 4, June 4
Bridge	Jan. 18, Feb. 10, Nov. 19
Brilliant, The	May 19
British Gun Boat	Sept. 10
Brophy, Annie	Nov. 21
Browne, Noel	April 11
Bull Post	Oct. 20
Butt, Issac	Feb. 6
Brugha, Cathal	Aug. 20
Brugha, Caithlín	Aug. 30
Cap of Maintenance	April 30
Carnegie, Andrew	Oct. 19
Cathedral Catholic	May 5
Catholic Emancipation	Sept. 7
Central Technical Institute	Jan. 12, Oct. 1
Cemetery	Mar. 15, April 2, Oct. 31
Chamber of Commerce	Sept. 23

Chancery Letters	April 3, April 26, May 8, May 14, June 26, Nov. 3, Nov. 13
Charles II	May 27
Charters	Feb. 8, Feb. 19, Mar. 25, May 7, May 26, June 16, July 3, Nov. 14
Cherry's Brewery	June 4
Cholera	July 2, Sept. 11
Christ Church	June 19, June 28, July 14
Chronicle	Jan. 19, Feb. 18, May 29, July 27, Aug. 9, Sept. 7
City Hall	Feb. 2, May 18
City of Waterford, The	Mar. 2, Sept. 19
Civil Survey	Sept. 26
Civil War	Jan. 25, April 23, July 21, Aug. 15
Clock Tower	April 5
Clooney, Patrick	Sept. 17
Clover Meats	Nov. 30
Clyde Shipping Company	Feb. 5, Sept. 19, Sept. 30, Dec. 15, Dec. 16, Dec. 17, Dec. 27
Coat of Arms	Feb. 16
Coliseum	Oct. 15
Collins, Michael	Mar. 26
Congreve Family	Feb. 12, May 24
Connerys	May 22, July 22
Conninbeg, The	Dec. 17, Dec. 27

Conscription	June 9
Corporation	Jan. 8, Jan. 13, Jan. 15, Jan. 27, Jan. 28, Feb. 1, Feb. 2, Mar. 5, April 22, May 3, May 4, May 27, June 18, June 27, June 29, Aug. 2, Sept. 7, Sept. 9, Sept. 13, Sept. 14, Sept. 16, Sept. 20, Oct. 10, Oct. 29, Nov. 29, Dec. 3, Dec. 18, Dec. 22
Cosgrave, W.T.	Aug. 26
Council Books of Munster	Feb. 1, July 19, Nov. 6
Court Case	June 5
Courthouse	July 12
Cromwell, Oliver	April 25, Aug. 10
Crotty, William	Mar. 18
CTI	Jan. 12, Oct. 1
Cullen, Martin (Snr.)	Mar. 12
Dáil Constituency	Feb. 25
Death Rate	Dec. 12
Deevy, Teresa	Jan. 21
De La Salle	April 13, Dec. 26
Denny, Henry	Jan. 3
De Valera, Éamon	Mar. 13, June 7
Dillon, Jonathan	Mar. 10
District Court	July 24
Dock Strike	Nov. 18

Dominican Friary	April 2, April 26, Aug. 29
Doonican, Val	Feb. 3
Dredger	June 3, Sept. 18
Edward VII	May 2
Edwards, Frank	Jan. 6
Elizabeth I	April 9
Emergency	Sept. 2
Emigration	May 20
Exchange, The	Feb. 2, Aug. 22
FAI Cup	April 18
Faithlegg	Mar. 1
Fanning Institute	Oct. 25
Farm Labourers	Dec. 8
Farrell, Walter	Oct. 3
Ferry	June 24, July 23
Ferrybank Church	Sept. 12
Fever Hospital	Oct. 9
Fire	July 28, Dec. 23
Food Parcels	Mar. 24
Food Riots	May 17, June 8
Formby, The	Dec. 15, Dec. 27
Foy, Bishop Nathaniel	Mar. 21, June 18
Franciscan Friary	Mar. 27, April 2, April 26, July 8
French Church	Mar. 27
French Vessel	May 19

Freeman	Feb. 6, Feb. 22, April 6, April 12, April 21, May 15, June 22, Aug. 28
Gallipoli	Jan. 9
Garda Station	June 23, Oct. 23
Garter Lane	Sept. 8
Gipsy, The	May 12
Goff, Sir William	Jan. 16, May 30, Nov. 23
Good Shepherd Sisters	April 1
Goold, Vere St. Leger	July 15
Grand National	Mar. 29
Graveyards	July 13
Graves	Nov. 8
Great Charter Roll	Nov. 14
Great Lewis, The	Jan. 26
Great Western, The	Dec. 24
Great Parchment Book	Sept. 28
Hallé Orchestra	April 24
Handwriting	May 29
Hanging	April 10, April 14, Oct. 21, Dec. 5
Hansard, Joseph	Nov. 15
Harbour Commissioners	July 17
Hearn, Francis	Oct. 21
Hearne, John	Dec. 29
Henderson, Bishop Charles	April 6
Henry II	Oct. 18

Hobson, William	July 30
Hogan, Edmund	Nov. 26
Holy Ghost Hospital	Oct. 28
Horn, John	Dec. 21
Housing	Sept. 29
Hurling	Sept. 5, Sept. 6, Oct. 4
Indiana, The	May 6
Infirmary	May 23
Inglis, Henry D.	Mar. 20
Iowa, The	Nov. 28
Jacob, Rosamond	Oct. 13
Jacobs	Sept. 21
Jail	Feb. 14, Mar. 4, Mar. 16, May 22
Jarvey Car	Feb. 23
John, King	June 20
Jute Factory	Dec. 20
Kelly, Bishop Michael	Feb. 13
Keily's Brewery	Nov. 20
King's Birthday	May 27
King's Coronation	Aug. 31
L&N	Nov. 5
Larkin, Fr. Bernard	Aug. 29
Leper House	Sept. 25
Library	Oct. 19
Lifeboat	Mar. 19, Sept. 30, Nov. 7, Dec. 7

Lincoln, Abraham	Mar. 10
Light Opera Festival	Sept. 3
Lord Waterford	April 27, Dec. 3
Lind, Jenny	Oct. 8
Mac Conmare, Donncha Rua	Oct. 6
McCleverty, William	Oct. 24, Dec. 10
McCormack, Count John	Mar. 23
Mahoney, Patrick	Oct. 30
Mail Coach	Aug. 17
Malchus, Bishop	Dec. 28
Malcomson, Joseph	April 15
Mall, The	Dec. 19
Manahan, Anna	April 12
Manning, Robert	Dec. 9
Martial Law	Jan. 5
Maritana	July 15
Mars, The	Mar. 31
Master McGrath	Feb. 21
Mayor	Jan. 8, Jan. 23, Feb. 12, Feb. 19, Mar. 5, Mar. 12, April 30, May 2, May 4, May 8, May 30, June 8, June 30, July 3, July 11, Aug. 19, Sept. 10, Sept. 14, Oct. 10, Oct. 29, Nov. 13, Dec. 6, Dec. 22, Dec. 25, Dec. 31

Meagher, Thomas Francis	Feb. 24, Aug. 3
Merchants' Guilds	Oct. 26
Mercy Convent	April 29
Merrie England, The	Feb. 7
Milford Haven	April 16, June 1
Militia	Nov. 28
Modern Bakeries	Dec. 23
Moore, John	Aug. 12
Mulcahy, Richard	May 10
Munster Express	July 7
Munster Packet	Jan. 14
Munster, Sebastian	Jan. 20
Murphy, James	Feb. 26
Newfoundland	Nov. 22
Newport, Sir John	Feb. 9
Newport's Bank	June 6
Newtown School	Aug. 1
Newspapers	Jan. 14, July 7, Aug. 21
O'Connell, Daniel	July 9
O'Connor, Peter	Aug. 5
O'Driscolls	Feb. 20, Dec. 25
O'Neill, Sir Neal	July 8
Olga, The	April 20
Papal Nuncio	May 15
Parish Courts	Mar. 14

Passage East Car Ferry	July 23
Passage to America	May 11
Pere Charles	Jan. 10
People's Park	Aug. 19, Nov. 25
Pernicious Literature	Dec. 14
Pickardstown Ambush	Jan. 7
Piracy	June 15, Dec. 18
Plague	Sept. 28
Pomona, The	April 28
Poor Law Union	Mar. 30
Portlairge, The	Sept. 18
Potamain, Brother	April 13
Power, Harry	Oct. 11
Power, Sir James	Jan. 23, May 2
Power, Canon Patrick	Mar. 8
Presbyterian Church	Oct. 22
Presentation Convent	June 10
Press Gang	Oct. 24, Dec. 10
Printing	Aug. 12
Public Lighting	Aug. 25
Railway	Jan. 31, April 4, May 21, July 11, Aug. 14
Rebellion	June 14
Redmond Bridge	Feb. 10
Redmond, Bridget	Jan. 24

Redmond, John	Sept. 1
Redmond, Willie	Mar. 13, June 7, Aug. 26
Reginald, The	Aug. 8
Reginald's Tower	June 17
Rice, James	Dec. 6
Richard II	May 13, Oct. 2
Roberts, John	Mar. 1, May 5, May 18, May 24, June 2, July 14, Aug. 1, Oct. 9
Roberts of Kandahar, Lord	Aug. 28
Roche, Hal	Feb. 28
Rockabill, The	Feb. 5
Ryland, R. H.	Jan. 1
Sabbath Day	Dec. 31
St. John's Church	Feb. 18
St. John's College	Oct. 27
St. John's Priory	June 12
St. Martin's Gate	Jan. 11
St. Olaf's Church	July 29
St. Patrick's Day	Feb. 27, Mar. 17
St. Thomas Church	Oct. 31
Seahorse, The	Jan. 30
Seduction	Nov. 9
Seven Years War	May 19
Sherlock, Don Pedro	April 19
Ship Building	Aug. 27, Dec. 21

Ship Launch	Feb. 7, Mar. 2, May 6, Nov. 28
Shipwrecks	Jan. 17, Jan. 22, Jan. 26, Jan. 30, Mar. 31, April 20, April 28, May 12, Sept. 19, Nov. 2
Shortis, Valentine	Nov. 4
Silkstone, The	Aug. 8
Snowcream	May 1
Staple of Waterford	May 8
Steamships	April 16
Strangman, Mary	Jan. 15
Strangman's Brewery	Jan. 4
Strongbow	Aug. 23
Submarine	Aug. 4
Suir	Jan. 18, Feb. 10, June 24, Aug. 18, Nov. 19, Dec. 4
Temperance	Dec. 11
Thackeray, William	July 14
Theatre Royal	Feb. 11, April 17, May 18, July 26, Oct. 8, Oct. 14
Thompson Hankey, The	Feb. 7
Timbertoes	Jan. 18
Tops of the Town	Feb. 4
Torrie, Adam	Nov. 5
Tower Hotel	May 28
Traffic Lights	Jan. 2

Tramore Bank Robbery	Aug. 7
Tramore Motor Races	July 5
Tramore Railway	April 4, July 11, Aug. 14, Aug. 24
Tramore Races	Aug. 16, Dec. 13
Tramore Sand Dunes	Dec. 13
Trams	Jan. 31
Tricolour	Mar. 7
Turkish Baths	Mar. 3
Undercroft	June 21, July 6
Urbs Intacta	June 3
Ursuline	Aug. 6
Van der Hagen, William	June 29
Victoria Cross	Oct. 30
Wadding, Luke	Oct. 16
Wallace, William Vincent	Mar. 11, June 11
Walton, Ernest	Nov. 16
Water Supply	June 13, Oct. 5
Waterford Dáil Constituency	Feb. 25
Waterford Giant	Feb. 26
Waterford Glass	Jan. 12, April 7, June 25, Nov. 1
Waterford United	April 18
Waterpark	Sept. 4
Wide Street Commission	June 2
Wild Man of Borneo	Mar. 29
William, King	Jan. 28

William Penn, The	July 10
Wimbledon	July 15
Wiseman, Cardinal N.	Feb. 15
WIT	Sept. 22
WWI	Jan. 9, Mar. 24, May 31, June 7, July 1, Aug. 4, Nov. 11
WWII	Feb. 17, Sept. 2
Wyse, Sir Thomas	July 4, Dec. 1
Wyse, William	April 30
X-Ray	April 13
Young, Arthur	Oct. 17